Jump
Start
the Adult Learner

*To my husband, Thomas, who has always believed in me
and encouraged me to reach my full potential in anything I do.
To my children, Sara, Daniel, Rebecca, Tony, and Alyssa, who have lovingly given
me the space I needed to develop my ideas and create this book.*

Jump Start

the Adult Learner

How to Engage and
Motivate Adults Using
Brain-Compatible Strategies

Laurie Materna

CORWIN PRESS
A SAGE Publications Company
Thousand Oaks, CA 91320

For information:

Corwin Press
A Sage Publications Company
2455 Teller Road
Thousand Oaks, California 91320
www.corwinpress.com

Sage Publications Ltd.
1 Oliver's Yard
55 City Road
London EC1Y 1SP
United Kingdom

Sage Publications India Pvt Ltd.
B 1/I 1 Mohan Cooperative
Industrial Area
Mathura Road, New Delhi 110 044
India

Sage Publications Asia-Pacific Pte Ltd
33 Pekin Street #02-01
Far East Square
Singapore 048763

Printed in the United States of America

Library of Congress Cataloging-in-Publication Data

Materna, Laurie.
Jump-start the adult learner : how to engage and motivate adults using brain-compatible strategies / Laurie Materna.
    p. cm.
Includes bibliographical references and index.
ISBN 978-1-4129-5293-4 (cloth)—ISBN 978-1-4129-5294-1 (pbk.)
    1. Adult education. 2. Learning—Physiological aspects. 3. Brain. I. Title.

LC5225.L42M365 2007
374—dc22

2006035950

This book is printed on acid-free paper.

Diagrams or templates have been created using Inspiration Software®, Inc., copyright © 2006, and Kidspiration Software®, copyright © 2006. Used with permission.

07 08 09 10 11 10 9 8 7 6 5 4 3 2 1

Acquisitions Editor:	Rachel Livsey
Editorial Assistant:	Phyllis Cappello
Production Editor:	Catherine M. Chilton
Copy Editor:	Cate Huisman
Typesetter:	C&M Digitals (P) Ltd.
Proofreader:	Jennifer Ang
Indexer:	Sheila Bodell
Cover Designer:	Lisa Miller

Contents

List of Figures   vii

List of Tables   ix

Preface   xi

Acknowledgments   xv

About the Author   xvii

Part 1: Brain 101   1

Chapter 1: How the Brain Learns   3

The Lower Brain   3

The Middle Brain   7

The Upper Brain   13

Whole-Brain Learning   16

Upper-Brain Processing   19

Brain Circuitry and Transmission of Thought   23

Chapter 2: Promotion of Learning   27

Promotion of Memory and Information Processing
    in Adult Learners   27

The Adult Brain   38

Part 2: The Resourceful Learning State   45

Chapter 3: Learning Styles and Multiple Intelligences   47

Preferred Learning Styles   48

Promoting Combination Learning   52

Kolb's Cycle of Learning Theory   52

Personality Preferences and Learning Style   53

Personal Application of Learning Styles Theory
    to Adult Education   54

Theories of Intelligence   56

Personal Application of Intelligence Theory
    to Adult Education   60

Chapter 4: Preparing the Brain to Learn   71

Promoting the Resourceful Learning State   72

Breathing Exercises   72

Powerful Peripherals   74

The Use of Aromas to Promote Learning   75

The Impact of Nutrition Upon Learning   76

The Role of Music in Learning   78

Creative Visualizations and Mind Calms   79

Balancing the Brain Through Movement Activities   84

Recipe for Success in Promoting a Resourceful Learning State   87

Part 3: Active Learning Strategies   **89**

Chapter 5: Key Metacognitive Learning Strategies   **91**

Metacognition and the Adult Brain   91

Knowledge Acquisition Strategies   94

Types of Graphic Organizers   95

Study Strategies to Promote Comprehension   122

Promoting Active Learning   126

**Chapter 6: Blending Taxonomies to Bring the
Learning Process Full Cycle**   **133**

Taxonomies in Education   133

The Materna Method   138

Application of Brain-Compatible Principles in the
Adult Classroom   162

Free Your Creative Spirit!   170

Resource A: Brain Warm-Ups   **171**

**Resource B: Active Learning Strategies for
Knowledge, Remembering, and Retrieval**   **175**

**Resource C: Active Learning Strategies for Comprehension
and Understanding**   **181**

**Resource D: Active Learning Strategies for Application
and Deeper Comprehension**   **187**

Resource E: Active Learning Strategies for Analysis   **193**

References   **199**

Index   **207**

List of Figures

Preface   **xi**

    Figure P.1 Benefits of Brain-Compatible Learning   xiii

Chapter 1: How the Brain Learns   **3**

    Figure 1.1 Major Brain Areas   4

    Figure 1.2 How Emotions Affect Learning   11

    Figure 1.3 Three Brains in One   12

    Figure 1.4 Diagram of Brain Lobes   13

    Figure 1.5 Cognitive Style Alert Scale   17

    Figure 1.6 Whole-Brain Teaching   20

Chapter 2: Promotion of Learning   **27**

    Figure 2.1 Formula for Long-Term Memory   29

    Figure 2.2 Memory Processing   30

    Figure 2.3 Working Memory and Long-Term Memory   33

    Figure 2.4 Impact of Multisensory Review on Learning   38

Chapter 3: Learning Styles and Multiple Intelligences   **47**

    Figure 3.1 Learning Style Inventory   50

    Figure 3.2 Kolb Learning Styles Progression   53

    Figure 3.3 Myers-Briggs Personality Preferences   54

    Figure 3.4 Silver and Hanson Learning Styles   55

    Figure 3.5 Active Learning Strategies to Expand Intelligences   66

Chapter 4: Preparing the Brain to Learn   **71**

    Figure 4.1 Recipe for Successful Learning   88

Chapter 5: Key Metacognitive Learning Strategies   **91**

    Figure 5.1 Concept Map Guidelines   98

    Figure 5.2 Academic Goal Setting   99

    Figure 5.3 Financial Management   100

    Figure 5.4 Effective Study Strategies   101

    Figure 5.5 Concept Map Patterns   102

    Figure 5.6 Basic Multibox Concept Maps   103

    Figure 5.7 Procedure Map for Completing a Project   105

    Figure 5.8 Procedure for Emergencies   106

    Figure 5.9 Procedure Templates   106

Figure 5.10 Process Map for Writing a Resume 107

Figure 5.11 Process Map Template 108

Figure 5.12 Cause and Effect Diagrams 109

Figure 5.13 Cause and Effect Templates 110

Figure 5.14 Venn Diagram Comparing Differences
Between Two Potential Job Offers 111

Figure 5.15 Venn Diagram Templates 111

Figure 5.16 Cycle Web Examples 112

Figure 5.17 Cycle Web Templates 113

Figure 5.18 Objective Overview Diagram 114

Figure 5.19 Objective Overview Templates 115

Figure 5.20 Research Design Tree 116

Figure 5.21 KWHL Diagram for Computer Operating Systems 121

Figure 5.22 KWHL Template 121

Figure 5.23 Concept Worksheets 127

**Chapter 6: Blending Taxonomies to Bring the
Learning Process Full Cycle** **133**

Figure 6.1 Marzano and Kendall's Model 139

Figure 6.2 Show-You-Know Diagram 143

Figure 6.3 Show-You-Know Worksheet 144

Figure 6.4 Learning Strategy KWHL 146

Figure 6.5 RSQC Grid 147

Figure 6.6 Big Picture Overview: Test Taking 148

Figure 6.7 Tree Diagram 154

Figure 6.8 Cycle Web 155

List of Tables

Chapter 1: How the Brain Learns   **3**

Table 1.1 Positive and Productive Classroom Rituals   6

Table 1.2 The Four Lobes of the Cerebrum   13

Table 1.3 Upper Brain Areas: Right/Left-Brain Specialization   16

Table 1.4 Flow and Downshift: Facilitators and Barriers to
the Natural Learning Process   21

Chapter 3: Learning Styles and Multiple Intelligences   **47**

Table 3.1 Gardner's Multiple Intelligences   58

Table 3.2 Personal Intelligence Profile   63

Chapter 5: Key Metacognitive Learning Strategies   **91**

Table 5.1 Medication Matrix   118

Table 5.2 Mineral Matrix   119

Table 5.3 Science Project Matrix   120

Table 5.4 Notes and Note-Taking Tips   124

**Chapter 6: Blending Taxonomies to Bring the Learning
Process Full Cycle**   **133**

Table 6.1 Anderson and Colleagues' Model   135

Table 6.2 Marzano and Kendall's Objectives   137

Table 6.3 The Materna Method: Brain-Compatible
Learning Strategies for the Classroom   140

Table 6.4 Biology Matrix   150

Table 6.5 Research Matrix   151

Table 6.6 Business Matrix   152

Table 6.7 General/Specific Analysis   156

Table 6.8 Defining Features Grid   157

Table 6.9 Pro/Con Grid   159

Preface

The Evolution of Brain-Compatible Learning

Over the last 40 years, more has been learned about how the brain works than ever before. While working on cures for brain injuries and neurological diseases, neuroscientists have actually discovered many other interesting details about brain structure and function in relation to learning. From the initial interdisciplinary research findings, a dynamic new focus on educational brain-compatible research has evolved. Since much of the early research was done on laboratory animals, however, many educators have been hesitant to apply these findings to the classroom. Traditional behaviorists argued that all education is brain-compatible and has worked well for decades—why fix it if it isn't broken! Educators with a more cognitivist or constructivist philosophy of education were more willing to try new approaches to teaching and learning, but were often viewed as risk-takers, lacking empirical evidence to support their effectiveness.

During the past 10 years, however, a number of scientists have been using magnetic resonance imaging (MRI), functional MRI (fMRI), and positron emission topography (PET) scans to study human brain function in greater depth. From coast to coast, neuroscientists are conducting research that can ultimately expand our understanding of how the brain functions.

Innovative and resourceful educators have recognized the value of this research and have begun working alongside neuroscientists and cognitive psychologists in efforts to transform these insights into practical applications for the classroom. Although the effectiveness of brain-compatible learning principles has been validated by the new research, many educators remain skeptical, hanging onto traditional models of instruction and educational philosophies. Despite the fact that traditional strategies and instructional methodologies are not netting the same results they once did, many educators are resistant to stepping out of the comfort zone of the old and familiar.

My personal exploration of brain-compatible teaching activities began in 1994. As an adult educator, I began to recognize a pattern of learning behaviors among a large percentage of adult students. Frustration, anxiety, and feelings of being overwhelmed with trying to keep up with the readings led to uncertainty over whether they were learning what they were expected to be learning. These perceptions of inadequacy were often validated through low test scores. The majority of students often had to repeat classes in order to receive a passing grade. Consequently, they reported feeling unmotivated and disinterested in the whole process of learning—they were simply doing whatever they needed to do to survive.

You could say that these students were a captive audience in the traditional instructional paradigm, where teachers primarily used the didactic lecture method of disseminating volumes of information to large numbers of students. There was certainly a disparity between the learning style of the students and the teaching style of most of the instructors I observed. Although my personal teaching style was more interactive, I was expected to fall in in lockstep fashion and teach the same way. I knew there had to be a better way to reach these students. After all, wasn't learning supposed to be a meaningful and rewarding experience?

As a result, I began exploring the impact of learning styles and the process of learning as well as brain-compatible learning principles. I soon discovered that my style of teaching and learning was naturally brain-compatible! As a student, I had recognized that my personal learning style was more visual and kinesthetic than auditory. I sailed through three nursing degrees by diagramming, tabling, and getting directly involved in whatever I was learning. I used diagrams and graphic organizers as a nurse to explain complicated medical treatments and diseases to my patients. Now, as a college professor, I began using the same approach with my students.

Although my professional colleagues were skeptical at first, the fruits of my labor soon became obvious. Students were demonstrating an increasing understanding of nursing concepts as a result of learning them in a more brain-compatible way. By the end of the first year, I was offering faculty workshops on creative learning methods that naturally engaged the brain to learn.

My passion for brain-compatible learning has since led me on a self-directed journey that has culminated with a doctoral degree in adult education. Every classroom became a dynamic learning lab as I applied my personal research on brain-compatible learning over the last 12 years. As a result, I have developed a wide variety of brain-compatible strategies appropriate for the sophisticated and self-directed adult learner. Brain-compatible strategies offer an alternative way of learning concepts that naturally engage the brain.

The bottom line is that when adult learners become empowered to use their personal learning strengths, creative potential becomes unleashed as the learner explores a variety of learning modalities. I have noticed that once learners understand how their brains actually learn, they gain more autonomy over their own learning. Consequently, learners become more invested in their learning, rising to the challenge with new energy, enthusiasm, and commitment.

Imagine how much different your teaching role would be if your students became interested, engaged, motivated, and responsible for their own learning. Imagine how easy it would be to assess learning outcomes if your students were able to demonstrate the ability to recall, comprehend, and apply complex information to other settings. I'm not talking about utopia; I'm talking about the realities of using a brain-compatible learning approach. Brain-compatible learning is a dynamic and interactive approach that promotes the brain's

Figure P.1   Benefits of Brain-Compatible Learning

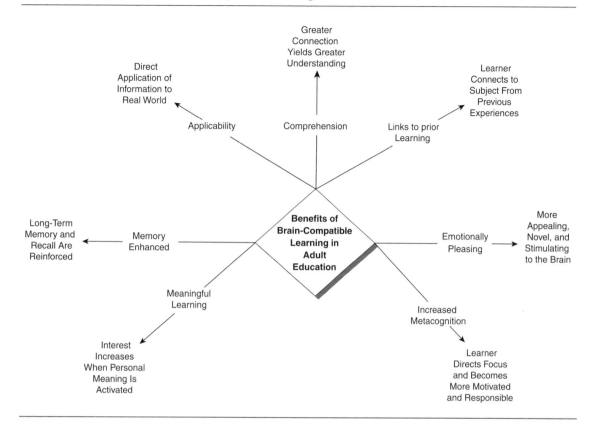

natural and infinite capacity to learn. A brain-compatible learning approach empowers both students and teachers to get the most out of the educational setting.

This book describes proven brain-compatible learning strategies along with useful information about how the adult brain learns best. The intent of this book is to promote awareness of how brain-compatible principles can be applied in any adult learning environment, formal as well as informal. It is not intended to be a complete reference on brain research; rather, it provides a more practical day-to-day application of brain research. For a more comprehensive understanding of how the brain learns, there are countless books on brain research and theory in any bookstore. However, educators who desire a more hands-on approach will appreciate the simplicity of this resource book.

Chapter 1 begins with a basic explanation of the structure and function of the brain as well as the principles of brain-compatible learning. Chapter 2 compares the younger brain with that of the adult learner and highlights benefits of using brain-compatible learning in adult settings. Chapter 3 introduces educators to the value of promoting and maintaining the resourceful learning state. Chapter 4 focuses on how educators can empower adults to make the most out of their unique blend of learning styles and talents. Chapter 5 features specific learning strategies that have been proven to be effective in both formal and informal

> "The mind is like a parachute—it functions best when open."
>
> —*Sir Robert Thomas Dewar*

adult learning situations. Chapter 6 demonstrates how lesson plans can be constructed using underlying principles of brain-compatible learning as a guiding framework.

Intrigued? I hope so! So, sit back and read on, leaving your mind open to new possibilities in a very old traditional educational paradigm.

Acknowledgments

With deep gratitude, I would first like to recognize the trust and faith extended to me by all of my students over the last 15 years as I have developed brain-compatible learning strategies for adults. Collectively, you have demonstrated the unique spirit of the adult learner for whom I have created this book. Without your enthusiasm and honest feedback, I would not have been as encouraged to develop my ideas.

I would also like to recognize the support of my faculty peers over the last 10 years at Milwaukee Area Technical College as I persistently shared ideas on how to use brain-compatible methodologies in the adult classroom. Your encouragement has helped me to direct my path in creating this book.

The contribution of reviewer David Sousa is gratefully acknowledged. Many thanks to all educators like him who have inspired me with their own works on brain-compatible teaching and learning.

About the Author

 **Laurie Materna**, PhD, has been a professor of nursing at Milwaukee Area Technical College, Milwaukee, Wisconsin, since 1996. She earned her doctoral degree in education through Capella University, Minneapolis, Minnesota, in 2000.

Among her areas of interest in brain research are the relationship between nutrition and learning, the use of graphic organizers to promote learning, and the development of learning styles and multiple intelligences in adult learners. Recognizing the unique learning needs of adults, she has integrated brain-compatible learning methodologies into nursing theory and clinical courses. In addition, Dr. Materna has coached many educators individually and through group in-service training sessions on developing brain-compatible strategies for specific classes.

Dr. Materna has spoken extensively on these areas to college and professional groups throughout the United States, and she presented at the Brain Expo in San Diego in January, 2005. She has also conducted focus groups among business and industry leaders to promote creative problem-solving and get employees to think outside the box. Dr. Materna has developed a brain-compatible nutritional snack, called Brain Fuel Energy Snack, based upon the nutrients required for optimal brain functioning.

You can obtain a 30-day free trial of the Inspiration 8.0 software program that was used to design the graphic organizers in this book from www.inspiration.com, or by calling 503-297-3004.

Please feel free to share your thoughts and personal application of brain-compatible learning strategies in the classroom. Send comments to

Laurie Materna, RN, PhD
Milwaukee Area Technical College
700 West State St.
Milwaukee, WI
e-mail: maternal@matc.edu

Part 1

Brain 101

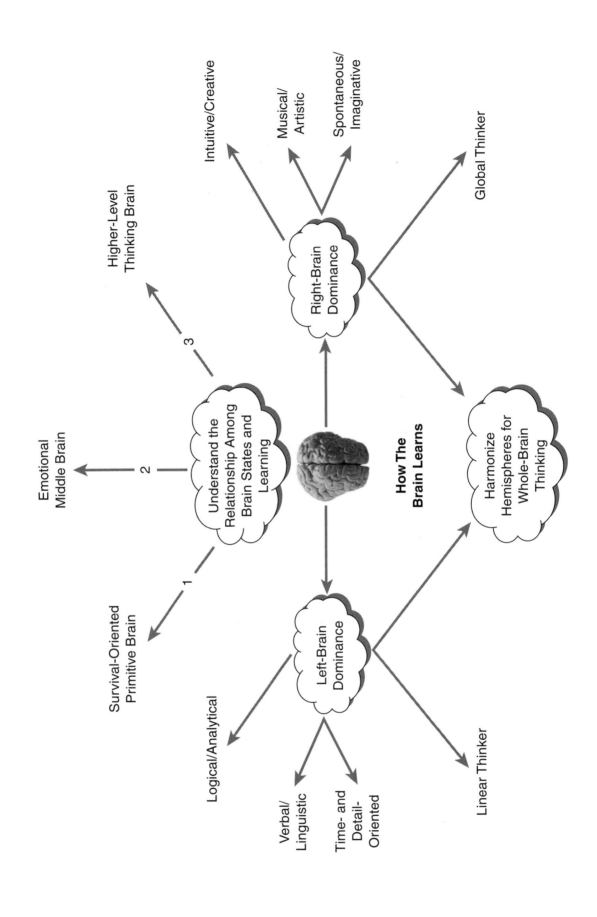

Intuitive/Creative

Musical/
Artistic

Spontaneous/
Imaginative

Higher-Level
Thinking Brain

Right-Brain
Dominance

Global Thinker

3

Understand the
Relationship Among
Brain States and
Learning

2

Emotional
Middle Brain

**How The
Brain Learns**

Harmonize
Hemispheres for
Whole-Brain
Thinking

Survival-Oriented
Primitive Brain

1

Left-Brain
Dominance

Logical/Analytical

Verbal/
Linguistic

Time- and
Detail-
Oriented

Linear Thinker

How the Brain Learns

A basic appreciation of how the human brain functions is essential for educators who strive to understand how brain research can be applied to learning. The intent of this chapter is to provide an educator's interpretation of structures in the brain as they relate to learning. From a neuroscientist's perspective, a basic explanation of the brain structures would be far more detailed than this simplistic perspective! Nevertheless, I suspect that a fundamental, nuts-and-bolts approach may be more appealing to most educators than a detailed neurological report. Those parts of the brain that have been linked to the learning process will be the focus of this description.

I strongly believe that once educators understand how information is processed, they will be more inclined to venture out of their comfort zone and begin using strategies that facilitate the natural learning process. Likewise, educating learners about how their brains learn best will empower learners to want to learn, which will actually make the educator's job easier. The traditional classroom atmosphere becomes transformed into an exciting and energetic learning environment where learners are stimulated and challenged to learn!

To help you understand how the brain works, the brain areas related to learning will be discussed as lower, middle, and upper brain structures, as shown in Figure 1.1. All three of these regions of the brain interact in very intricate and complex ways. At times, however, one particular region may be more dominant than the rest of the brain during the learning process.

THE LOWER BRAIN

The lower areas involved in the learning process include the brain stem and the cerebellum. Following is a brief description of how each of these areas is involved in the learning process.

Figure 1.1   Major Brain Areas

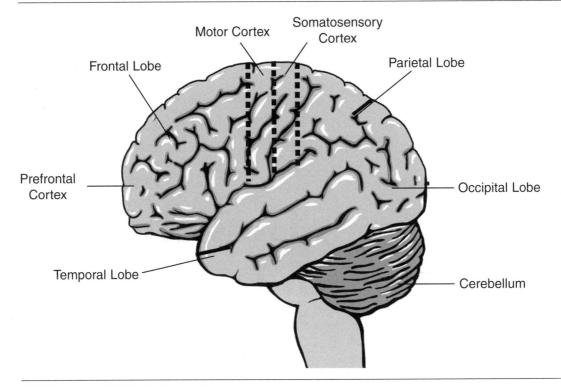

SOURCE: Sousa (2001). Used by permission.

The Brain Stem

The brain stem is positioned on top of the spinal column and is said to be the oldest part of the human brain from an evolutionary perspective. It is responsible for processing vital body functions such as heartbeat, respiration, temperature, and blood pressure. This structure focuses on survival and maintenance of the body. Like other lower and midbrain brain structures, it is responsible for the fight or flight response, enabling humans to run when danger is encountered in nature. Likewise, when the learner encounters threats within the classroom, the brain perceives this as a dangerous situation, and the survival mechanism takes over. At this point, all energies are directed toward self-preservation rather than processing new information.

The educator who understands the defensive nature of the lower and midbrain structures acknowledges that this instinctive response manifests in immediate behaviors. However, once the learner reregisters the threat as non-life-threatening, rational thought processes take over, and a more appropriate response is often generated. On the other hand, if the learner continues to perceive the environment, instructor, or content to be personally threatening, it may not be possible to shift out of lower brain functioning into the higher cognitive levels of creativity and problem-solving.

This survival mechanism actually takes precedence over logical thinking. Learning theorist Leslie Hart (1983) coined the term *downshifting* to describe this phenomenon. Alternatively, Mihaly Csikszentmihalyi (1990) coined the term *flow* to describe the optimal functioning state of the brain. Flow is that highest level of learning brought about by active engagement in a challenging and stimulating learning experience. Once a learner enters the flow state, intrinsic motivation and commitment to learning predominates. The learner finds the subject to be personally meaningful and therefore becomes personally committed to learning. Educators can eliminate downshifting and promote flow within the learning environment by promoting the resourceful learning state (Chapter 4) and utilizing many of the active learning strategies described in Chapter 5.

The lower brain also controls learner behaviors such as territorialism, ritualistic attention-getting behaviors, and social conformity behaviors. Have you ever noticed, for example, how learners will file into a classroom and sit in the same seat or general area along with the same group of learning peers every class period? When forced to move into a new territory, there is an obvious display of discomfort and annoyance. Settling-in socializing at the beginning of class and packing-up rituals at the end of class are prime examples of ritualistic behaviors expressed by learners.

The Cerebellum

Just below the rear of the cerebrum is the cerebellum. This area is integral to movement, as it coordinates motor tasks, balance, and posture. It also stores kinesthetic memories of past activities for future reference, such as riding a bike or typing on a keyboard. Recent research reveals that the cerebellum also works with the cortex in processing information and coordinating thoughts (Leiner & Leiner, 1997).

Based on their research, Henrietta and Alan Leiner have found that the cerebellum contains more neurons than all of the other parts of the brain combined and can process the information it receives from other parts of the brain quickly and efficiently. The lateral part of the cerebellum is able to communicate with the cerebral cortex by sending out signals through a segregated bundle of nerve fibers. As a result of this bundling of fibers, the cerebellum is able to communicate complex information back and forth to the cerebral cortex at lightning speeds. Information from sensory, motor, cognitive, language, and emotional areas of the cerebral cortex is transmitted through more than 40 million nerve fibers. The combination of movement and thought yields full activation and integration of the brain, thus expanding brain circuitry significantly. The result is that memories are etched into many more areas of the brain, making them easier to retrieve.

Educational implications of this research suggest that the cerebellum is integral in mental performance as well as motor performance and sensory function. The Leiners theorize that the cerebellum makes predictions, based on past performance, about the internal conditions necessary in other regions of the brain to perform motor tasks. The cerebellum automatically prepares those internal conditions in the involved areas of the brain for optimal performance. In other words, the cerebellum actually monitors other areas of the brain and intervenes automatically to improve performance. Experimental evidence has shown that the cerebellum allows motor tasks to be performed automatically and accurately after mental and motor rehearsal. However, because the cerebellum is also connected to regions of the brain associated with mental and sensory tasks, it can also automate mental and sensory skills.

In another study, Karni et al. (1995) demonstrated activation in the primary motor cortex during hand movement activities. These studies validate other findings on neural plasticity and changes in neural structure in response to visual and motor learning (Eriksson et al., 1998; Gould, Beylin, Tanapat, & Shors, 1999) and also validate the principle that the brain processes information by activating multiple brain centers. In addition, recent fMRI (functional magnetic resonance imaging) research related to the role of the cerebellum in motor skill learning indicates that the cerebellum works in concert with activation of motor-related cortical regions to initiate movement sequences (Doyan et al., 2002).

These researchers have contributed significantly to the current understanding of the cerebellum. The implication of these contributions for adult education is that they could certainly make the classroom a more productive environment. If a learner can perform mental tasks without conscious attention to detail, more areas of the brain can be accessed for cognitive processing. By combining movement with mental and sensory rehearsal of new learning, concepts are more likely to be retained automatically.

Meeting the Needs of the Lower Brain in the Adult Classroom

Although the time-honored behaviors of the lower brain may interrupt the flow of class, educators cannot dismiss these instinctive rituals. They can, however, acknowledge the need to express such behaviors by incorporating opening and closing activities, such as collaborative group previews before the introduction of new material and wrap-up reviews at the end of the class period. Eric Jensen (2000) has introduced many classroom rituals to get younger students excited about learning.

Following his lead, I have developed a modified list of positive and productive classroom rituals that can be incorporated into the adult learning environment (see Table 1.1).

Table 1.1   Positive and Productive Classroom Rituals

Start of class	• Write warm-up brainteasers on chalk board. (See Resource A for a collection of brainteasers.) • Greet learners at door; allow five socializing minutes.
During class	• Group learners by teams for collaborative work. • Celebrate learner contributions with positive feedback.
End of class	• Use review games to reinforce concepts. • Conduct a visualization exercise that highlights the major concepts that were covered in the class. • Have students do free-flow journaling covering major concepts learned. • Play background music while learners share self-assessment of learning.

To integrate movement into learning, I have at least two brain breaks an hour during my presentations. Brain breaks give adult learners the opportunity to process information using the kinesthetic-tactile preference, by getting up, moving around, and discussing topics with others. When learners combine movement with mental and sensory rehearsal of new learning, using visual and auditory modalities, they are more likely to retain concepts automatically.

> "The more we use our brains, the more brains we have to use."
>
> *–G. A. Dewey*

Here are several movement strategies that I have adapted to the adult learning environment:

- Offer a group stretching and breathing exercise every 30 minutes.
- Integrate hands-on activities into the lesson plan.
- Invite learners to get up and move around as needed to keep energized.
- Create cooperative group activities such as role-playing or skits of concepts.
- Walk and talk to review concepts during class breaks.

THE MIDDLE BRAIN

After the brain stem and cerebellum, the next brain area to evolve was the limbic system, also known as the middle brain, which includes the amygdala, hippocampus, hypothalamus, pineal gland, thalamus, and nucleus accumbens. The middle brain controls the hormonal system and is responsible for maintaining immunity as well as the primal drives for food, sex, and nurturing. The middle-brain structures that have been linked to learning are the thalamus, hippocampus, and amygdala.

According to neuroscientist Richard Restak (2003), every emotional response and perception can be linked to the limbic structures within the middle brain. Additionally, Restak maintains that these structures work with the prefrontal cortex to mediate the emotional response to violence and aggression. In other words, when an aggressive or violent emotional response occurs to an event that is perceived as a threat, the prefrontal cortex is activated to act as sort of a shock absorber, tempering the actual response to a socially acceptable level. Functional neuroimaging techniques, used to map the neural networks activated in response to emotions, have linked the circuitry of the amygdala with that of the anterior cingulated cortex (Restak, 2003). As a result, according to Restak, individuals who have sustained damage to the anterior cingulated cortex show little emotional response.

The Thalamus

The thalamus initially processes all sensory information except for smells. In other words, all incoming information, including sights, sounds, and tactile stimuli, is interpreted in this area first before being sent on to other areas of the brain for processing. Thus the thalamus contributes significantly to a learner's ability to pay attention. According to Robert Sylwester (1995), the thalamus acts as a relay center between the sense organs and the cortex where higher-level processing takes place, thereby determining what is worth attending to. The thalamus holds important information within our attention and short-term memory systems while ignoring less important sensory information, such as environmental sounds and activity.

The Hippocampus

The hippocampus is responsible for making meaning out of stored memories and converting information from working memory to long-term memory. This process varies in individuals and may take several weeks to several months. The hippocampus is constantly comparing and contrasting stored memories with incoming information in an attempt to make sense out of the new information. The hippocampus primarily stores factual or semantic memories, while the amygdala focuses on emotional memories (Restak, 2003). Recent fMRI studies by Dr. Michael Zeineh have demonstrated subdivisions within the hippocampus that undergo distinct changes as learning occurs (Zeineh, Engel, Thompson, & Bookheimer, 2003). The fMRI studies showed that certain parts of the hippocampus integral to memory and recall became highly active during the time that subjects were asked to remember specific criteria. The left prefrontal cortex also interacted significantly with the hippocampus during information encoding and retrieval, according to Zeineh.

Conversely, Restak (2003) explains that MRI studies of persons suffering from depression actually show atrophy of the hippocampus, which explains why depression often leads to memory problems. Treatment with antidepressants, according to Restak, prevents the atrophy and actually increases the hippocampal volume by allowing neurons to branch out. Research such as this may have important implications for development of additional drugs to improve memory.

The Amygdala

The amygdala stores the emotional component of a long-term memory. When the memory is recalled, the attached emotions are experienced with it, positive as well as negative. Although other areas of the brain also process emotion, the majority of emotional processing, especially the processing of fear, occurs between the amygdala and the cortex (Dolan, 2002). Neuroscience researchers Larry Squire and Eric Kandel, in their book *Memory: From Mind to Molecules* (1999), have contributed significantly to the body of research on emotional processing of information. In particular, they have shown that negative emotions have a detrimental effect upon learners of any age.

Functional MRI studies led by neuroscientist Ahmad R. Hariri have demonstrated that responses to fearful stimuli result in a strong bilateral amygdala response, particularly in the prefrontal and anterior cingulate cortices (Hariri, Bookheimer, & Mazziotta, 2000; Hariri, Mattay, Tessitore, Francesco, & Weinberger, 2003). In another study, both positive and negative stimuli were found to activate amygdaloid and basal forebrain regions (Liberzon, Phan, Docker, & Taylor, 2003), validating the theory that these regions are involved in general emotional processing.

Neuroscientist Turhan Canli examined responses in the brain relative to personality types. He found that women with extrovert personalities exhibited greater brain activity in the amygdala with positive stimuli than with negative stimuli. In contrast, women with introvert personalities, as well as women who had depressed or neurotic personalities, exhibited no brain activity in the amygdala in response to positive stimuli but had high levels of brain activity in response to negative stimuli (Caine, Caine, & Crowell, 1999). These studies indicate that individual differences in brain response to emotional stimuli are linked to personality and emotional well-being. Extroverts also exhibited greater blood flow to the amygdala than the other personality types. In another study (Canli, Zhao, Brewer, Gabrieli, & Cahill, 2000), Canli and colleagues found that individual experiences of intense emotional stimuli correlated with memory of those stimuli. Their findings demonstrated that activation in the left region of the amygdala enhances memory of the emotional intensity of experiences.

These studies help to validate the role of emotions in learning and memory. Implications for educators are huge: They should keep the learning environment free from threat, and be aware of their own body language and gestures that may suggest negativity. Adult learners who have previously experienced threat and negativity in the classroom are especially vulnerable to hints of displeasure from instructors.

Emotions and Memory

The role of emotions in learning has been researched widely by neuroscientists and psychologists (Clore, 2000; Damasio, 1994, 1999; Dolan, 2002; LeDoux, 1996; Milner, 1999; Pert, 1997; Restak, 2003; Schacter, 2001; Squire & Kandel, 1999) over the last decade. Results indicate that although the middle brain area is considered the root of all emotion, it actually influences all areas of the brain as well as the body, binding them together through a chain reaction of brain chemicals referred to as neurotransmitters. Neurotransmitters are responsible for communication between neurons. According to Candace Pert, dopamine, serotonin, acetylcholine, and norepinephrine are the predominant neurotransmitters that influence behavior of learners (Pert, 1997).

Once these neurotransmitters are released in response to emotions perceived in the learning environment, the body's response, which can be measured through EEGs (electroencephalograms) and MRIs as well as through changes in vital signs and skin color, temperature, and feel, may be sustained for an indefinite period of time. Psychologist Daniel Schacter suggests that emotional events become emblazoned in our memories because of the simultaneous release of stress hormones and neurotransmitters, which mark the event with special significance and give it prominence in the memory pathways (Schacter, 1996). Schacter asserts that emotional memories generally receive greater attention and become elaboratively encoded, giving the memory an emotional boost. This emotional boost extends to both positive and negative memories, with negative memories being recalled in greater detail. Response to emotionally charged events become strengthened and reinforced when people simply discuss the events with other people (Schacter, 2001).

Emotions and Learning

In the learning environment, the brain immediately attends to emotionally activated stimuli, influencing pathways used to process information at higher cognitive levels. According to neuroscientist Joseph LeDoux, if the emotion is positive, the brain becomes aroused, focusing attention, memory, and higher-level thinking skills on the learning. Alternatively, if the emotion is negative, the brain downshifts to the primitive survival-mode brain state, and learning may become inhibited (LeDoux, 1996). Dr. Antonio Damasio (1994) argues that emotions are not separate from the body and actually affect the way a person feels and thinks about learning. From this perspective, it can be summed up that emotions influence all learning.

The intensity of the emotion, according to Peter Milner, may assist in the recall process. Stronger emotions promote greater recall, while engaging too few emotions in the learning process tends to cause learners to quickly forget material unless it is rehearsed repeatedly (Milner, 1999). Therefore, according to Raymond Dolan (2002), when learners elicit a strong emotional response during learning, they may not require any rehearsal for total recall to be initiated. Gerald Clore (2000) maintains that the best learning environments provide both positive and negative feedback in the form of a challenging activity. In this way, learners use what they already know and build upon that knowledge as they rise to the challenge of learning something new.

Daniel Goleman (1995) states that emotional intelligence has far more influence over how a person responds to any given situation than rational intellect. The middle brain is integral in the learning process, because emotional arousal activates the release of those neurotransmitters, which initiate attention and burn the memories into long-term storage. For example, when individuals remember something that involves strong emotions, it is generally remembered in vivid detail. Likewise, any learning activity that generates strong emotions most likely will yield the same results.

The middle brain also acts as an emotional clearinghouse for the brain. When new information is taken in that is emotionally pleasing, it is transferred through to the cortex (thinking brain). However, if the incoming information is perceived in a negative way, the middle brain prohibits this information from reaching the thinking brain and downshifts to the primitive brain to preserve self-integrity (see Figure 1.2). Consequently, if learners are stressed, anxious, or concerned, even at the subconscious level, they are less likely to learn effectively, as their attention is directed to survival.

Paul MacLean brought the nation's attention to the role of emotions in the learning process in the late 1970s. MacLean's work suggests that emotions are critical to learning and that educators detract from the meaningfulness of the content for learners if they ignore the emotional component of the content being taught. So closely tied are emotions and learning that MacLean claims that the middle brain insists that learners feel that something is true before it is believed and integrated into long-term memory (MacLean, 1978).

According to MacLean, the middle brain tempers humans' basic primitive responses by inhibiting ritualistic behaviors. As a result, our instinctive and rational behaviors are linked in this region of the brain. Subsequently, when

Figure 1.2   How Emotions Affect Learning

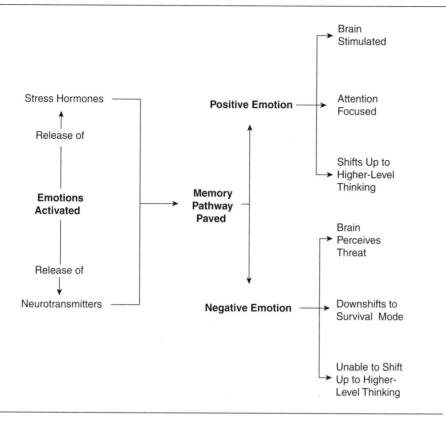

the middle brain experiences strong emotion (positive or negative), the brain focuses on that emotion over and above any other incoming information.

Since MacLean's seminal research on emotions and learning was first published, educators as well as psychologists have promoted using a positive emotional climate to enhance learning as well as personal competence (Jensen, 2000; LeDoux, 1996; Levinthal, 1988; Mills, 1987; Schacter, 2001; Sousa, 2001; Sylwester, 1995). The general consensus is that when learners feel emotionally balanced and challenged in a nonthreatening manner, they feel good emotionally as well as physically. The overall attitude of the teacher also plays a huge part in the learner's emotional well-being. Negative nonverbal expressions and gestures on the part of the teacher convey the message, "I really don't want to be here!" This can be quite devastating for learners of all ages. However, adult learners, who are trying to balance home, work, family, and school, may be put on the defensive or become quite insulted. Either way, the learner tends to downshift to the primitive survival state, where little if any learning takes place (see Figure 1.3).

Meeting the Needs of the Middle Brain in the Adult Classroom

Considering the influence of emotions upon learning, I have found that taking the time to consider the emotional needs of the learner is critical, especially in

Figure 1.3 Three Brains in One

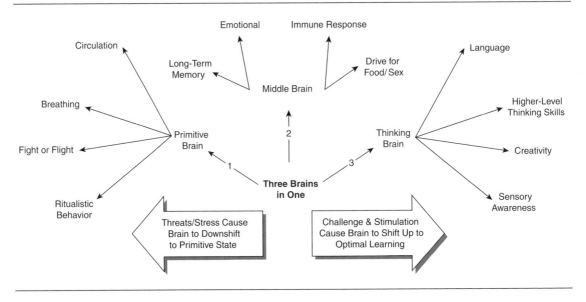

the adult learning environment. Adults live multidimensional lives and often come into class with excessive baggage in terms of family and work-related concerns. During times like this, they are more concerned with their own personal lives than with taking in the lesson of the day. If the educator does not take the time to de-stress the learners, they may be stuck in their own emotional brains. When this happens, it is almost impossible to shift up into the thinking brain.

Here are a few methods I have used for creating an emotionally balanced learning environment:

- Have upbeat music playing at the start of class, as learners are coming in.
- Greet learners by name as they come in; exchange pleasantries.
- Ensure that the learning environment is adequately lit and thermoregulated.
- Introduce objectives for the learning unit at the start of class, and reinforce what was covered in the previous class to set the context for new learning.

> "Our feelings are our most genuine and direct paths to knowledge."
>
> *–Audrie Lorde*

- Encourage voluntary sharing of opinions, personal experiences, and ideas at appropriate times. Ensure that learners have the full attention of the rest of the class, and thank them for sharing afterwards.
- Pay attention to the impact of your own verbal and nonverbal body language on learners' facial and body expressions, behaviors, and verbal responses (or lack of responses).
- Set realistic assignment expectations, and be flexible with deadlines.
- Encourage input from adult learners in planning class activities and assignments.
- Elicit feedback in the form of course evaluations, share results, and use feedback to modify the learning environment as necessary.

THE UPPER BRAIN

The upper brain region is the most recent part of the brain to develop. The wrinkled gray matter that is often associated with images of the brain is called the cerebrum. It is covered by a thin layer called the neocortex, where most thinking occurs. The outer surface of the cerebrum is divided into four lobes: the frontal, occipital, parietal, and temporal (see Figure 1.4). Each of these lobes is responsible for specific brain functions, as shown in Table 1.2.

Right and Left Hemispheres of the Upper Brain

The cerebrum is further separated into left and right hemispheres by a thick band of nerve fibers called the corpus callosum. This band communicates

Table 1.2   The Four Lobes of the Cerebrum

Lobe	*Location*	*Function*
Frontal	Across front of cerebrum	Higher-level thinking Home of working memory
Occipital	Across middle back of cerebrum	Visual processing
Parietal	Across upper back of cerebrum	Sensory and language processing
Temporal	Above ears, both sides	Hearing, memory, meaning

Figure 1.4   Diagram of Brain Lobes

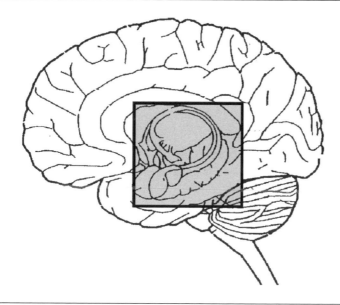

SOURCE: Sousa (2001). Used by permission.

between hemispheres, combining left- and right-brain processing specialties into whole-brain learning. Neuropsychologist Elkhonon Goldberg (2001) points out that the two hemispheres are not mirror images of each other, as the right frontal lobe is wider, protruding over the left lobe. The left occipital lobe is wider and protrudes over the right occipital lobe. Additionally, the frontal cortex is thicker on the right as opposed to the left hemisphere (Goldberg, 2001). Goldberg maintains that brain chemistry is also asymmetric. Dopamine is more widespread in the left hemispheres, while norepinephrine is more common in the right hemisphere (Goldberg, 2001).

Cognitive researchers suggest that the two halves of the brain possess very distinct characteristics. The left hemisphere has long been linked to language skills, while the right has been associated with spatial processing. Although the left hemisphere is the dominant side in most people (even left-handed people), information is not processed exclusively in the left hemisphere. In fact, the brain processes information not only from the left to right, but also from the brainstem to the cortex and from the back to front of the brain. Goldberg and Costa (1981) have researched the theory that the right hemisphere is more adept at processing novel information and the left hemisphere more adept at processing routine and familiar information. Thus they contend that because the brains of humans possess a powerful drive for learning, it is possible that the structural and chemical differences between the two hemispheres may have evolved as a result of a greater push to acquire more knowledge and skills over the years.

Functional MRI images of specific changes in brain regions during visual learning activities have revealed an initial progression from right-brain processing, specifically in the frontal and parietal regions, to bilateral brain processing (Seger et al., 2000). Left hemispheric activation resulted from abstract visual stimulation, and left frontal activation was evident when successful learning occurred. Interestingly, studies measuring activation for conceptual priming tasks demonstrate a decrease in activity in the left frontal cortex (Demb et al., 1995), while studies measuring perceptual priming tasks demonstrate decreases in activity in the occipital cortex (Poldrack, Desmond, Glover, & Gabridi, 1998). Results from these studies indicate that the brain processes different kinds of information in different ways and that different types of learning activities are linked to specific memory storage systems, resulting in specific neural restructuring.

With significant advances in image technology, neuroscientists are able to look inside the living brain and determine activity patterns in response to emotions, behaviors, and learning activities (Canli et al., 2001; Greene et al., 2001; Restak, 2003). With this in mind, it is helpful for educators to understand the processing characteristics of both hemispheres of the brain, and to offer whole-brain activities that engage both hemispheres.

Brain Dominance

Nobel Prize winner Roger Sperry initiated studies in the 1960s on the differences between the brain's right and left hemispheres. His discovery that the left hemisphere processes information logically, rationally, and analytically, in a sequential manner, while the right hemisphere processes information intuitively, by integrating, synthesizing, and recognizing relationships has paved the way for many researchers in this area. Ned Herrmann significantly enhanced Sperry's earlier studies by further defining hemispheric function and dominance (1989). Going back to Goldberg's (2001) theory that the right brain processes novel information and the left brain processes routine information, the once-novel soon becomes the routine, and changes in routine become somewhat novel. Goldberg contends that there is a dynamic interaction between the two hemispheres that may be controlled in part by cognitive processes and in part by anatomical differences among individuals. Evidence obtained through MRI and positron emission tomography (PET) backs up these associations of novel processing with the left hemisphere and routine processing with the right hemisphere (Goldberg, 2001).

Left-Brain Thinkers

Goldberg's (2001) theory of left-brain processing supports what Herrmann (1989) found: The left hemisphere is where the majority of conscious thinking processes occur. It is accessed for writing, reading, and speaking. Thinking in the left brain follows a linear and sequential pattern leading from the parts to the whole. Because of this, the left-brain-dominant thinker prefers to deal with inputs one at a time. The left-brain-dominant thinker needs to analyze all of the facts before understanding how concepts come together. The left hemisphere specialties include verbal expression as well as analytical and detail-oriented thinking. The left brain more readily recognizes words, numbers, and letters. Persons with left-brain dominance are more linear types of learners and prefer a step-by-step build-up of information. Left-brain-dominant learners are generally detail oriented and prefer a structured and orderly learning environment with minimal changes in learning outcomes.

Left-Brain Teachers

Teachers with left-brain dominance tend to teach the same way they learn, presenting detailed lecture notes and following an outline provided to the class. Minimal visuals are used during the presentation. They stay focused and keep track of the time. If time allows, learners are given problems or scenarios to solve independently. Group discussion or individual questions from learners are discouraged, as this cuts into the time needed to deliver the content. These teachers' classrooms are orderly and well managed. Left-brain-dominant learners love this type of structured, predictable environment, while right-brain-dominant learners are begging for illustrations and diagrams.

Right-Brain Thinkers

The right hemisphere of the brain is where the majority of nondominant cognitive functions occur, including awareness of feelings (Herrmann, 1989) and processing of novel information (Goldberg, 2001). It is here where options are explored, images are visualized, and imagination is nurtured. Right-brain thinking perceives concepts from whole to parts. Because of this, the right-brain-dominant thinker can handle many inputs one at a time. Persons with right-brain dominance are more global types of learners and prefer the big-picture approach to learning. As a result, this type of thinker is more likely to understand where the lesson is going before receiving all of the details. The right hemisphere specialties include melody, pattern recognition, intuition, and spontaneous thought. The right brain more readily recognizes faces, places, and objects. Right-brain-dominant learners prefer an open, spontaneous learning environment and are much more tolerant of ambiguity and unpredictable learning outcomes.

Right-Brain Teachers

The right-brain-dominant teacher is very much like the right-brain-dominant learner. Information is presented using many visuals, diagrams, and hands-on models. Discussion and hands-on learning is welcomed and even encouraged. Learners are frequently engaged in projects and may even be given the opportunity to solve problems outside of the classroom. The classroom itself could be inside, outside, or just about anyplace that is conducive to learning. Right-brain-dominant learners connect well with this style of teaching, while left-brain-dominant learners are often frustrated and asking for more structure. Table 1.3 summarizes the differences in right- and left-brain specialization.

The test in Figure 1.5 will help you see where you are in terms of brain dominance. It may help you understand why you have a preference for some of the teaching activities you are most comfortable with!

WHOLE-BRAIN LEARNING

As mentioned previously, both right and left hemispheres are highly interactive while learning and are continuously communicating with each other through the corpus callosum. Learners truly need the interaction of both hemispheres to process information effectively. Left-brain processes, such as writing and giving a speech, are enriched and supported by creative right-brain processes such as

Table 1.3   Upper Brain Areas: Right/Left-Brain Specialization

Left-Brain-Dominant Learner	Right-Brain-Dominant Learner
Prefers using logic, math, and language skills	Spatially oriented
	Recognizes patterns readily
Analytical	Intuitive
Time oriented	Creative/musical
Linear, sequential thinker	Spontaneous, global thinker
Perceives parts to whole	Perceives whole to parts
Prefers inputs one at a time	Prefers multiple inputs
Remembers words, numbers, letters	Remembers places, faces, objects
Prefers structured learning	Prefers open, unstructured learning
Intolerant of changes in lesson	Tolerant of ambiguity in lesson

Figure 1.5   Cognitive Style Alert Scale

The Alert Scale of Cognitive Style

Circle the one sentence that is most true in each pair. Do not leave any items uncircled.

1. A   It's fun to take risks.

    B   I have fun without taking risks.

2. A   I look for new ways to do old jobs.

    B   When one way works well, I don't change it.

3. A   I begin many jobs that I never finish.

    B   I finish a job before starting a new one.

4. A   I'm not very imaginative in my work.

    B   I use my imagination in everything I do.

5. A   I can analyze what is going to happen next.

    B   I can sense what is going to happen next.

6. A   I try to find the one best way to solve a problem.

    B   I try to find different answers to problems.

7. A   My thinking is like pictures going through my head.

    B   My thinking is like words going through my head.

8. A   I agree with new ideas before other people do.

    B   I question new ideas more than other people do.

9. A   Other people don't understand how I organize things.

    B   Other people think I organize well.

10. A   I have good self-discipline.

    B   I usually act on my feelings.

11. A   I plan time for doing my work.

    B   I don't think about the time when I work.

12. A   With a hard decision, I choose what I know is right.

    B   With a hard decision, I choose what I feel is right.

(Continued)

Figure 1.5 (Continued)

13. A   I do easy things first and important things later.

     B   I do the important things first and the easy things later.

14. A   Sometimes in a new situation, I have too many ideas.

     B   Sometimes in a new situation, I don't have any ideas.

15. A   I have to have a lot of change and variety in my life.

     B   I have to have an orderly and well-planned life.

16. A   I know I'm right, because I have good reasons.

     B   I know I'm right, even without good reasons.

17. A   I spread my work evenly over the time I have.

     B   I prefer to do my work at the last minute.

18. A   I keep everything in a particular place.

     B   Where I keep things depends on what I'm doing.

19. A   I have to make my own plans.

     B   I can follow anyone's plans.

20. A   I am a very flexible and unpredictable person.

     B   I am a consistent and stable person.

21. A   With a new task, I want to find my own way of doing it.

     B   With a new task, I want to be told the best way to do it.

To Score

Give yourself one point for each time you answered "A" for questions
1, 2, 3, 7, 8, 9, 13, 14, 15, 19, 20, 21
Give yourself one point for each time you answered "B" for questions
4, 5, 6, 10, 11, 12, 16, 17, 18
Add all points
0–4 = strong left brain
5–8 = moderate left brain
9–13 = middle brain
14–16 = moderate right brain
17–21 = strong right brain

SOURCE: Crane (1989). Reprinted with permission of Dr. Loren D. Crane.

visualization, intuitive insight, and pattern recognition. Right-brain processes, such as producing a work of art or a piece of music, require a significant amount of analytical left-brain thinking in the early planning stages. All in all, whole-brain learning uses the creative-intuitive mind as well as the critical-logical mind to accomplish a variety of learning goals.

Whole-Brain Teaching

Learners who find themselves in class with a teacher who has similar brain dominance, as well as learners who find their teacher has a different approach to teaching than they have to learning, will benefit from whole-brain learning activities. Ideally, strengthening the hemisphere that is less dominant will help learners (and teachers) to become more well rounded in their processing abilities.

To do this, based on your personal brain dominance, select at least two or three new teaching activities that you could get comfortable with. For example, if you traditionally use PowerPoint or overhead presentations, add a little color and graphics to go with the text. Conversely, if you don't use any structured type of content delivery system, try putting at least the main points in outline format for students who need the structure. Shorten the lecture portion of the class, and add more hands-on activities. Offer learners the option to work in groups and discuss learning objectives.

Figure 1.6 has some general guidelines for reaching both right-brain-dominant and left-brain-dominant learners. Part 3 of this book is full of dynamic whole-brain learning strategies. Have fun and be creative; everything else will follow!

Engaging both hemispheres simultaneously is a sure way to reach almost any type of thinker. In fact, making learners aware of how to combine left- and right-brain specialties will empower and prepare learners for almost any type of learning environment. Likewise, engaging adults in the natural process of learning will promote higher brain processing (flow) and prevent learners from shifting down into the defensive, survival-oriented primitive brain state (downshifting).

Flow and Downshift

Generally speaking, when adults are processing information at a higher cognitive level, they are utilizing their upper brains. Problem-solving activities that require analysis, synthesis, and evaluation along with a touch of creativity and flexibility will engage both the right and left hemispheres as well as promote whole-brain thinking. Just as important, however, educators must recognize those activities that cause learners to downshift from higher-level upper-brain processing to lower levels of primitive brain functioning. As Table 1.4 shows, almost every learning environment that promotes downshifting can be turned around to facilitate flow.

UPPER-BRAIN PROCESSING

The upper-brain areas control writing, speech, and language centers. Much of the processing of sensory data takes place in the upper brain. It is also here that

Figure 1.6   Whole-Brain Teaching

Whole-Brain Teaching

Before you change anything, let students know the importance of incorporating a whole-brain approach.

- Offer both structured outlines and graphic organizers for students to follow during presentations.

- Incorporate more visuals and hands-on learning props in the classroom.

- Demonstrate the big picture and separate it into parts; then review by incorporating the parts into the whole.

- Offer learners the option of working alone or in small groups to problem-solve.

- Be attentive to cues from learners who are left-brain-dominant or right-brain-dominant learners.

- Offer both structured content delivery and open group discussion during the class period.

- Encourage both right-brain-dominant and left-brain-dominant learners to share in discussion and activities.

- Be flexible in assigning projects; they might include diagrams, role-playing, debate, panel discussions, or individual writing or speaking assignments.

- Interact with learners one-on-one as well as in small groups.

Most important, be tolerant of and receptive to the differences you notice in learners!

Table 1.4   Flow and Downshift: Facilitators and Barriers to the Natural Learning Process

Facilitating Flow: The learner . . .	*Downshifting: The learner . . .*
1. participates in planning personal learner outcomes.	1. has no choice in personal learning outcomes.
2. perceives the learning environment as a low threat and a high challenge.	2. perceives the learning environment as threatening and without challenge.
3. is in a relaxed and resourceful learning state.	3. is in a state of high anxiety and frustration over learning.
4. feels that his or her personal life experiences contribute toward learning new material.	4. does not receive credit and validation for personal life experiences.
5. is able to collaborate with peers to learn new concepts.	5. is required to sit quietly and listen to a lecture.
6. helps decide how learning will be evaluated.	6. has no effect on the decision as to how learning will be evaluated.
7. appreciates that outcomes are explained in a meaningful whole before being broken down into parts.	7. is frustrated by outcomes that are broken down into trivial fragments that the brain cannot assign meaning to.
8. is able to pace his or her learning experiences.	8. must keep up with the pace of the instructor.
9. is able to learn new content in preferred learning modality.	9. is forced to absorb information through auditory channels.
10. understands the relevance of the content being taught.	10. has no idea what the relevance of the content is to learning.
11. is able to associate previous learning with the new content being taught.	11. cannot associate the meaning of previous material to the new content being taught.
12. is given the time to actively process and assign meaning to new information.	12. passively sits through a didactic lecture without interaction or application of learning.
13. uses multiple sensory channels to process information.	13. is given new information through one sensory channel.
14. gets excited and emotionally involved in the new content.	14. becomes bored, and his or her mind drifts away from the content.
15. is stimulated by novel and unique learning experiences.	15. is subject to learning in the same way for every unit of study.

higher cognitive skills such as analyzing, problem solving, reflection, visualization, and creative thinking take place. Different regions tend to handle different areas of cognitive function. For example, the frontal lobe controls abstract reasoning, while the parietal lobe processes information from the senses, the temporal lobes process hearing and language, and the occipital lobe processes sight. Although it was once assumed that each of these areas functioned independently, recent PET scans and fRMIs indicate that a vast majority of the brain is active at any given time (Canli et al., 2001; Doyan et al., 2002; Hariri et al., 2000, 2003).

This dynamic interaction allows the brain to quickly access information throughout the brain related to a single thought. The more novel and challenging the stimulation is, the more the brain thrives and grows. What an empowering thought for educators and learners: We all have the ability and brain capacity to learn an infinite amount of knowledge—at any age!

Early research by Karl Pribram (1971) maintains that the structures within the cerebral cortex work together to detect and make patterns out of incoming information. It is within the cortex that raw information is deciphered, reorganized into patterns and relationships, and indexed for future reference. This, in fact, is one of the foundational principles of brain-compatible learning: the natural ability and propensity of the brain to elicit patterns of meaning. All people bring their own personal experiences into the learning environment, and the brain depends heavily upon these experiences or perceptions in developing patterns of association. Once new information is patterned and associated with personal experiences, learners are able to relate this information from one area to another and truly derive meaning from the information.

The cerebral cortex is also responsible for conscious and unconscious thought processes. German researchers Gert Pfurtscheller and Andrea Berghold (1989) found that the nonconscious mind actually acts before the conscious mind directs the body to act. In other words, before the brain is even consciously aware of thinking about an activity, the nonconscious mind is already acting upon that activity. More than 99 percent of all learning, according to Pfurtscheller and Berghold, is nonconscious. Implications for education are profound: Learners are unconsciously absorbing, interpreting, and acting upon environmental cues over and above the actual lesson presented to their conscious minds.

The Dangers of Multitasking

As a result of this dynamic interaction of cerebral activity, the human brain is able to multitask several activities at one time. However, Richard Restak (2003) warns us that multitasking may not be as efficient as we once thought. Restak asserts that switching back and forth from one task to another demands considerable energy and actually reduces the effectiveness with which we complete a single task. Most adults can relate to how difficult it is to focus attention on both talking on a cell phone and driving at the same time. Although society tends to promote multitasking, and most adults do multitask in order to meet the demands of their multiple life dimensions, they are not functioning at an optimal level. In terms of learning new information, the brain works most efficiently when working on one thing at a time.

Meeting the Needs of the Upper Brain in the Adult Classroom

The key to stimulating the upper brain is to get learners actively engaged in the process of learning. Here are some suggestions that I have successfully used for actively engaging the upper brain in the adult classroom setting:

- Avoid didactic lecturing if possible. An energetic and interactive discussion is much more stimulating.
- Provide frequent opportunities for learners to apply concepts in dynamic and collaborative groups.
- Structure debates, discussions, and simulations into the presentation.
- Use stimulating music and colorful and interactive media (short video clips).
- Limit the use of a long series of slides or transparencies.
- Interact with the audience; ask critical thinking questions.
- Move around while presenting, using animated gestures and fluctuating your voice throughout the presentation. Infuse your energy into your learners!
- Integrate colorful graphic organizers to demonstrate links between previous learning and new learning.
- Use figurative language, analogies, mnemonics, and metaphors to emphasize points.
- Eliminate distractions that may force attention away from the topic at hand.
- Be ENTHUSIASTIC and everything else will follow!

> "Anyone can learn anything . . . the only difference is that some take more time than others."
>
> —*Benjamin Bloom*

BRAIN CIRCUITRY AND TRANSMISSION OF THOUGHT

Throughout all regions of the brain, hundreds of billions of microscopic cells and interconnecting fibers are responsible for the transmission of thoughts, ideas, and responses, both physically and mentally. However, only 10 percent, or approximately one hundred billion cells, are neurons. The remaining 90 percent of brain cells, referred to as glial cells, support the neurons by supplying nutrients, repairing the brain following injury, and attacking invading bacteria.

Neurons are linked throughout the body, composing two major nerve networks. The central nervous system consists of the brain and spinal column, while the peripheral nervous system is the network of nerves throughout the rest of the body. A bundle of neurons is called a nerve. Nerves carry electrochemical signals, called nerve impulses, back and forth between the brain and the rest of the body. These nerve bundles can be thinner than a strand of hair or as thick as a nautical rope.

Neurons have a central cell body, branching extensions called dendrites, and a long wire-like extension called an axon. Axons are insulated by a protective myelin sheath that also helps conduct messages efficiently. Some axons may be as long as the length of the human body. The dendrites, which branch out from the center, pick up electrical activity from neighboring neurons and carry the signals toward the cell body, while the axons carry the signals away. The enlarged, distal end of each axon is called the synaptic knob. It is within this knob that neurotransmitters are manufactured, stored, and released. Each neuron is programmed to produce a specific type of neurotransmitter, which receptors on the dendrites respond to in response to thought.

In a split second, the neurotransmitters are quickly absorbed by the dendrites and transferred to the neuron center of the cell. Structurally, these connections, called synapses, change with repeated stimulation, thereby influencing the relationships between neurons. Each time the brain thinks a thought, these connections are fired up, modifying the electrochemical wiring. The more novel and stimulating the thought is, the more likely it will activate a new connection. Likewise, meaningless and trivial information is rejected by the brain or at best forms only a weak connection. Only those connections that are meaningful, rich, and deeply carved into the brain tissue trigger the electrochemical process that promotes long-term memory.

According to science writer Rita Carter, who wrote *Mapping the Mind* (1998), new neural connections are possible with every incoming thought and sensation; however, the thoughts begin to degenerate and disappear if they are not transferred into long-term memory. Those thought patterns that do connect with other memories form patterns of association that are constantly shifting and modifying as the brain continues to interact with the steady influx of new stimuli throughout life. Carter maintains that this dynamic feedback process ensures that patterns of thought related to survival are permanently laid, while connections that are less crucial fade away. Recent brain-scan imaging clearly demonstrates that incoming information is split into unique paths within the brain, branching out to either the right or left hemisphere (Seger et al., 2000).

Remarkably, each of the billions of neurons in the brain is capable of firing off an infinite number of messages simultaneously, allowing learners to multi-process, interpret, and store sensory data instantly. Over the years, more than half of a person's original brain cells decay through a naturally occurring process called pruning. However, recent neural research (Eriksson et al., 1998; Gould et al., 1998, 1999) reveals that new connections are produced in the hippocampus of adult learners in response to the challenge of learning. Although it was once believed that the total number of neurons gradually declined as humans aged regardless of mental stimulation, this new finding validates that the brain not only creates new cells throughout a lifetime but that the new cells live longer and grow stronger when the brain is actively engaged in new learning. This research is particularly exciting in terms of adult learning and supports the need for promoting learning activities that naturally engage adults' motivation, interest, and attention by drawing upon personal experiences.

Elkhonon Goldberg (2001) suggests that cognitive exercises designed to match specific cognitive functions provide the stimulation required to protect from degeneration and keep the adult brain cognitively fit. For example, activities requiring complex decision-making and memory skills exercise the frontal lobes, activities requiring visualization and imagining exercise the occipital lobes, activities that require hands-on and linguistic skills exercise the parietal lobe, and activities that require listening and perception exercise the temporal lobe.

To an adult educator, this amazing potential for brain cell plasticity at any age is one of the most exciting developments in brain-based research that has emerged over the last four decades. Barring structural damage or illness, individuals have the ability to become more intelligent every time they use their brains and stimulate their minds. It is stimulation and use that deepen and broaden the dendrite connections, thus increasing intelligent thought. That means the capacity of the human brain to learn is practically infinite! It is this complexity of neurons and dendrite connections that allows the brain to simultaneously process data continuously from our senses and to store and catalog every experience we have ever had throughout our lifetime.

Brain Synergy

The bottom line is that all parts of the brain interact and work together through neural connections in a very complex and synergistic way. The strategies in Part 3 of this book are designed to address the natural learning requirements of each area. Indeed, the avoidance of threat and bodily harm, the search for emotionally satisfying experiences, and the innate need for novelty and stimulation are the driving forces behind learning. Educators who are aware of the brain's ability to learn develop greater awareness of a wide variety of factors that ultimately may influence learning.

> "The limits to learning are largely self-imposed."
>
> —Colin Rose

Although it would be impossible to influence all of these variables, much can be done to respond to the brain's quest for meaning and challenge by understanding how information is processed and memories are stored and recalled in adult learners.

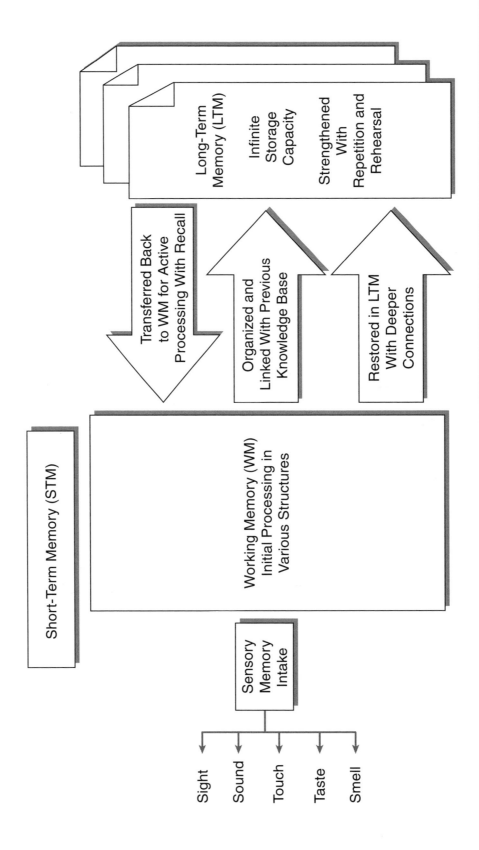

SOURCE: Adapted from Wolfe (2001).

Promotion of Learning

PROMOTION OF MEMORY AND INFORMATION PROCESSING IN ADULT LEARNERS

Learning is a dynamic and complex process that occurs quite naturally every moment of our lives. From the time we are born (some may argue even before birth), humans are taking in data through all available senses, determining what is worth remembering, and letting go of the rest. How does this happen? Why are some things more memorable than others are? Let's review the natural process of creating, transferring, and retaining information in long-term memory as well as the physiological effects of aging upon the adult brain. By understanding this process, educators will appreciate how the use of brain-compatible techniques promotes long-term memory in adult learners.

Creation and Storage of Memories

According to neuroscientists who have studied memory storage, when memories are created, they are not isolated to a single cell, but rather, stored throughout the brain areas in several cells (Courtney, Ungerleider, Keil, & Haxby, 1996; Funahashi, Bruce, & Goldman-Rakic, 1989). For example, auditory memories are stored in the temporal lobes of the neocortex, while visual memories are stored in the visual cortex. Kinesthetic memories are stored within the cerebellum. Personal learning styles impact how information is remembered. According to Colin Rose, author of *Accelerated Learning Action Guide* (1995), the two most dominant learning styles are visual (40–65 percent of learners) and auditory (approximately 25–30 percent of learners). The least dominant learning style, constituting only 5–15 percent of all learners, seems to be kinesthetic-tactile (Rose, 1995).

Think about your own personal experiences in trying to remember something very important, like your phone number, social security number, or a combination to a safe deposit box. Most people focus their energies on learning (selecting and attending) and rehearse and repeat the information over and over until they know it. Some people may repeat the information out loud (auditory learners), others may write it over and over (visual learners), while others may find it most helpful to finger a dial-pad or combination lock to get a feel for the information (kinesthetic-tactile learners). Better yet, using all of these modalities (multisensory learning) will increase the likelihood of getting the information into long-term memory. Ideally, using teaching methods that address all three learning styles will assist learners in creating memories using all three memory styles, thus yielding more well-rounded learners as well.

Encoding—or forming a permanent memory, visually, auditorily, and kinesthetically—increases the number of places in the brain where the memory is stored. Because the brain undergoes actual physical and biochemical changes when it stores memories, existing neural pathways are strengthened, and new neural pathways are created. These complex neural networks become more dynamic as more and more memories are created. Encoding memories in a multisensory way enriches the neural pathways and ensures stability of the memory as well as the probability of recall when needed.

These neural connections are further strengthened when the learner rehearses the memory. Practice and repetition increase the sensitivity of the neural dendrites to the initial stimulation. By simply thinking about an event or process over and over, for example, the connections are essentially etched into the brain cells. This mechanism is termed long-term potentiation (LTP): the biological process of strengthening synaptic plasticity to enhance memory formation (Squire & Kandel, 1999). Repeated firing of neurotransmitters binds a group of neurons together, forming a memory trace or network. LTP primarily occurs within the hippocampus, the area of the brain most responsible for transferring memories into long-term storage. As a result of repetition, the neural pathways that the memory travels upon become a well-traveled path, paving the way for neurotransmitters to connect with every future repetition.

Activation of LTP is contingent upon regular rehearsal of the thought process. The lasting effects are more pronounced when the initial stimulus is strong (as in multisensory encoding) and will eventually fade over time if not practiced consistently. However, the more connections that are made between existing memory networks and new learning, the more likely it is that the memory will be stored in multiple networks, increasing the opportunity for recall. Once learners buy into this phenomenon and experience how it works, they become empowered to use strategies of repetition and rehearsal and build upon previous memories by attaching personal meaning and relevance to what they are currently learning.

I encourage learners to use multisensory techniques to review material within 24 hours of learning, again within 48 hours, and again within 72 hours of the first learning (see Figure 2.1). According to my own personal observations working with nursing students, this intense three-day review has proven to get more information into long-term memory than other approaches

Figure 2.1 Formula for Long-Term Memory

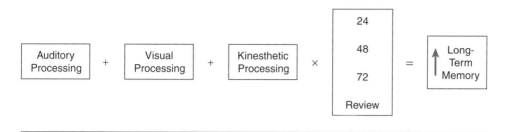

to learning. Most students report that by the third review, they experience a gut feeling of "knowing" the material and rely less and less on notes. Richard Bandler suggests that this "knowing" is achieved when learning is reinforced in a multisensory way with repetition over time (Bandler, 1988). My grade book test scores further indicate that this review strategy really works!

As more new information is learned, I encourage students to continue to integrate this newly learned knowledge with previously learned knowledge so that it develops stronger and deeper links and associations within the long-term memory networks. Daniel Schacter (1996) refers to this process as consolidation. With frequent recall of information, consolidation can last for decades.

Types of Memory

In order for memories to be created, they must first enter the brain. Understanding how information enters and is processed in the brain is helpful for educators in promoting learning strategies that ensure that what is taught becomes what is learned. Several models have been devised to explain the types of memory and the process of memory formation from initial input to permanent storage, but basically, there are two types of memory: short-term and long-term. Short-term memory is designed to hold information just long enough for immediate recall. Long-term memory is designed to hold important information infinitely (see Figure 2.2).

Short-Term Memory

Short-term memory, which includes sensory memory and working memory, is a kind of holding pen for processing bits and pieces of information that humans are exposed to every day through their senses of sight, hearing, touch, smell, and taste. The auditory, visual, and kinesthetic senses are of primary concern to most educators; most of what is learned in formal educational and informal workplace settings is the result of auditory, visual, or kinesthetic-tactile stimulation.

Sensory Memories

Of the three sensory memories, visual memory, or iconic memory, is the shortest and least reliable (Sperling, 1960). Iconic memory is what causes the brief (less than a second) afterimage of something that is observed. Memory that originates from hearing, referred to as echoic memory, lasts just a tad

30

Figure 2.2 Memory Processing

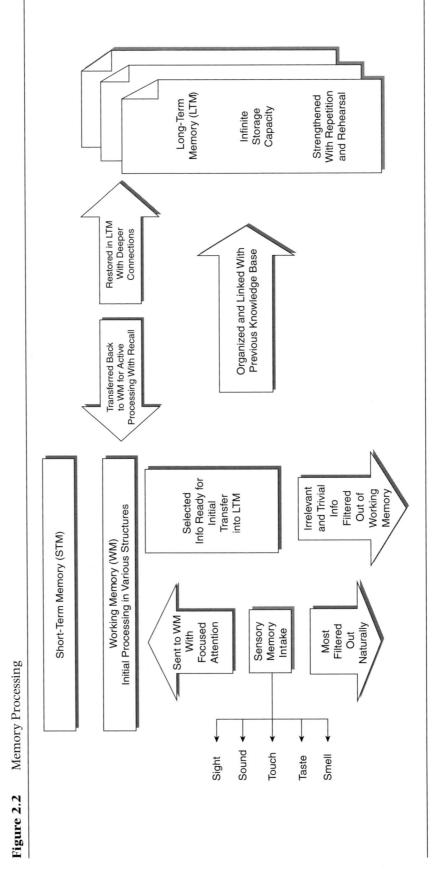

SOURCE: Adapted from Wolfe (2001).

longer than iconic memory. That is why information that is heard or repeated out loud by the learner is more likely to be remembered than what was merely observed. However, information that is observed visually and then repeated out loud is doubly encoded, because it is stored in different memory networks throughout the brain, providing the learner is not overly stressed.

Stress affects the formation of visual and auditory memories because the hippocampus, the main memory processor, is located within the limbic system and is greatly influenced by the amygdala. Perceived stress sends signals from the limbic system to the prefrontal cortex causing a disruption of memory formation (Schacter, 2001). That is why, when learners are stressed, they often forget what was previously read or discussed. These sensory memories never had a chance to develop!

Kinesthetic memory tends to be the most enduring and least affected by stress, as it is stored outside the neocortex, in the cerebellum. Initially, kinesthetic memories require conscious thought and concentration. Over time, kinesthetic skills become automatic and are applied with less and less attention and awareness. Learning using all three modalities triples the probability of forming long-term memories in learners.

Sensory memories are initially processed in the prefrontal lobe of the cortex in what is referred to as working memory. Select areas of the temporal, parietal, and occipital lobes; the cerebellum; and the motor cortex are also activated. Some sensory memories are stored within the prefrontal lobe just long enough to use them (as in a phone number or address you are trying to locate). The majority of sensory memories are filtered out unless efforts are made to intentionally remember the information.

Working Memory

The working memory is the area where prior memories are recalled from long-term memory consciously, or triggered into recall unconsciously, and processed. During this processing, prior memories are reorganized and restructured with new learning and transferred back to long-term memory with even greater connections.

Working memory, however, is limited in capacity, being able to process only seven bits of information at a time, according to watershed research conducted by George Miller (1956). Miller, founder of the field of cognitive psychology and psychology professor at Princeton University, coined the phrase "chunking" to describe the concept of linking isolated pieces of information to form one chunk as opposed to four to five pieces of information. By increasing the number of chunks (seven chunks of information, each made up of six or seven pieces of information), the capacity of working memory can be greatly increased.

Broadbent (1971) argued to modify Miller's initial assessment, proposing that the amount of information that can reliably be stored in short-term memory is more like three to four chunks. However, recent studies corroborate the value of chunking information as an effective information-processing technique for aiding in memory retention (Gredler, 2001; Joyce & Showers, 2002).

New research on working memory also indicates that mental training exercises may promote reasoning and problem-solving (Cowan, 2005; Klingberg et al., 2005; Martinussen, Hayden, Hogg-Johnson, & Tannock, 2005; Pernille,

Westerberg, & Klingberg, 2004). The bottom line is that practice and rehearsal actually enhances the limited potential of working memory. Grouping information into larger chunks has been shown to increase efficiency of working memory within the prefrontal and parietal lobes in both children and adult learners (Pernille et al., 2004).

Working memory is also time-limited, being able to process information for approximately 10 to 20 minutes for most adults, according to Alan Baddeley and Graham Hitch's 1974 working memory model (Baddeley, Hitch, & Andrade, 2002). Peter Russell (1979), author of *The Brain Book*, further suggests that focus can be maintained for longer than 20 minutes if the individual applies the concept in a different modality (such as talking about the information or applying the knowledge directly). Alternatively, things that a person is highly concerned with or worried about may stay "on the mind" in working memory for hours or even days. Unfortunately, such overprocessing is seldom effective and tends to interfere with the processing of other things.

The brain is naturally wired to transfer information critical for survival into long-term memory. Likewise, emotional attachment to new information tends to fix the memories into long-term storage (more about that later). Textbook information is more difficult to get into the long-term memory banks, but it can be transferred if learners determine that the information makes sense to them personally and is relevant, according to educator David Sousa (2001). If the learner determines the information to be trivial or useless, the information is most likely to be filtered out.

Once short-term memories are determined to be worth remembering, they are further processed in the limbic system, which is termed the emotional brain. Within the limbic system, it is the hippocampus and amygdala that are primarily responsible for transferring memories into long-term storage within the neocortex. Specifically, the hippocampus region processes factual information, while the amygdala processes emotional information. The cerebellum regulates final processing of kinesthetic memories.

Neuropsychologist Elkhonon Goldberg, who has investigated the role of the frontal cortex and working memory, asserts that the frontal cortex rapidly initiates recall of stored information into working memory instantaneously and effortlessly for both complex and routine day-to-day problem-solving in healthy individuals (see Figure 2.3). Deterioration of such recall and ability to problem-solve is one of the first signs of mental deterioration. Goldberg contends that working memory and the frontal cortex work hand-in-hand to process information (Goldberg, 2001).

Long-Term Memory

Semantic and Episodic Pathways

The factual information processed in the hippocampus travels along explicit memory pathways and is referred to as declarative or conscious memory. Declarative memory includes semantic (content) and episodic (context) memories. Semantic memories develop from words, numbers, and symbols. Episodic memories develop from events one experiences in life. Once these memories are processed, they are stored in various sites throughout the neocortex. When you recall semantic memories such as a scientific process, facts, or formulas, if the

Figure 2.3   Working Memory and Long-Term Memory

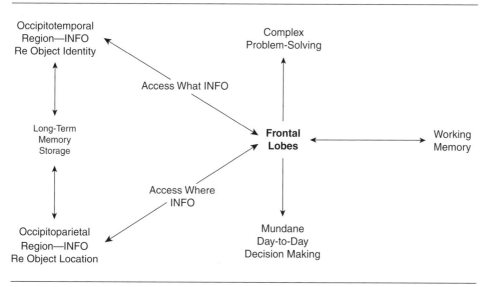

NOTE: In a dynamic two-way interaction, the frontal lobes instantaneously select several stored memories from long-term memory and recall them into working memory just long enough to make appropriate decisions. Once the information is no longer required, the memories are restored in appropriate brain regions until they are recalled again.

context in which you learned it (in a study group with a peer) is recalled, the memory becomes almost effortless. Episodic memories are easier to recall, as they become part of our autobiographical history.

Memory studies have shown that episodic memories have been recalled from when subjects were as young as 18 months old (Schacter, 2001). Semantic memory is not very stable over time, according to memory studies in which individuals were asked to remember lists of words (Schacter, 2001). However, with frequent review and rehearsal, semantic memories can be retained in long-term memory. Eric Jensen (2000) recommends getting learners involved in real-life scenarios to link episodic and semantic learning, thereby making it more durable.

Working with adult nursing students, I must agree that getting learners personally involved in real-life scenarios combines and strengthens episodic and semantic learning. Learners are much more likely to remember clinical situations where they have applied theory personally, such as administering cardiopulmonary resuscitation in a life-threatening emergency. This retention generally withstands the test of time, as learners transfer these skills from semester to semester.

> "People get wisdom from thinking, not from learning."
>
> —*Laura Riding Jackson*

The Emotional Pathway

Emotional information processed by the amygdala travels along implicit memory pathways and is referred to as nondeclarative or unconscious memory. Emotional memories, both negative and positive, are the most enduring and powerful memories. Although emotional memories are stored in various sites throughout the neocortex, they are strongly linked to the amygdala. When an especially strong emotion is felt, a surge of adrenaline is released that is thought to permanently fix the emotional experience in the brain. Try integrating emotional appeal (humor, music, games) with semantic content to fix the information into your students' long-term memory. Joseph LeDoux warns that too little emotion causes a state of underarousal, and too intense emotion causes a state of overarousal (LeDoux, 1996). Neither of these states contributes to a productive learning experience.

The Procedural Pathway

The implicit memory pathway is also shared with procedural memories. Procedural memories (muscle memory) are accessed through the cerebellum, which is considered the center for movement in the brain. Procedural memories are stored within the cerebellum and are best recalled unconsciously. Thinking too much about how to do a specific skill can often interfere with performance. Physically going through the motions of doing the skill activates muscle memory most efficiently. Like emotional memories, procedural memories are very enduring. Although they do not cause a surge of adrenaline to fix them into long-term memory, they are less resistant to degenerative changes over time, as occurs within the hippocampus, because they are stored within the cerebellum.

Engaging Multiple Memory Pathways

Because semantic content can be dry and rather unexciting to the brain, but is nevertheless a part of advancing knowledge, learning such content via a brain-compatible approach that engages multiple memory pathways is advocated by many leading educators (Allen, 2002; Jensen, 2000; Sousa, 2001; Sprenger, 1999; Wolfe, 2001). The well-known acronym SEEP, which stands for Semantic, Episodic, Emotional, Procedural, is a handy mnemonic for educators who want to ensure that factual learning reaches the long-term memory banks. Adding the letters MS in front of this acronym further prompts educators to consider the role of multisensory leaning styles and the importance of making the new information sensible to the learner. Although the criteria for making meaning out of new learning are dependent upon the individual learner, they will most likely be met when learners have information presented through multiple modalities.

M	Multisensory
S	Sensible
S	Semantic
E	Episodic
E	Emotional
P	Procedural

With a little planning, semantic learning activities can be presented in a way to appeal to multiple senses, paired up with episodic events, infused with a little emotional appeal, and incorporated into a kinesthetic activity. This process stimulates multiple pathways for both processing and recall of information. For example, if semantic information is first introduced in a multisensory way (discussion, visuals, and a hands-on activity), it is more likely to make sense and have meaning to the learner. Additionally, actively engaging learners in applying the information (procedural) in collaborative work groups (episodic) within an enjoyable and nonthreatening setting (emotional) will promote a greater chance of activating multiple pathways and satisfying criteria for transfer into long-term storage.

Retention of Long-Term Memory

If the information makes sense and is meaningful to the learner, when it is reviewed (semantic), the other aspects of memory—including where the learning took place and the other persons involved (episodic), how the learner felt about the learning (emotional), and how familiar the learner is with applying the information (procedural)—will flow effortlessly into working memory. Since multiple pathways have been activated in the storage of this information, if the semantic information cannot be recalled immediately, accessing the episodic, emotional, and procedural memory pathways may stimulate recall of the semantic pathway.

It is the ability to recall information from long-term memory that indicates that learning has taken place. Retention of learning refers to the storage and retrieval of information from long-term memory. Aside from emotional and kinesthetic memories, most learning takes time and effort on the part of the learner. If information is not transferred to long-term memory, it cannot be recalled accurately; therefore, it is not actually learned.

Rehearsal Strategies

Rehearsal and review of information over time are critical in order to get information from working memory into long-term storage. However, the type of rehearsal strategy used determines the longevity of the memory and the pathways in which the memory is stored. The two common types of rehearsal are referred to as rote and elaborative.

Rote Rehearsal

Rote rehearsal is one way to get information stored. Rote memory is most effective for memorizing facts and skills to the point where recall is automatic. It is a fairly simple process that involves repetition. For example, when trying to remember facts for a test, it is possible to recite the facts over and over in working memory until the test is taken. However, once the information is applied to the test, most is filtered out. The real test is when it comes time to retrieve the information for direct application weeks, months, or years from the time it was memorized, and odds are that the memory will have faded or failed completely by then.

Some types of rote memory endure and get information into long-term memory, such as telephone numbers, identification codes, lyrics to a poem or song, and steps in a procedure. However, the items that are stored in rote memory may have little or no meaning to the learner and may not even make sense. There is little or no relationship between rote files of information, as they are seldom linked to existing memories.

Elaborative Rehearsal

Elaborative rehearsal, on the other hand, is a more sophisticated strategy, whereby the learner links new information to existing memories. Elaborative rehearsal strategies ensure meaningful relationships between past learning and new learning in a way that make sense to the learner.

Like rote rehearsal, elaborative rehearsal involves repetition. However, the meaning of the information changes with each repetition as the links between new and previous learning build stronger and deeper relationships. Unlike rote rehearsal, elaborative rehearsal almost always results in a rich interconnection of associations that share multiple memory pathways. Elaborative rehearsal strategies take advantage of the MSSEEP model discussed previously.

Making the Most of Elaborative Rehearsal

According to educator David Sousa (2001), shorter periods of rehearsal and review are more productive than intense cram sessions. The brain is most receptive to 20-minute increments of new information, with the first and last parts made most memorable. Sousa recommends making the most of this by reviewing the most important information first, and by summarizing at the end of each 20-minute session.

Personally, I have found that strategy to work well with adult learners. Try limiting lecturing to 20- or 30-minute sessions, with the first and last parts of the learning session most exciting and stimulating. The end of each session should include a review of the most essential points.

Here is an opportunity to get really creative: I like to challenge my learners to come up with an acrostic, mnemonic, or acronym to summarize the main ideas of a presentation (more about that in Part 3). This helps promote active involvement in the review process. Another dynamic technique to cement learning in a fun way is to bring the concepts together into visualization (let me take you through a journey of the cardiovascular system) or to review with a story (Once upon a time there was a very diseased heart. . . .). Again, learner involvement in these reviews increases the odds that the learners will begin to internalize these new concepts.

Sometimes it takes more than just repetition and rehearsal to make that critical connection into long-term memory. Sometimes the information has to be spiced up a little or reorganized into a format more conducive to the learner's primary learning modality. For example, suppose learners have to remember a series of activities that led up to an historical event. They have read the chapter describing the events over and over and over. They think they know this infor-mation. However, when the time comes to show they know, they recall bits and pieces at best. What happened? Reading is primarily a visual modality, and relying on one modality exclusively does not ensure transfer into long-term memory.

By incorporating a brain-compatible approach to this same situation, learners can strengthen learning potential through a variety of activities, such as developing a timeline or diagram to depict the events leading up to the historical date (kinesthetic-tactile modality), discussing or debating the process with a colleague or classmate (auditory modality), or visualizing themselves in that timeframe (visual modality), making the event personally meaningful. The bottom line is that the more information that is handled, the more modalities that are employed in handling the information, the more time that is invested in handling and reviewing to develop an understanding, the more likely learners are to transfer the information into long-term memory.

I encourage my adult learners to attach personal relevance and interest to that which they find the hardest to learn. Within 24 hours of the first attempt at learning new information, I teach my adult learners to incorporate this strategy during the 24-, 48-, and 72-hour reviews. Depending upon the amount of material that is reviewed, learners break each study session into 20- to 30-minute increments. They review the new material first, find ways to connect it to previous learning in a multisensory and meaningful way, and then summarize what was learned at the end of the session. I encourage them to separate each learning session with a brain break, including water, stretching, and breathing exercises (more about that in Part 2). That gives a total of 72 hours to learn the information using three different modalities.

The more multisensory stimulation that is involved, the more retention can be predicted (see Figure 2.4). Colin Rose, who developed the *Accelerated Learning Action Guide*, validates concepts of accelerated learning by stating that learners remember 90 percent of what they see, hear, say, and do, as compared to only 20 percent of what they read, 30 percent of what they hear, 40 percent of what they see, 50 percent of what they say, and 60 percent of what they do (Rose, 1995).

Multisensory Teaching to Enhance Retention

Just as it is important to recognize each learner's brain dominance, it is important for educators to use multisensory techniques to promote learner retention. According to my personal experiences, combining lectures (auditory stimulation) with videos, graphic organizers, demonstrations, prereading assignments (visual stimulation) and hands-on practice, group work, teaching others, and prelecture worksheets (kinesthetic-tactile stimulation) increases significantly the percentage of information retained.

That is certainly a very empowering proposal for both educators and adult learners! Once educators understand how much more meaningful and memorable their lessons can become when they integrate multisensory teaching modalities throughout shorter teaching sessions, they are freed up from the constraints of the didactic lecture. Teaching actually becomes fun—the passion to teach returns! Once learners understand how powerful their memories can become by reviewing using multisensory techniques on a regular basis over a

Figure 2.4   Impact of Multisensory Review on Learning

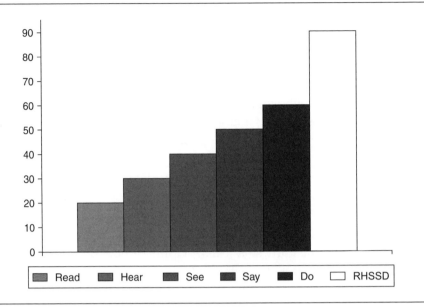

SOURCE: Adapted from Rose (1995).

NOTE: RHSSD indicates "read, hear, see, say, do."

set amount of time, they are no longer dependent upon what is being presented by the teacher. They begin to exert more control and take greater ownership over their own learning outcomes—the passion to learn returns!

THE ADULT BRAIN

Despite the renewed passion to learn, conventional wisdom has it that as a person starts to age, senility is inevitable—certainly a grim prospect for adults who are investing time and energy into their education. While some older adults do become senile, the majority of adults are able to maintain their mental capacities until the day they die. Most cases of senility are the result of hardening of the arteries, causing diminished cerebral blood flow, or neurological diseases, such as stroke, which cause physical damage to the brain. Fortunately, elderly people who are in good physical health generally remain cognitively intact throughout life.

Age-Related Memory Loss

The healthy human brain does go through some normal physical changes, however, with the most noticeable effect being upon short-term memory. Long-term memory and recall declines only slightly as adults age, along with the ability to problem-solve and multitask. Psychologist Daniel Schacter (2001) refers to these changes of omission (failing to bring to mind a fact, idea, or event) and commission (an incorrect form of memory), as common malfunctions that plague all aging adults.

Although the effects of normal adult aging on the brain are subtle and difficult to detect using conventional neuroimaging techniques, new technology is making these subtle changes more obvious. Diffusion tensor imaging (DTI), an MRI method, has been used to demonstrate vulnerability of the frontal white matter to normal aging, validating age-related declines in information processing (Benedetti et al., 2006; Sullivan, Adalsteinsson, & Pfefferbaum, 2006). PET studies reveal normal age-related decline in both presynaptic and postsynaptic dopamine markers (Volkow et al., 1998).

Ted Spiker (2003) summarizes several important contributions that neuroscience has made to the study of memory in adults: Michela Gallagher of Johns Hopkins University in Baltimore, Maryland, is researching age-related memory loss in hopes of developing memory loss drugs. Her research is helping educators understand normal memory losses in adult learners. Bruce Miller of the University of California, San Francisco has explored behavioral changes in relation to brain structure and function in neurodegenerative diseases, such as Alzheimer's disease, in hopes of promoting early intervention drug therapies. His research has given educators insight into how part of the limbic system of the brain, the amygdala, controls emotions in learners. Ron Hayes of the University of Florida is developing diagnostic tests in hopes of tracking brain-damaging chemicals that are released in response to head injury. His research promotes an understanding of the biology and physiology of brain structures. Herbert Benson, of Harvard Medical School in Boston, Massachusetts, has studied the effects of the mind-body relationship since the early 1960s. His continued research has contributed to educators' understanding of how stress and anxiety affect cognitive performance and learning (Benson, Malhotra, Goldman, Jacobs, & Hopkins, 1990).

Woodbury (2004) summarizes how scientists have focused research on the maintenance and promotion of memory. Edward Zamari, a researcher at the University of Alabama at Birmingham, promotes challenging mental stimulation in adults to increase connections between neurons, resulting in greater recall of memories. Robert Sapolsky of Stanford University has found that keeping stress levels under control promotes greater memory and recall. Matt Walker of Harvard University has found that sleep is essential in the formation of memories. Antonio Convit of New York University School of Medicine has researched the relationship between glucose levels and memory. He advocates weight control with exercise and diet to control blood sugars, thus promoting memory and recall. Findings from this research give credence to a more holistic approach to education in terms of promoting memory among adult learners.

The Effect of Aging on the Brain

By the time people reach young adulthood, they have lost approximately half of their synaptic connections (Khalsa, 1997), although most of those connections have withered away naturally from lack of use. PET scans reveal that at the age of 30, the brain begins to shrink noticeably, causing slight cognitive decline. Fortunately, because of the brain's amazing plasticity, new synaptic connections continue to be formed, so the cognitive decline is not that pronounced.

Starting at age 40, however, there is a two percent decrease in brain weight with every added decade of life (Khalsa, 1997). Although this may not sound like much, the brain areas that are affected the most are the areas that are primarily associated with memory. The hippocampus and the amygdala, located in the limbic system of the cerebrum, have shrunk by 25 percent by the time a person reaches 70 years of age (Khalsa, 1997). As previously mentioned, these two structures are responsible for storing some short-term memories and sending memories into long-term storage within the neocortex. The hippocampus is responsible for the storage of semantic memory, while the amygdala is responsible for the processing of emotional memories. As a person ages, the hippocampus loses the ability to transfer short-term memories into long-term storage. That is why short-term memory is more susceptible to effects of aging. Psychologist Daniel Schacter (2001) refers to this gradual loss, which becomes most notable in an individual's sixties and seventies, as transience. However, the same individuals tend to recall long-term memories more efficiently because they are safely stored within the neocortex.

Because of these age-related biological changes, adults tend to become stressed while trying to learn new information. This becomes a vicious cycle. Enduring long periods of stress causes the release of cortisol, which further affects the ability of the hippocampus to transfer memories. Glucose is the brain's power source, and cortisol decreases glucose supply to the brain. As a result, new concepts are difficult to remember and existing memories are more difficult to recall. Excess cortisol levels further interfere with neurotransmitter function, thus reducing synaptic transfer between cells. Attention and focus are impaired as well as creativity and cognitive processing. Moreover, cortisol has been implicated with free-radical production, which causes severe dysfunction of brain cells. The memory centers in the hippocampus and amygdala regions are most susceptible to free-radical destruction.

In addition, the myelin sheath, the protective covering that insulates each axon, declines more in the limbic areas than other parts of the brain, thus decreasing the speed of impulse transmission between neurons. The result of these changes is a noticeably slower ability to process, transfer, and retrieve information as efficiently as the younger brain.

Another primary cause of age-related memory impairment is the gradual decline of the neurotransmitter acetylcholine, which is the primary carrier of memory. According to neuropsychologist Elkhonon Goldberg (2001), studies of Alzheimer patients have shown a decrease in acetylcholine, especially in the temporal region of the neocortex, where most long-term memories are stored. Because memories are stored not in one cell but in several cells throughout the brain, acetylcholine is needed to trigger the thought process between cells. Without sufficient acetylcholine on board, brain cells cannot communicate as efficiently with each other when a person tries to recall a memory. Concentration and focus in older adult learners is diminished as well with declining production of acetylcholine.

At around the age of 50, people are less able to multitask and learn new complex skills. Memory continues to decline, especially auditory and visual memory, while kinesthetic memory seems to remain intact (Khalsa, 1997). As previously mentioned, kinesthetic memory is stored in the cerebellum, which is less vulnerable to degenerative changes than the neocortex and the hippocampus, where most visual and auditory learning is processed. As memory begins to decline, an individual's creativity also begins to wither. This may be in part because creativity requires the ability to recall and focus on memories in an inventive way.

By the time people reach their sixties, there is a significant decline in cognitive function as well as memory (Khalsa, 1997). The ability to memorize new facts and to focus and concentrate is affected dramatically. Older learners may experience difficulty in matching names to faces, remembering phone numbers, and learning new information. The nervous system also begins to slow down, thus decreasing speed and agility in performing tasks.

Although these changes may seem quite dismal and frustrating, adults can learn to activate neural connections and build upon previously learned information using the brain-compatible strategies tailored to the adult brain that are described in Part 2 of this book.

The Benefits of Using Brain-Compatible Learning for Adults

The use of brain-compatible learning strategies is especially conducive to the way the adult brain learns. The healthy adult brain is richly woven with intricate connections formed throughout a lifetime of experiences. Having a more extensive base of previous life experiences yields more potential new associations to link with new learning opportunities. Adults are by far more self-directed and autonomous learners than their younger counterparts. They seek out relevant information to expand their knowledge base in order to improve productivity at work and quality in living. Brain-compatible learning strategies offer adults the opportunity to apply concepts directly and to modify the application to fit their needs.

According to Donnalee Markuson (2003), creator of "Designs for Strong Minds," a program based on brain and neuromuscular functioning, adult learners are molded by experiences, both physically and mentally. When a past experience is recalled, a blend of past and present memories is brought forth from various neurons throughout the cerebrum into the working memory. In working memory, past experiences are combined with present events to produce future effects. These past experiences include emotions, values, sensations, conditioned responses, and motivation. Once this blend of experiences is brought forward, knowledge is processed through higher-level cognitive skills such as planning, decision-making, discussing, solving problems, calculating, visualizing, composing, writing, designing, and many other learning activities.

When these messages or newly formed ideas are inconsistent with personal experiences and values, they are quickly forgotten and filtered out. Alternatively, when new learning is strongly valued based on past experiences, strong connections between neurons are forged and transferred into long-term memory. Consequently, knowledge builds upon what the brain already knows. Since drawing upon past experiences facilitates new learning, adult learners bring a multitude of personal resources to the learning environment. Educators who recognize this relationship can facilitate opportunities for adults to learn by encouraging interactive activities that draw upon past experiences.

Because they are by nature self-directed and motivated to learn, adult learners are more likely to direct a stronger focus of attention to learning activities that incorporate previous knowledge and experiences. The rich neural network formed by past knowledge and experiences connects to newly learned concepts, thereby creating multiple opportunities for the adult to construct, retain, and retrieve new material.

I have observed in teaching adults that some learning activities seem to challenge old patterns of behavior and thinking. As a result, learners may become aware of feelings of ambiguity and uncertainty, as the working memory strives to seek out more information to make sense of the activity. Educators who recognize this response to be a natural reaction of the brain will provide opportunities and time for learners to discuss and process the concepts. Once new insights are integrated and valued by the learner, new connections are stimulated, thus increasing the knowledge base in that area. Working memory improves with activities that require adult learners to use higher-level cognitive processes that facilitate absorption and creation of knowledge. When working memory is activated to pull previous knowledge and experiences from long-term memory, the previous knowledge is actually being relearned and restored back into long-term memory with stronger connections than it had before it was activated (Sousa, 2001).

From a developmental perspective, adult concerns of personal integration and valuing cause many adults to return to school to increase their levels of competence and explore their own values and ethics related to work. Because the underlying motivation of all adult learning is the need to make sense out of the world, to find meaning, and to be effective at those aspects of life most highly valued, the stakes are rather high. When adult learners are able to connect their own values and perspectives to the learning experience, their motivation to learn is ignited. These intrinsic variables provide the primary source of motivation, which drives all adult learning.

Adults possess an innate desire to construct or reconstruct meaning to make sense out of what they are learning (Taylor, Marienau, & Fiddler, 2000). Educators can promote this development by using strategies that actively engage learners in a topic, getting them to draw upon previous knowledge, to reflect upon their assumptions, and to understand from a new perspective that reconstructs previously held ideas. Deeper levels of personal transformation and understanding often result from learning experiences that challenge the way learners think, moving them beyond knowledge acquisition to knowledge construction. Robert Kegan (2000) refers to this as transformative learning—learning that creates a change in knowing, as opposed to behavioral learning, or learning that creates a change in behavior.

From a brain-compatible perspective, learning becomes meaningful when it moves from memorization of facts and acquisition of skills to more active and collaborative authentic learning experiences. Group collaboration especially is essential in adult education, since adults want to share their experiences and interact with others both academically and professionally (Mentkowski and Associates, 2000). Stephen Brookfield and Steve Preskill (1999) argue for teaching approaches that convey dignity and respect by allowing learners to become actively involved in the design, process, and evaluation of their own learning.

From my personal experiences in working with adult learners, I have found such teaching approaches to be an integral element of working with adult learners. Once adult learners have invested time and energy into their education, they want to become actively involved. Denying that level of participation is a sure recipe for disaster in any adult learning setting. Eliciting involvement and feedback from adult learners certainly demonstrates respect and increases the likelihood that the lesson will be considered more meaningful and valuable to the learner.

Although many adult education programs are based upon behavioral outcomes, brain-based principles and strategies can be easily integrated into the traditional adult education program. Higher-level cognitive skills, such as critical thinking and problem-solving, can be enhanced through brain-compatible learning strategies. By promoting visual, auditory, and kinesthetic memory pathways, an extraordinary amount of complex information can be stored in long-term memory and accessed more efficiently in any adult educational environment.

> "It is the supreme art of the teacher to awaken joy in creative expression and knowledge."
>
> —*Albert Einstein*

All individuals have the capacity to become excellent learners. For all practical purposes, the capacity of the human brain is limitless. Most people, however, only use a fraction of their true potential, because they do not know how to learn using their preferred learning style and their full range of talents or intelligences. In Chapter 3, learning styles and multiple intelligences will be explored as well as teaching and learning strategies that naturally complement the unique needs of adult learners.

Part 2

The Resourceful Learning State

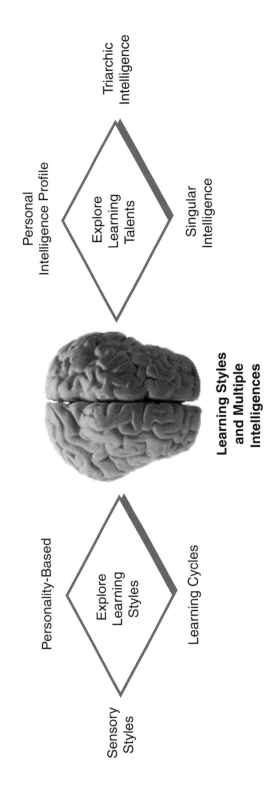

Triarchic
Intelligence

Personal
Intelligence Profile

Explore
Learning
Talents

Singular
Intelligence

**Learning Styles
and Multiple
Intelligences**

Personality-Based

Explore
Learning
Styles

Learning Cycles

Sensory
Styles

3

Learning Styles and Multiple Intelligences

The way adult learners feel about learning is vitally important to their academic success. When adults feel confident about their ability to learn as well as comfortable, secure, and respected in their learning environment, they are in an optimal state to learn. This optimal or resourceful state of learning involves positive emotions as well as a belief in and commitment to the use of personal learning styles and strengths. Educators who are proponents of brain-compatible research (Allen, 2002; Caine & Caine, 1994; Hyerle, 2004; Jensen, 2000; Marzano, Pickering, & Pollock, 2002; Sousa, 2003; Tate, 2004; Wolfe, 2001) as well as educators and psychologists who have researched learning styles and preferences (Dunn, 1988; Kolb, 1984; McCarthy, 1987; Myers, 1962; Silver & Hanson, 1998; Silver, Strong, & Perini, 2000) support the belief that all learners are unique and have their own unique learning profile, including a combination of innate learning talents (Gardner, 1999; Perkins, 1995; Sternberg, 1997).

As previously discussed in Chapter 2, environmental information is continuously being taken in through our five primary senses. Each individual has his or her own learning style that reflects the way information is processed and used to form new ideas. Depending on the dominant learning style of the individual, the same information can be assigned different meanings. I have certainly seen that happen in a classroom full of adults!

All learners bring their own unique experiences, memories, and attitudes into the learning environment. Imagine how boring it would be if every learner were a carbon copy of the others. It would be like teaching robots! Educators can celebrate this uniqueness by respecting and encouraging learning differences.

I have found that learners gain as much from sharing experiences as they do from learning on their own.

Empowering learners to recognize their unique styles can help them to capitalize on personal strengths and build upon weaker areas. Becoming aware of personal strengths and areas to develop will make individuals aware of just how they learn. Although adult learning styles and preferences are multifaceted, adult educators can attempt to address the main learning styles as much as possible within the formal or workplace educational setting to ensure that all learners' needs have been met.

> "The only truly educated person is the one who has learned how to learn."
>
> —*Carl Rogers*

PREFERRED LEARNING STYLES

When you observe a group of adult learners, it becomes quite obvious that there is an incredible variety of learning preferences, styles, and talents within the group. All individuals develop their own learning styles, and this affects the way they interpret, interact, and make sense out of their world. An individual's learning style is the way that he or she begins to process, internalize, and concentrate on new material. Each person's learning style is as unique as the person's fingerprints.

According to David Kolb (1981, 1984), developer of the Learning Style Inventory, a person's learning style is influenced by genetics and personal life experiences as well as the usual day-to-day stressors. Although they are relatively stable, learning styles change as a result of developmental and environmental stimuli (Cornett, 1983). Rita and Kenneth Dunn (1992) developed a model that examines multiple variables that affect how learners respond to their environment, including seating, interaction with peers, cognitive skills, reasoning skills, and many more.

Neuropsychologist Elkhonon Goldberg (2001) maintains that the way we process and organize information within our frontal lobes determines our individual learning styles. Psychologist Daniel Schacter (2001) suggests that the attention-splitting demands of modern technology (watching television while a news crawler is run across the bottom of the screen, for example) actually affect the way we attend to and learn new information. Robert Steinberg argues that while thinking and learning styles differ widely among individuals, they are nevertheless as important as levels of ability and should be addressed as such by educators (Steinberg, 1990).

There is a great deal of consensus among learning style researchers that learners at all age levels develop more positive attitudes toward education and achieve more when taught and counseled through their primary style rather than through a style that is secondary or underdeveloped, especially when confronted with new materials or experiences (Dunn, 1988; Kolb, 1984; Letteri, 1980; Roberts, 1977; Trayer, 1991).

Some people learn best by doing (kinesthetic-tactile learners), while others learn best by listening (auditory learners) or watching (visual learners). Most learners also possess one or more highly developed abilities or natural intelligences that further promote optimal learning for that individual. For example, you may have noticed some learners who are more talkative and able to relate to other people, while other learners are more quiet and reflective and have a natural propensity for solving mathematical formulas and reasoning things out logically. These profiles demonstrate the variety of learning styles and intelligences or abilities in individuals.

No two individuals in any given class will have the exact same combination of learning styles and intelligences. Everyone learns things in his or her own way, having a specific preference that they have acquired over time. Educators also have a preferred learning style, which is generally the modality that they feel most comfortable teaching and presenting through. Studies by a variety of educators (Rose, 1995; Thomas, Ratcliffe, Woodbury, & Jarman, 2002; Wyman, 2001) suggest that 40–65 percent of learners are visually dominant, while 25–30 percent are primarily auditory, and 5–15 percent are primarily kinesthetic learners. When these statistics are applied to the traditional lecture hall presentation (primarily an auditory style of presentation) used in most adult learning environments, it is clear that only 25–30 percent of the learners (the auditory ones) are receiving the information through their preferred sensory modality. However, the majority of learners, primarily visual or kinesthetic, are desperately trying to visualize or physically manipulate or replay the information in order to effectively process it in their preferred learning modality. These odds are truly overwhelmingly stacked against the majority of learners!

With a little planning, however, it is possible to broaden teaching modalities to respond to a wider variety of learning styles. Educators who understand their own personal learning style and natural learning abilities tend to use a wider variety of learning activities and strategies in the classroom.

This section will help you to understand your own learning styles and abilities as well as those of your learners. Once you recognize the various learning styles and abilities in yourself and your learners, you will be able to implement learning strategies that will promote the process of learning.

Auditory, Visual, and Kinesthetic-Tactile Learning Styles

Organizing learning styles around sensory systems is one of the most common and familiar ways of classifying them. The visual, auditory, and kinesthetic-tactile sensory systems are the primary classes of internal sensory channels that distinguish learning styles. To learn more about them, before proceeding further, stop and take the Learning Style Inventory, shown in Figure 3.1. Read each statement and select the response that best describes you. Go through each statement quickly and select the response that comes to mind first.

Add totals for all styles and compare with the cutoff score for each category. If your score is equal to or higher than the cutoff score, you exhibit a preference for that particular learning style. The higher the score, the stronger the preference. If you have high scores in two or more areas, that means you have a preference for multiple learning styles, which means you are a combination learner/educator.

Figure 3.1 Learning Style Inventory

Learning Style Inventory

	Yes	No
1. I remember more easily if someone tells me new information than if I read it myself.		
2. I would rather read about doing an unfamiliar skill than learn it by practicing it.		
3. I would rather watch a film about a new procedure than read about it in a book.		
4. I would rather develop a model of new concepts than read about them in a book.		
5. I prefer to read out loud when I am having difficulty understanding information.		
6. I would rather draw a model and label each part than practice terms orally.		
7. I understand new material presented orally when I read about it ahead of time.		
8. I would prefer using a new piece of computer software to reading about how to use it in a manual.		
9. If I have to mix a formula, I would rather have someone explain how to do it than rely on written directions.		
10. If I had to use a new piece of equipment, I would rather have someone explain how to do it first than practice doing it myself first.		
11. If I have to go to a new town that I am unfamiliar with, I would rather get written directions than oral directions.		
12. I prefer to listen to new information presented orally before actually reading it myself.		
13. If I were planning on buying a new computer, I would prefer to try it out rather than have someone explain how it works.		
14. When I am having difficulty understanding steps in a procedure, I prefer to have written directions rather than to have someone explain how to do it.		
15. I prefer to listen to books on tape rather than to read books.		
16. When learning the spelling of new words, I prefer to practice by reciting out loud rather than writing the words several times.		
17. Given the choice, I would prefer to read about an experiment rather than to do it.		
18. If I am having difficulty solving a formula, I prefer to work through sample problems rather than have someone show me how to do the problem.		

Scoring: Tally your responses as follows:

Auditory: Count the number of YES responses to items 1, 3, 5, 9, 10, 12, 15, and 16 and the number of NO responses to items 6, 7, 11, 13, 14, and 18. Place these totals on the chart below under Auditory.
Visual: Count the number of YES responses to items 2, 7, 11, 14, and 17 and the number of NO responses to items 1, 3, 4, 5, 9, 12, and 15. Place these totals on the chart below under Visual.
Kinesthetic: Count the number of YES responses to items 4, 6, 8, 13, and 18 and the number of NO responses to items 2, 10, 16, and 17. Place these totals on the chart below under Kinesthetic.

	Auditory	Visual	Kinesthetic
Yes			
No			
Total			
Cutoff score	8	7	5

Combination Learner

Being a combination learner/educator is actually beneficial, as this type of learner/educator is able to be more flexible in diverse learning environments. Consider the characteristics of auditory, visual, and kinesthetic-tactile learning styles illustrated below. You may recognize yourself in all of the descriptions; this means that you most likely have some potential to develop and respond to other learning styles as well. Even though your scores on the Learning Style Inventory may indicate that you are dominant in one particular modality, discipline yourself to build competence in less dominant styles as well, so that you evolve into a flexible combination learner, which makes you a combination educator. Trust me; you will meet the needs of many more learners this way!

The Visual Learner

Visual learners obviously learn best by seeing things. Visual learners love to read and to examine pictures and graphics, such as diagrams and tables. Visual learners are also quite receptive to demonstrations, videos, and films. The visual reader generally reads content silently prior to hearing a lecture to understand it more thoroughly. This type of learner relies heavily on writing notes during a lecture and while studying. The use of learner-generated maps and diagrams also aids visual learners. When visual learners are trying to recall information, they generally can see or visualize in their mind's eye what they are trying to recall. During a test, the visual learner reads each item silently while visualizing solutions.

The Auditory Learner

Auditory learners learn best by hearing information presented to them. They most likely prefer to listen to a presentation about new information rather than reading about it. A true auditory learner actually understands new information better after hearing it first and then reading about it. An auditory learner prefers to tape the lecture and listen to it afterwards. Another strategy used by auditory learners is to read text passages or instructions out loud. Auditory learners love to discuss what they have read with others to help them understand the material. When auditory learners are trying to recall information, they tend to rely on auditory recall—hearing in their heads what was said in a lecture. During a test, auditory learners can subvocalize questions to stimulate recall.

Kinesthetic-Tactile Learner

Kinesthetic learners learn best by getting physically involved in doing things. This type of learner prefers hands-on activities such as experiments and practice demonstrations. Kinesthetic learners get actively involved in their learning by creating maps and flash cards to reinforce concepts. When kinesthetic learners are trying to recall information, they focus on the self-study strategies that they have personally created to help them learn. During a test, a kinesthetic learner would benefit by shifting positions and doing movement exercises quietly to stimulate recall.

PROMOTING COMBINATION LEARNING

Using a combination of learning styles is most beneficial for almost any type of learning environment. Relying too much on your preferred learning style to teach may become counterproductive. For example, a kinesthetic-tactile learner may become frustrated when forced to sit quietly through a lecture-style presentation, while an auditory learner may be in heaven! Conversely, auditory learners may feel out of their element in a laboratory situation where they are expected to perform skills.

Combining teaching strategies that promote learning across all styles is the most obvious solution. From a brain-compatible learning perspective, combining auditory, visual, and kinesthetic-tactile learning creates multisensory learning. Individuals have separate memories for what is heard, seen, and felt. Therefore, promoting activities that activate seeing, hearing, and feeling facilitate much more productive, efficient, and long-lasting learning. In Part 3 of this book, you will find several multisensory learning strategies to try out in your classroom.

KOLB'S CYCLE OF LEARNING THEORY

In my research on learning styles, David Kolb's learning theory also seems to have much relevance for adult learners (Kolb, 1984). Kolb suggests that learning involves a cycle of four processes, each of which must be present for learning to occur most completely. The core of the model is a simple description of the learning cycle: how experience is translated into concepts that eventually guide the learner in making choices for new learning experiences.

The cycle begins with the learner's involvement in a specific learning experience. The learner then reflects upon this experience from a variety of viewpoints in an effort to attach personal meaning to the activity. From this reflection, the learner draws logical conclusions to which he or she adds relevant theory. These very conclusions then guide decisions and actions that lead to new concrete experiences.

Kolb argues that learners, if they are to be effective, need four different kinds of abilities: concrete experience, reflective observation, abstract conceptualization, and active experimentation abilities (see Figure 3.2). Any individual may have strengths in particular areas of the cycle and will need to develop the skills to operate along the full range of the cycle if he or she is to be optimally effective (Kolb, 1981).

Based upon the instructional design of experiential learning, educators Marilla Svinicki and Nancy Dixon proposed several activities that support different phases of Kolb's learning cycle. It is their belief that by constructing learning sequences that lead students through the full cycle, an instructor can foster a more complete learning experience than could be gained from one perspective (Svinicki & Dixon, 1988).

In terms of adult education, learners could be assigned to read a certain portion of text and reflect upon the content prior to class, attend a lecture, and participate in small group case studies to apply the concepts in class. Another cycle would be to attend a lab, write a journal entry about the lab experience, demonstrate the skill to a peer, and then to apply the skill in the work setting. Yet another cycle might be to observe a specific scenario or clinical situation, reflect and brainstorm questions related to the observation, write a descriptive analysis of the situation, and then apply this analysis to a case study.

> "Education is learning what you didn't even know you didn't even know."
>
> *—Daniel Boorstin*

PERSONALITY PREFERENCES AND LEARNING STYLE

Another popular way to examine learning styles is to consider how personality structures affect thinking and response to learning. Based upon psychologist

Figure 3.2   Kolb Learning Styles Progression

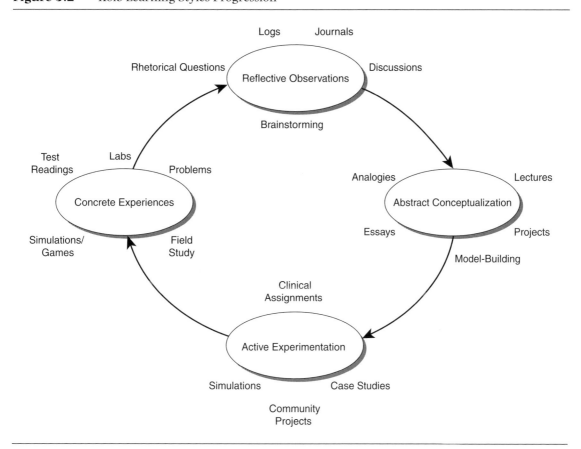

Carl Jung's initial 1923 research on personality types, Isabel Myers (1962) developed the Myers-Briggs Type Indicator (MBTI), which is widely used today. As Figure 3.3 shows, the MBTI is based upon four scales that identify eight personality preferences.

Harvey Silver and J. Robert Hanson (1998) used the MBTI as a springboard for developing their own four-style model. Using four combinations of two of the MBTI categories, sensing/intuitive and thinking/feeling, they came up with four specific learning styles:

- Mastery
- Understanding
- Interpersonal
- Self-expressive

Using these four styles, they linked learner characteristics to each style, as shown in Figure 3.4. For a more detailed description of how this learning style model was integrated with multiple intelligences profiles, refer to *So Each May Learn: Integrating Learning Styles and Multiple Intelligences* (Silver, Strong, & Perini, 2000).

PERSONAL APPLICATION OF LEARNING STYLES THEORY TO ADULT EDUCATION

I have found that within the adult classroom setting, learners are generally not familiar with what their own learning style is. Although they are well motivated to learn and tend to be self-directed in their learning activities, they often

Figure 3.3   Myers-Briggs Personality Preferences

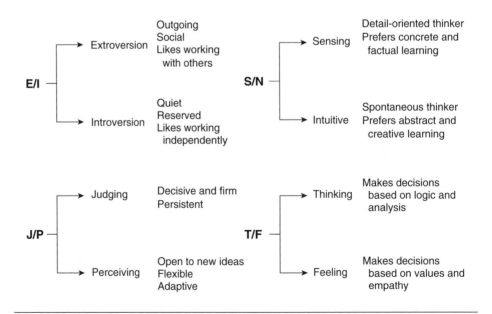

SOURCE: Adapted from Myers (1962).

Figure 3.4   Silver and Hanson Learning Styles

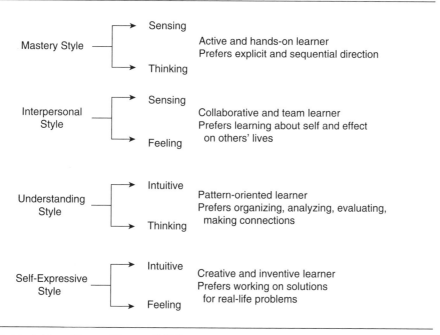

SOURCE: Adapted from Silver and Hanson (1998).

will rely on their strongest sensory modality to process information. This may work well for many; however, when the auditory learner meets up with a visually oriented teacher, the learner comes out short!

Having an awareness of their own personal learning styles can help learners focus on their strengths and build upon their less developed sensory channels. I always offer learners the opportunity to take a self-scoring learning style inventory at the start of class. Knowing your learners' personal preferences is also a great way to hone your own teaching methods to meet the needs of the learners.

For example, if I knew that 90 percent of my class were highly visual learners, I would certainly include a large variety of visual representations of the information I presented. However, I would also include activities to provide opportunities for the same learners to discuss, give opinions about, or debate the content—to build upon their auditory skills. Likewise, I would have learners develop their own graphics or demonstrate proficiency in hands-on practice to build their kinesthetic-tactile skills. However, if I knew that the majority of my class were strong auditory learners, I would offer more explanation and group discussion to cover content. To build this same group's visual skills, I would provide opportunities for them to create a diagram, graph, or table of the information to review. In this situation, the hands-on activity of creating the visual representation will also enhance kinesthetic-tactile skills. Generally, by the end of the semester, my learners become well rounded within the full combination of modalities.

Using a combination of teaching methodologies to transition learners through Kolb's cycle of concrete, reflective, abstract, and active learning will further ensure that learners give adequate attention to all three sensory channels. For example, having learners read a scenario or excerpt from a book (concrete/visual), discuss it or brainstorm ideas within collaborative work groups (reflective/auditory), develop a group presentation or an alternative solution to the problem (abstract/auditory/visual/kinesthetic-tactile), and finally apply the solution or skill in a real-life setting (experimentation/ kinesthetic-tactile) is one way that Kolb's cycle and sensory preferences can be integrated into the adult learning environment.

While personality structures can also be addressed in the classroom, I have observed that most adult learners naturally seek out peers of similar personality structures. For example, learners who are quiet and reflective naturally pair up, while learners who are opinionated and challenging tend to find each other quickly! As an optional outside assignment, I distribute a list of Internet sites learners can go to to take a variety of learning style inventories to find out on their own how their unique personality structures determine how they process information.

THEORIES OF INTELLIGENCE

The study of human intelligence is truly a complex subject that has been under debate for as long as man has been able to think! From the early research of French psychologist Alfred Binet in the 1900s came the fundamental version of the standardized intelligent quotient (IQ) test, which continues to be highly regarded even today (Swiegers & Louw, 1982). Although this test measured primarily how capable a person was in English language and math skills, it soon became the standard by which everyone's intelligence was measured. For years educators and school systems have been labeling and categorizing children according to their IQs. Consequently, students have been perceived by their teachers as either below average, average, or above average in intelligence and dealt with accordingly. Below average learners did not stand a chance to grow and develop their natural abilities to learn when judged solely by IQ.

While there is no clear agreement on what constitutes IQ or how to measure it, many psychologists and educators have attempted to summarize the findings and put their own personal spin on intelligence. As a result, two distinct conclusions have been reached. The first, supported by one group of psychologists (Eysenck, 1982; Jensen, 1993, 1997; Spearman, 1904), is that all intelligence is derived from one general factor, referred to as *g*. This singular dimension of intelligence is challenged by another group of psychologists (Gardner, 1983; Perkins, 1995; Sternberg, 1977, 1988) who argue that there are different types of intelligences.

Singular Intelligence Theories

Psychologist Charles Spearman (1904) postulated that if an individual were highly developed cognitively, that person would display positive correlations among a variety of cognitive abilities. Spearman referred to this positive correlation among tests as positive manifold, or general intelligence factor (*g*). This theory was retested and supported by Arthur Jensen (1997).

Psychologist Hans Eysenck (1982) found that there is a high correlation between a person's reaction time and his or her intelligence. His theory is based on the assumption that an individual requires an intact nervous system in order to react to various motor and sensory stimuli. The quicker the reaction, the more highly functioning the brain and sensory organs are. Conversely, slower reactions indicate impairment in neurological functioning, which in turn translate to lower intelligence according to Eysenck. Jensen (1993) supported this theory by arguing that speed of information processing is the actual speed of transmission through nerve pathways, and faster processing time equates to better reaction time, thereby equating to higher intelligence.

Multiple Intelligence Theories

Arguing that a single dimension or score on an IQ test cannot quantify the complexity and wide range of human capabilities, proponents of multiple intelligences argued against the singular intelligence theory. The most notable theorist, Howard Gardner, proposed his original seven intelligences in 1983, and then later added an eighth intelligence in 1997.

Gardner expanded the traditional and widely accepted concept of intelligence to also include such areas as music, spatial relations, and interpersonal knowledge as well as mathematical and linguistic ability. He defined intelligence as "the capacity to solve problems or to fashion products that are valued in one or more cultural settings" (Gardner & Hatch, 1989).

Table 3.1 identifies Howard Gardner's eight intelligences, provides examples of persons who commonly demonstrate each intelligence, and includes a brief description of the character traits of each intelligence.

Gardner suggests that these eight intelligences rarely operate independently but instead are used concurrently and typically complement each other as individuals draw upon them to solve problems (Gardner & Hatch, 1989). Although we all have the potential for using these inherent intelligences, they seem to be present in varying degrees among learners. Gardner suggests that these intelligences are not fixed but rather dynamic and expanding throughout life.

Triarchic Theory of Successful Intelligence

Robert Sternberg's (1977, 1988) triarchic theory of successful intelligence contrasts with Gardner's theory, as it does not take specific human abilities into account but rather the interaction of experiential, contextual, and componential behaviors exhibited in social situations and environments. Like Gardner, Sternberg believed that the standard IQ test measured a very narrow range of human abilities. He geared his research to thinking behaviors, while Gardner focused on natural abilities. According to Sternberg, successful intelligence is determined by a person's ability to think and behave in ways that will develop personal and career-related excellence. True successful intelligence is a balanced blend of analytical, creative, and practical thinking behaviors:

Table 3.1   Gardner's Multiple Intelligences

Intelligence	Example	Characteristics
Logical-mathematical	Mathematicians, scientists, accountants, bookkeepers, statisticians, engineers, computer analysts, inventors	• Ability to compute and apply higher math concepts to everyday life, construct arguments, and apply logic to complex arguments
Linguistic	Journalists. writers, poets, philosophers, professors, clergy, counselors, lawyers, playwrights, actors, administrators, contractors, politicians, salespersons	• Ability to use language to describe and express, build trust, develop arguments, persuade, and influence • Ability to express self in writing, drama, comedy
Musical	Musicians, composers, music teachers, technicians, choral/band/orchestra conductors, music critics, music directors, collectors, performers, music therapists	• Ability to understand and develop music, interpret music, and create performances and compositions • Ability to relate and express self with music and to use music to help others
Spatial	Sculptors, artists, designers, photographers, painters, architects, builders, cinematographers, illustrators, interior designers, seamstresses, tailors, sailors, surgeons, mechanics	• Ability to visualize and perceive through use of hands or other body parts • Ability to arrange objects, color, line, shape, form, and space • Ability to interpret and graphically represent ideas and to transform ideas into creative expressions
Interpersonal	Teachers, sales clerks, clergy, politicians, doctors, nurses, counselors, social workers	• Ability to perceive emotions of others and respond accordingly
Intrapersonal	Anyone who has personal insight	• Ability to have personal insight and understand own emotions and responses
Bodily-kinesthetic	Athletes, dancers, sports enthusiasts, mechanics, surgeons, sculptors	• Ability to use parts of body to excel in various careers or hobbies
Naturalistic	Naturalists, surveyors, environmentalists, archeologists, biologists	• Ability to understand and classify patterns in the natural environment

SOURCE: Adapted from Gardner (1999).

Experiential intelligence (creative intelligence): Ability to deal with different situations, and to develop new ideas for dealing with situations

Componential intelligence (analytical intelligence): Ability to process information effectively using abstract thinking and logical reasoning skills

Contextual intelligence (practical intelligence): Ability to do well in both informal and formal educational settings, ability to adapt to the environment, street smarts, and ability to change behaviors in a new environment

Sternberg maintains that successfully intelligent people define goals for success and demonstrate achievement by using their personal strengths and also by identifying and correcting their limitations.

Learnable Intelligence

David Perkins has conducted numerous research studies in the areas of teaching and learning for understanding, creativity, problem-solving, and reasoning within specific disciplines as well as in organizations. Perkins (1995) suggests that every person can become more intelligent through study and practice and through access to and utilization of appropriate resources. He has worked with Howard Gardner in Project Zero at the Harvard Graduate School of Education since 1967. Perkins also strongly supports Gardner's theory of multiple intelligences. His own analysis of the study of intelligence focuses on three dimensions of intelligence:

Neural intelligence: Efficiency and precision of the neurological system

Experiential intelligence: Accumulation of life experiences in different areas

Reflective intelligence: Metacognitive abilities or personal strategies for problem-solving and self-management

Perkins maintains that neural intelligence can be adversely affected in utero (for example, where there is drug use by the mother) or during the growing-up years (for example, where a child is exposed to lead poisoning or has insufficient nutrition) as well as in adulthood (for example, where there is a lack of mental stimulation). Experiential intelligence is adversely affected by lack of stimulation within the learning environment. Growing up in a rich learning environment increases experiential intelligence, according to Perkins.

Reflective intelligence enhances both neural and experiential intelligence. Metacognitive strategies to improve personal learning are examples of reflective intelligence. Perkins believes that the learner, through integration of higher-level thinking skills, can control this particular intelligence.

PERSONAL APPLICATION OF INTELLIGENCE THEORY TO ADULT EDUCATION

Although general intelligence theories are well grounded within a biological explanation of neural processing speed, these theories do not take into account the wide variety of natural human talents, such as musical, physical, and social abilities that cannot be measured with psychometric evaluations. As for the multiple intelligence theories, Gardner's theory has the strongest biological link to brain processing capabilities. By studying the brains of individuals with disabilities, Gardner localized areas of the brain related to the impairment in functioning and related them to the specific intelligences that he identified.

The only drawback for teachers is that applying Gardner's theory specifically to the individual's actual brain functioning is simply not possible in the classroom setting. However, by observing the way individuals use their natural talents to learn and process information, educators can begin to understand the diversity of learning strengths and styles. I have come to appreciate the ideas that human intelligence goes well beyond verbal and computational skills and that not all learners have the same balance of natural intelligence. In my observations of adult learners over the years, I have noted some unique characteristics that I will share as typical learner profiles of persons exhibiting Gardner's intelligences:

• **Logical-mathematical profile:** These learners are extremely detail-oriented and analytical. They need to examine things from all angles and perspectives. A logical-mathematical learner moves cautiously and cannot be rushed into making decisions or accepting information. They need to think about the material presented and apply it to their own life experience to it before they accept it. In a collaborative group process, they are most likely to weigh the pros and cons of any given situation.

• **Linguistic intelligence profile:** Linguistic learners are extremely verbose; they love to discuss and debate issues. This type of learner has developed mastery over the art of communication. This learner can also articulate and express himself or herself rhetorically or poetically. They learn best by verbalizing to themselves (thinking out loud) and to others. They love getting together for collaborative projects and are not shy about expressing their opinions or taking on the facilitator role for the group.

• **Spatial intelligence profile:** Spatial learners are very much drawn to visual images and often recreate theoretical content in the form of diagrams or tables. They learn best by manipulating and creating mental images in order to solve problems. My spatial learners are quick to visualize concepts and can recreate them graphically. In a group collaborative process, they will often volunteer to map or diagram the details of a project.

• **Musical intelligence profile:** Learners who are dominant in musical intelligence appreciate music or song as a complement to learning. They have the ability to put concepts into lyrics, poems, and songs in order to learn information. In a collaborative group process, these learners contribute by keeping the rhythm of the group in balance and by coming up with jingles or limericks to remember information.

- **Bodily-kinesthetic intelligence profile:** These learners are easy to spot. They are the ones that are consistently moving or tapping a pen against the desk. They learn best by moving and practicing content through hands-on demonstrations. They are extremely coordinated and demonstrate a close relationship between the mind and body. In a collaborative group process, these learners express themselves with their hands and arms and will definitely keep things flowing along.

- **Interpersonal intelligence profile:** These learners are very sociable and absolutely love getting together in a collaborative group process. They learn best by interacting with others and contribute quite a bit in a group, as they will often draw out the quieter members by asking them what they think about the topic.

- **Intrapersonal intelligence profile:** Intrapersonal learners are reflective and metacognitively in tune with themselves. They may appear quiet on the outside, but they are generally thinking things through. These learners contribute to the collaborative group process by summarizing, synthesizing, and reflecting on the process.

- **Naturalistic intelligence profile:** These learners observe and make connections to the environment. They are sensitive to what is happening on a global level. They tend to bring a broader perspective to the collaborative group process.

I have found that when I encourage learners to consciously work to promote underdeveloped intelligences, they have greater opportunities to explore material more creatively. Promoting the use of the full range of intelligences promotes balanced learning, allowing learners to grow and develop in all dimensions of their lives. In addition, understanding the full scope of your own intelligences will promote greater appreciation of other learners' unique intelligences as well.

Traditionally, our current system of education has promoted the development of two of these intelligences to a far greater degree than the other six, specifically, linguistic intelligence and logical-mathematical intelligence. The exploitation of these two intelligences began innocently enough—after all, what better way to measure whether a student has learned anything than by having him or her demonstrate total recall and analysis? Therefore, those students who were more talented in the use of words and abstract reasoning have been rewarded with higher grades and considered to be more intelligent.

Ironically, if these same students are called upon to use their bodily-kinesthetic, spatial, interpersonal, intrapersonal, musical, or naturalistic intelligences to demonstrate learning outcomes, they may fall far short of the mark. These other abilities or intelligences are often not recognized as valid enough to measure. As a result of the focus almost entirely upon linguistic and logical-mathematical intelligences, many learners are forced to memorize information in order to prove that they know it.

Adult learners, returning to school years after being on their own, developing and using their natural strengths, find it even more difficult to accept traditional assessment. They need to be recognized for what they have learned throughout life. These natural talents can be validated and used to measure achievement in several areas.

Just as it is important for adults to understand their own unique learning styles, recognizing your own learning attributes or intelligences as an educator will promote a greater understanding of learner intelligences. The profile of Gardner's multiple intelligences shown in Table 3.2 will assist you in understanding your own dominant intelligences and give you insight into your learners' abilities.

Your Personal Profile of Intelligences

Using Table 3.2, you can explore the many ways you prefer to learn. As an educator, understanding your own unique learning strengths will help you to become aware of the learning strengths of your learners. The activities and skills described in these tables will help you to fine-tune your personal intelligence awareness. Check off those activities that sound most like you in each of the areas. If there is a similar activity or skill that you excel at in a particular area, write it in at the bottom in the space provided. This will more accurately reflect your personal learning strengths.

Once you have completed the learning profile, count all check marks in each intelligence, and transfer the total amount to the first column. The more check marks you have in a particular area, the stronger that particular intelligence is. If you have checked items in both the activities and skills for a particular area, this is an especially strong natural talent that will greatly benefit you as you learn.

Use what you learn about your profile to assist learners in identifying their dominant learning styles and intelligences. Have them select their dominant learning style (for example, auditory) plus one style to develop (for example, visual), and have them write these on the Personal Learning Strategies Plan at the end of this chapter. Next, have learners identify and write in several strategies to complement their dominant style and the style to develop.

Learners should then identify at least two natural learning intelligences (for example, spatial-linguistic and musical) and an intelligence to develop (for example, linguistic) and place this information on their personal plans as well. Again, have them identify and write in several strategies that complement their dominant intelligences and the intelligence they would like to develop.

Next, have students personalize their plans by making a commitment to taking at least five action steps to implement the selected strategies into their current study strategies.

Instruct students to sign the plan and treat it as an official contract to improve their own learning. Encourage them to implement the plan every day for 21 days in order to integrate the new strategies into their lifestyles and make the strategies habitual.

Now that you have determined your personal strengths, you may have a better understanding of how students process information in different ways. Use the profiles in this chapter to assist your adult learners to tap into their own

(Text continues on page 69)

Table 3.2   Personal Intelligence Profile

Total for Each Intelligence	Activities I Like	Skills and Attributes That Are Typical of Me
Bodily-kinesthetic	____ most sports ____ dancing ____ do-it-yourself projects ____ wrestling/playing ____ delicate handwork ____ cooking/baking ____ other: ____	____ physically involved when problem-solving ____ highly skilled physically in my job or hobby ____ highly skilled in sports ____ a kinesthetic learner ____ most likely to move around while studying ____ most likely able to remember what I have done physically ____ other: ____
Total: ____		
Linguistic	____ argue/debate ____ word puzzles ____ writing ____ reading/literature ____ poetry/prose ____ giving instructions ____ other: ____	____ fluent and expressive ____ good at explaining ____ a list-maker ____ appreciative of language ____ an auditory learner ____ most likely able to remember what I hear or read ____ most likely to discuss material with others while studying ____ other: ____
Total: ____		
Logical-mathematical	____ keeping budgets ____ planning trips ____ statistics ____ planning timetables ____ math activities ____ science activities	____ good at solving problems ____ detail-oriented and orderly ____ good at seeing patterns and relationships ____ appreciative of logical explanations ____ a logical and analytical learner ____ most likely able to remember what I hear and do ____ most likely to design formulas for what I am studying ____ other: ____
Total: ____		

(Continued)

Table 3.2 (Continued)

Total for Each Intelligence	Activities I Like	Skills and Attributes That Are Typical of Me
Intrapersonal	_____ keeping a journal _____ challenging myself to achieve goals _____ predicting my personal outcomes in life _____ being aware of my personal attitudes _____ being aware of how I feel about others _____ spending time alone _____ other: _____	_____ most content doing projects alone _____ appreciative of time alone to work and think _____ good at understanding my own feelings _____ perceptive of how others feel _____ a reflective learner _____ most likely to remember what I have the opportunity to reflect upon alone _____ most likely to prefer studying alone _____ other: _____
Total: _____		
Interpersonal	_____ listening to ideas expressed by others _____ working with others _____ managing or supervising activities _____ being a parent/teacher/counselor _____ being asked to help others with problems _____ belonging to clubs/organizations _____ other: _____	_____ a good liaison between people with problems _____ interested in helping others _____ involved in clubs/groups _____ comfortable working with a team _____ a sociable and collaborative learner _____ most likely to remember something that I discussed with others _____ most likely to study with a group _____ other: _____
Total: _____		
Musical	_____ listening to and playing music _____ singing songs _____ tapping my fingers or feet to music _____ dancing to music _____ musical rhymes, raps, slogans _____ music playing in the background _____ other: _____	_____ appreciative of all kinds of music _____ good with rhythm and melody _____ able to play a musical instrument _____ an auditory learner _____ most likely to remember something that is put to music _____ most likely to have music playing while studying _____ other: _____
Total: _____		

Spatial	
___ reading maps	___ good with directions
___ using diagrams	___ a keen observer
___ putting things together	___ a good visualizer
___ driving	___ appreciative of all forms of art
___ planning gardens	___ a visual/kinesthetic learner
___ sewing	___ most likely able to remember what I see
___ making models	___ appreciative of videos, charts and diagrams when learning
___ drawing/coloring/painting	___ most likely to doodle or draw while studying
___ other: ___	___ other: ___
Total: ___	
Naturalistic	
___ outside activities	___ appreciative of the changing seasons
___ getting my hands in the dirt	___ comfortable getting my hands dirty
___ walking barefoot on the grass/sand	___ environmentally sensitive
___ recycling projects	___ most likely to conserve on paper while writing
___ nature sounds	___ most likely to have nature sounds playing while studying
___ taking care of animals	___ most likely to have windows and plants in my learning environment
___ walking and hiking in the woods	___ an auditory, visual, and kinesthetic learner
___ playing in the snow/snow sports	___ most likely to remember what I see, say, hear, and do
___ swimming and water sports	___ other: ___
___ other: ___	
Total: ___	

SOURCE: Adapted from Gardner (1999).

Figure 3.5   Active Learning Strategies to Expand Intelligences

Bodily-kinesthetic	Act out or role-play what you are learning. Write it out. Keep a journal. Make note cards or flash cards. Walk or exercise while studying. Use your finger to scan material while reading. Get actively involved.
Linguistic	Brainstorm and write down or record everything you know about a topic. (Use your own words) Prioritize 3–5 most important points on note cards. Summarize only essential points on each card. Recite from note cards out loud. Tape yourself speaking and play back often. Talk to yourself about what you are learning while driving. Talk to others about concepts.
Logical-mathematical	Analyze topic from multiple perspectives. Write out questions as you read. Hunt for evidence to support concepts while reading. Make a flow chart, map, table, or diagram of what you have learned. Organize information sequentially.
Intrapersonal	Keep a learning log—record how your learning experiences are helping you meet your goals. Take time to reflect on how you can personally use the new information you have just learned. Compare and contrast what you are learning with what you already know about a topic. Think of analogies to make abstract concepts concrete.
Interpersonal	Teach someone else what you are learning. Discuss what you are learning in a group setting. Compare notes and ideas on a subject with someone else. Brainstorm solutions to problems with a group of peers. Involve yourself in creating a group learning project.
Spatial	Create a learning map of major concepts in a unit. Visualize yourself performing or working with a theoretical concept. Use graphic organizers. Make a poster, cartoon, chart, or videotape of topic. Create a timeline of events, steps, or dates to learn. Create a visual image of abstract concepts—make them real, put a face and name to them.

Musical	Play background music while learning. (Baroque and classical music work best.)
	Substitute new concepts for the lyrics in a familiar song. Write a song or rhyme about what you are learning.
	Hum to stimulate recall.
Naturalistic	Walk and talk outside to discuss new concepts.
	Place plants or trees in your learning environment.
	Use outside aromas, such as pine, to stimulate learning.
	Study with the windows open. Play tapes of nature sounds.

SOURCE: Adapted from Gardner (1999).

Personal Learning Strategies Plan	
Dominant learning style:	Strategies:
Style to develop:	Strategies:
Dominant learning strengths: 1. 2.	Strategies:
Learning strengths to develop:	Strategies:

Personal commitment (5 definite strategies I will use):

1.

2.

3.

4.

5.

I will implement the above strategies every day for at least 21 days.

Signature:_____

Date:_____

unique strengths. Familiarize yourself with the specific strategies shown in Figure 3.5 for helping your learners explore information using their unique talents. You can actually promote more comprehensive and holistic study habits if you encourage them to round out their personal profiles by strengthening those areas that they are less proficient in.

"If we succeed in giving the love of learning, the learning itself is sure to follow."

—*John Lubbock*

In the next chapter, we will discuss how to prepare adult learners to sharpen their study skills by getting them into a resourceful state of mind.

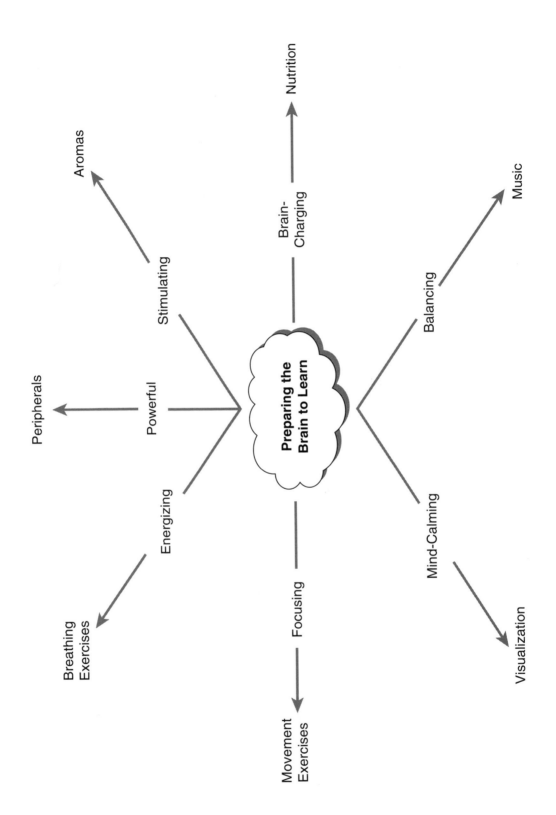

Preparing the Brain to Learn

Brain-Charging → Nutrition

Stimulating → Aromas

Powerful → Peripherals

Energizing → Breathing Exercises

Focusing → Movement Exercises

Balancing → Music

Mind-Calming → Visualization

4

Preparing the Brain to Learn

Preparing the learner to understand and process information is just as important as preparing the lecture or lesson plan. Yet, how much time do you devote to considering the environment or the state of the learner? Although there may not be much that most educators can do to alter the actual teaching environment, they can prepare their learners to be in the resourceful learning state. This is done by helping learners to shift up to the thinking brain.

The optimal or resourceful state of learning involves positive emotions, which appeal to the emotional middle brain. Remember from Chapter 1 that emotions and long-term memory are functions of the middle brain. New information entering the brain travels to the middle brain first, where it is processed for emotional content by the amygdala. If the new information is transmitted to the middle brain in a way that positively appeals to the learner's emotions, this information is then transferred to the neocortex, or thinking part of the brain, along with any long-term memories associated with it. Therefore, new information that is presented in ways appealing to the emotions can have a profound and positive impact upon learning.

Alternately, when negative emotions or fear are present, the middle brain suppresses the transfer of new information. In such situations, students will often regress into a primitive brain state, becoming defensive and protective of their own identities. In this mode, information is filtered out of the emotional brain and may never reach the thinking part of the brain. Unfortunately, students with previous negative learning experiences may not even realize, on a conscious level, that this is happening. On a subconscious level, these learners may feel threatened by a new learning experience, which affects their brains in the same way as other negative emotions. When learners feel insecurity either consciously or subconsciously, the brain is less receptive to learning, and much less of the brain's potential is available to learn.

PROMOTING THE RESOURCEFUL LEARNING STATE

The resourceful state for learning is an optimal brain state in which the learner is alert and focused on learning, while the body is calm and centered. This term was initially developed by Colin Rose, who created Accelerated Learning Techniques, a system for learning large amounts of information quickly (Rose, 1995). Mihaly Csikszentmihalyi, a Chicago psychologist, coined the term "flow" to mean a state of deep concentration and attention, when individuals are free of stress and strain; going about tasks smoothly, quickly, and efficiently; and experiencing enhanced productivity (Csikszentmihalyi, 1990).

Once learners understand the need for this optimal learning state and how to get there, they are truly empowered to take charge of their own learning. Educators can be instrumental in supporting the resourceful learning state by promoting a calm and positive classroom environment before starting the learning session.

This chapter introduces some active strategies I have used to promote the resourceful state of learning and to empower adult students to prepare their brains for learning. Not all of these techniques will be conducive to every learning environment; you may find one or two that will fit your teaching style or environment comfortably. The best gauge of effectiveness is the feedback you get from your learners. Whenever I use one of these techniques on a new group of learners, I first explain why I am doing it (i.e., to help you focus and center your mind before we start) and then ask for written feedback at the end of the session.

I find the feedback to be most valuable in helping me to refine the strategy for that particular group of learners. Over the years, I have introduced adult learners to a variety of techniques that can be used either during a class or during study time to promote optimal learning. Some of the most effective techniques, per learner feedback, are breathing exercises, use of peripherals, aromas, nutrition and hydration, music, visualization exercises, and movement exercises. These resourceful techniques can be used quite effectively in both large and small groups.

> "How we learn is often what we learn."
>
> —Bonnie Friedman

BREATHING EXERCISES

The brain requires a continuous supply of oxygen in order to function at optimal learning capacity. While the process of breathing is natural and automatic, breathing patterns change with certain behaviors. The shallow type of breathing that learners engage in while passively sitting through a lecture is not at all conducive to optimal learning. Breathing deeply and rhythmically will assist in relaxing both the mind and the body. Oxygen is needed by every cell, muscle, bone, and organ. An adequate supply of oxygen provides the brain with the glucose needed to power it up.

When any part of the body is tense, the whole system is thrown off balance. Negative emotional states can often be overcome by a change in breathing patterns. Since the oxygen we breathe provides the energy needed to center and focus, I generally start a learning session with some form of breathing exercise. Breathing exercises are also effective study strategies that learners can use to make the most of their study time. Following are three exercises that can easily be adapted in any teaching environment.

Diaphragmatic Breathing

In order to fully oxygenate the brain and charge the cells, I encourage learners to do deep diaphragmatic breathing at least once an hour. At the start of every presentation, I lead learners through a cycle of five diaphragmatic breathing exercises to get their brains primed for learning. I also schedule a brain break halfway through the presentation if it is longer than one hour. In addition, I empower learners to give themselves a brain break when they start to feel sluggish (underoxygenated) during the presentation. Diaphragmatic breathing exercises can be done rather subtly and without distracting other learners. This type of breathing quickly calms an anxious mind and centers the body for learning.

Directions for Diaphragmatic Breathing

Have learners stand with feet about a foot apart, hands placed over diaphragm (upper abdomen). Instruct learners to breathe in deeply through the nose and out through the mouth, concentrating on raising their diaphragm with every inhalation. After a few practice breaths, I have learners close their eyes and continue to breathe for a cycle of five breaths.

Ratio Breathing

Ratio breathing increases the ratio of parasympathetic to sympathetic nervous system activity, thereby decreasing internal anxiety and producing more harmonious functioning of the circulatory and digestive system. Since blood supply is enhanced with ratio breathing, greater amounts of oxygen are circulated to the brain, which increases the brain's effectiveness at using glucose and its overall efficiency. This exercise is especially beneficial for learners who tend to have test taking anxiety. I generally teach learners how to breathe in deeply using the diaphragmatic muscles for a few cycles before beginning ratio breathing.

Directions for Ratio Breathing

Breathe in deeply through the nose, raising diaphragmatic muscles for three seconds, hold breath for twelve seconds, and exhale through pursed lips for six seconds. A deep cleansing breath is recommended between each breathing cycle.

Repeat five times and end with a deep cleansing breath. Follow with the Alternate Nostril Breathing exercise, below.

Alternate Nostril Breathing

This particular breathing exercise helps to boost the supply of oxygen to both hemispheres of the brain. When both hemispheres are fully stimulated and ready to learn, the whole brain is engaged. Naturally, when the logical left hemisphere and the creative right hemisphere are both involved, the learning experience is enhanced by effective use of the whole brain.

Directions for Alternate Nostril Breathing

Begin by completely exhaling through both nostrils, as in blowing the nose. Close off the left nostril by pressing the thumb or forefinger against the opening and breathe in slowly and deeply through the right nostril. Hold the breath for five seconds and then breathe out through the right nostril while holding the left nostril closed. Next inhale deeply and slowly through the left nostril while holding the right nostril closed. Hold the breath five seconds and then breathe out through the left nostril while holding the right nostril closed. Continue alternating nostrils for five cycles. End exercise by breathing slowly and deeply through both nostrils and clearing secretions away with a tissue if necessary.

> "The gift of giving inspiration to others is the gift of life itself."
>
> —Karen Giardino

POWERFUL PERIPHERALS

The brain absorbs sensory information from the environment whether we want it to or not! The use of peripherals set to the theme of the new unit of study actively engages the learners and keeps their attention focused on the topic at hand. Peripherals are tangible objects used to enrich the learning environment by creating atmospheres, relevant content, and motivation. Typical peripherals are posters, plants, puzzles, and theme-related props. Peripherals engage the visual, auditory, and kinesthetic learning styles to reinforce content at a subconscious level. Strategically placed around the classroom, peripheral posters of key unit concepts keep the learners' minds focused when they naturally start to stray and become distracted.

Learner-generated posters and mind maps are the best peripherals to use, in my experience, because they are personally meaningful to the learners. Eric Jensen maintains that a passive approach to the learning environment can actually detract from learning (Jensen, 2000). The stark sterility of the typical classroom becomes transformed into a familiar and comfortable learning environment with the inclusion of color, models, and a few other well-planned peripherals that tie into the unit of study.

Adult learners are generally willing to bring in peripherals from their work settings or hobbies. This is a great opportunity for spontaneous and refreshing learner presentations to keep the theme flowing.

I have learners create a poster representing the key concepts of a unit of study and bring it in to display during the study unit week. This assignment becomes more meaningful and less threatening if learners are allowed to select the units for which they would like to present a poster. The poster then becomes part of the presentation on that unit, and the learner who created it has the honor of explaining its relevance. By making such presentations part of the course requirements, learners know in advance that they will be expected to rotate through a schedule of providing peripherals. Peripheral development can also become a collaborative group project as well, promoting social interaction and interpersonal skills. The best part of using peripherals, however, is that learners often donate their posters to the instructor after the unit of study has ended. The instructor then acquires a creative arsenal of peripherals to use with subsequent classes. Having an assortment of markers, pencils, paints, construction paper, glue, tape, and other materials on hand for small group work is a convenient way to promote spontaneous peripheral development.

THE USE OF AROMAS TO PROMOTE LEARNING

Barring any structural defects to the nose, mental clarity and skill performance can be greatly enhanced through the use of certain aromas or fragrances. The olfactory portion of the brain is closely related to the middle brain, where emotions are felt. Certain scents can trigger emotions, which impact the brain's ability to transfer long-term memories from the middle brain to the thinking brain.

Recent scientific research links use of aromas and fragrances to enhanced cognitive processing. Inhaled fragrances go directly to the brain by way of electrical impulses, which travel through olfactory membranes of the nasal cavity, where they are transmitted by the olfactory bulb to the amygdala, the brain's emotional control center. Certain scents that are memorable to learners can evoke emotions even before the individual is aware of them.

Within the limbic system, the hypothalamus is directly stimulated through the inhalation of fragrances, as well. The hypothalamus controls heart rate, blood pressure, and breathing and has a balancing effect on stress hormones (Heuberger, 2001). In a manner of speaking, the brain's neurochemistry is altered in a positive way through aromas and fragrances. Certain fragrances, such as sandalwood, clove oil, melissa, myrrh, and frankincense, have been found to increase oxygen in the brain by as much as 28 percent (Higley & Higley, 1998). Increased oxygen in the brain improves hypothalamus activity, improves the immune response, and increases energy and mental alertness, which leads to improved mental performance in the classroom and on the job.

Lavender induces a relaxed state, making learners feel relaxed and think calmly. Jasmine has been known to generate excitement, thus naturally boosting the brain's ability to think. Some aromas, such as spiced apples and the smell of the seashore, can significantly reduce anxiety and blood pressure to optimize the brain for learning. Floral scents boost creativity and productivity, while lemon fragrances increase mental alertness and responsiveness.

Eucalyptus and peppermint are natural stimulants that can refresh and increase energy levels in weary learners.

I have personally used a combination of gardenias and jasmine potpourri to get learners in the right-brain state to do some very creative group work and special projects. Likewise, I tend to use eucalyptus and peppermint during the long afternoon hours when energy levels are beginning to taper off. One of my favorite aromas is that of a special blend of clove, lavender, and lime oils that stimulates mental clarity and energy. I use this blend with a recording of calming ocean sounds to promote relaxation during mind calms and visualizations.

THE IMPACT OF NUTRITION UPON LEARNING

Every time we make choices of what to eat, we are also choosing how effectively we learn. Proteins, carbohydrates, vitamins, and minerals are transformed into membranes and chemicals that are used by the brain to remember, think, and feel. The amino acids tyrosine and tryptophan often compete with each other for the brain's full attention. The brain uses tyrosine to make dopamine and norepinephrine, which in turn provide the brain with the ability to think quickly and alertly, react fast, and access long-term memory. Tryptophan, which the brain uses to make serotonin, tends to slow reaction times down, impair concentration, and make learners sleepy.

If tyrosine gets to the brain first, the production of dopamine and norepinephrine that it stimulates will accelerate mental capacity. However, if tryptophan gets into the brain before tyrosine, the serotonin it generates will go to work slowing mental productivity down to a halt. Researcher Judith Wurtman, who wrote *Managing Your Mind and Mood through Food*, suggests eating protein foods, which are naturally higher in tyrosine, during the first few bites of a meal and saving the carbohydrates for the last part of the meal. By selecting a high-protein snack food (meat, peanuts, cheese, or yogurt) rather than a high-carbohydrate snack (potato chips, candy bar, or soda pop), learners can boost their natural production of dopamine and norepinephrine to optimize learning potential (Wurtman, 1988).

Vitamins are also important for optimal brain functioning. The B-complex vitamins (1, 2, 3, 6, and 12), found in food sources such as fish, chicken, pork, eggs, soybeans, oats, whole wheat breads and cereals, leafy green vegetables, and peanuts are recommended as well to convert carbohydrates and protein into pure mental energy. Vitamin C is another vitamin that enhances the use of protein to produce the necessary neurotransmitters to enhance memory. Good sources of Vitamin C include citrus fruits, green peppers, and broccoli, all best eaten when raw for the maximum effect.

Minerals are just as important as vitamins in boosting mental performance. In particular, insufficient amounts of boron, copper, and iron have been linked to impaired memory, thought, and mood. Raisins and apples are especially rich in boron, while copper is abundant in fresh fruits, vegetables, and seafood; meat sources are high in iron. While research continues in the area of nutrition and mental function, scientists recommend eating a well balanced diet, paying particular attention to the vitamin and mineral sources discussed in this section.

Fats are especially important nutrients for the brain, as brain cells are made up primarily of fat. Although we need fat in our diets to maintain our brain cells, the type of fat taken in does matter. Diets rich in saturated fats, such as those in animal protein and palm oil, have a negative effect upon thinking, while diets rich in monounsaturated fats, such as olive and canola oils, have a positive effect upon thinking, because they improve brain circulation.

Excessive intake of saturated fats tends to raise blood pressure and cholesterol levels, causing a disruption in the flow of blood to the brain, resulting in impaired memory and concentration. Another consequence of saturated fat intake is increased free-radical production, which actually kills off neurons. On the other hand, diets rich in polyunsaturated fats tend to lower blood pressure and cholesterol levels, resulting in improved circulation throughout the body. Improved circulation to the brain, especially, increases concentration and ability to process information efficiently by increasing the supply of oxygen, nutrients, and glucose to neurons. Another benefit of improved brain circulation is increased cellular metabolism, which protects neurons from free-radical damage.

Since our need for protein is equally important, nutritionists suggest getting primary protein sources from leaner cuts of red meat, chicken, pork, and fish, while avoiding highly marbled and fatty cuts of red meat. Soy products are ideal for meeting the brain's demand for protein, since they are low in fat and high in amino acids that make up the neurotransmitters. In addition, soy protein contains antioxidants that help destroy free radicals and eliminate them from the body. Soy products boost the high-density lipoprotein levels (our good cholesterol), reduce triglycerides, and stabilize blood sugar. The balancing of cholesterol and triglyceride levels promotes a healthier body, while a stable blood sugar keeps the brain alert and focused. Blood sugar that is too low or too high causes learners to become anxious and unable to concentrate.

Water is absolutely vital: The human body is 90 percent water, the brain is 75 percent water, and total body weight is 70 percent water. We rely upon water for all sorts of bodily processes, including circulation of nutrients and oxygen to the brain. When blood flow to the brain is increased, learners are naturally able to process information more efficiently. Fresh water is the ultimate brain beverage. One of the easiest and most inexpensive ways to get the most out of students' learning potential is to encourage BYOB (bring your own bottle *of water,* that is!). Even the strictest establishments will allow water to be brought in. Fresh water is naturally packed with minerals and is free of both sugar and fat—appropriate for any diet!

For small groups, I bring in a five-gallon camp thermos filled with cold, fresh water, and I encourage learners in larger presentations to bring in their own containers. Feedback from learners indicates that drinking water during learning sessions keeps minds sharp and focused. I encourage my learners to drink at least eight ounces of fresh water every hour while attempting to learn new and complex material.

Stress to your learners the importance of considering nutritional intake over the course of the day to ensure an even balance of nutrients for optimal

"To energize the body is to energize the mind."

—*Laurie Materna*

brain processing. Starting with breakfast, learners should take in a balance of protein, complex carbohydrates, and unsaturated fat at least every four to five hours.

THE ROLE OF MUSIC IN LEARNING

Music can also be used to set the stage for learning, especially if the tempo is slightly lower than the heart rate, as it is in baroque and classical music. According to Richard Restak (2003), this type of music activates the parasympathetic nervous system, which is the part of the autonomic nervous system allowing the heart to slow down. Not only does this music have an impact on the heart, it lowers blood pressure temporarily, dilates the blood vessels in the brain, and allows more blood and oxygen to be available for brain activity. These combined relaxation effects of baroque and classical music actually prime the student's brain for learning by synchronizing the beta and alpha brain waves. Restak (2003) attributes these changes to activation of and interaction between the amygdala, auditory cortex, cerebellum, and prefrontal cortex.

Interestingly, Restak maintains that the auditory cortex as well as the cerebellum and the corpus callosum are larger in adult musicians than in the rest of the population (Restak, 2003). Since this "Mozart effect" was popularized in 1993, codiscoverer Gordon Shaw has linked scientific evidence to the impact of music on the brain. Using behavioral and neurophysiological studies, Shaw has researched the relationship between music and how the brain works. Results indicate that music enhances spatial-temporal reasoning and mathematical skills in elementary school children (Graziano, Peterson, & Shaw, 1999) and in patients with Alzheimer's disease as well (Johnson, Cotman, Tasaki, & Shaw, 1998). Matteris, Silvestrini, Troisi, Cupini, and Caltagirone (1997) demonstrated that cerebral blood flow increases in the two middle cerebral arteries with greater flow to the right artery during melody recognition tasks. These results suggest that activation of the right hemisphere occurs while listening to music.

Here are a few baroque and classical artists whose compositions I have brought into the classroom:

- Georg-Friedrich Handel
- Johann Sebastian Bach
- Georg-Phillip Telemann
- Antonio Vivaldi
- Tomaso Albinoni
- Wolfgang Mozart

"Music leads to integration . . . to solid learning, to first-rate thinking, and to a wealth of creativity."

—Ole Anderson

I generally play the music while students are filing into a classroom and then turn it down to a barely audible pitch while presenting content. During group work, I turn the music up again to stimulate creativity. The wonderful thing about this type of music is that students don't even have to like the music to benefit from its effects. I encourage students to listen to this same type of music while studying to increase brain processing. A great resource for students is the book *Learn with the Classics: Using Music to Study Smart at Any Age*, by Ole Andersen, Marcy Marsh, and Arthur Harvey (1999).

CREATIVE VISUALIZATIONS AND MIND CALMS

Visualizations and mind calms are powerful learning strategies that can be utilized to promote success among learners by bringing about a state of relaxed alertness, inducing creativity and imagination, and promoting competence in learning. The human mind thinks in pictures, so naturally, by visualizing a memory that evokes positive and enjoyable feelings, a corresponding biological state will be induced. In contrast, a person who focuses on negative experiences that evoke inferiority and incompetence will in turn conjure up that very same destructive biological state. There is no question which one is the preferred learning state!

Scientific studies of the effects of visualization and meditation have demonstrated increases in the areas of the cortex associated with the perception of incoming information and an increase in the functional relationship between the two hemispheres (Lyubimov, 1992). Evidence from electroencephalograms (EEGs), which measure electrical signals in the brain, indicate that meditation leads to an increase in alpha rhythms (Delmont, 1984; Dillbeck & Vesely, 1986; Echenhofer & Coombs, 1987) as well as increased beta activity (Corby, Roth, & Zarcone, 1978; Peper & Ancoli, 1979; West, 1980). Other studies indicate that meditation is related to control of brain function. For example, Delmont (1984) concluded that meditation begins with activation of the left hemisphere, followed by activation of the right hemisphere. Using positron emission tomography (PET), scientists measuring the rate at which glucose is metabolized in the cerebrum have demonstrated increased frontal lobe activity in response to external or mental stimulation (Herzog et al., 1991).

Although primarily based upon meditation, studies like these clearly indicate that imagery and deep breathing exercises directly influence the synchronization of brain waves. Specifically, these activities elevate both alpha waves, which facilitate auditory and visual learning, and beta waves, which promote higher-level cognitive learning such as problem-solving.

Visualization is a powerful method that is not used to the extent that it could be in adult educational settings. Adult learners have a great wealth of mental movies filed away in their imaginations. Unfortunately, most classroom learning is predominantly composed of left-brain activities and requires very little application of visualization. Consequently, the creative and imaginative right brain often drifts off and daydreams during traditional classroom activities.

Visualizations can be used as a preclass activity to energize or calm students, to promote a positive learning state, or to stimulate creativity. The following visualizations are scripted to be read to learners and can be easily applied in almost any adult educational setting in a relatively short amount of time.

Positive Learning Visualization

Think back to a time in your life when you were successful at learning something: riding a bike, flying a kite, baking a cake, writing a paper, acting in a play, speaking to a group—whatever it was, transport yourself now to that very place in time. Tap into those very same feelings: competence, poise, self-confidence, and being on top of the world! Visualize yourself smiling, experiencing all of these same feelings and ready to do it all over again.

Energizing Visualization

Seeing what you want in your mind's eye will help you gain the energy to get it. So, picture something that you want—really badly! A degree, a new job, a promotion, whatever it is—visualize yourself having it. Think of yourself as successful in getting everything you work toward. Belief is biology: You have to see yourself with what you want before you will get it!

Calming Visualization

First, focus your gaze on an object; any object in the room will do. Close your eyes and visualize the same object. Then open your eyes to confirm the visualization. Continue until the closed-eyes version of the object is a mirror image of the real thing.

Creativity Visualization

Take a few moments to think about one or two concepts that you will be learning. Close your eyes and imagine these concepts coming to life. What are they doing, saying, and feeling? Can you put a face to them, give them a name? How would they want you to remember them? Open your eyes and jot down what you thought during that brief interlude with these concepts.

Mind Calms

Mind calms are centering exercises that increase relaxation and sharpen the learner's mental focus, thereby allowing the learner to enter a resourceful state of relaxed alertness. In this state of relaxed alertness, the brain is able to function more creatively and far more productively than when the mind is full of worry or tension. Mind calms bring the mind back to the body and allow the learner to let go of the everyday distractions outside of the classroom or workplace setting, so they can attend to learning. It is highly recommended to precede mind calms and visualization exercises with a breathing exercise to relax the mind and the body.

> "Imagination is more important than knowledge."
>
> *—Albert Einstein*

In the boxes on this and the following pages are a few mind calm exercises that I have used with large lecture hall presentations as well as small informal work discussion groups. For all these exercises, have learners sit in a comfortable, open position, with feet flat on the floor and without any crossing of extremities. Have them close their eyes as you begin to read the script.

Beginning of Class Centering Exercise

This particular exercise is ideal for starting a new class, especially on a Monday or before a major unit exam. It is best done with dim lights while playing a recording of soothing nature sounds, such as sea sounds or falling rain.

Script

You are relaxed and comfortable, as you sit anticipating this upcoming learning experience. Take a deep breath and focus your attention on your breathing. Breathe in slowly and deeply through your nose and exhale fully through your mouth.

As you sit comfortably now, think about all the events that led you to being here today. Think about all of the people in your life and all of the arrangements you had to make in order to be here today. (PAUSE) Think about how you felt when you awoke this morning, and the feelings you had as you traveled here. Take yourself back to that moment in time; imagine arriving at school this morning, getting off the bus or out of your car, and walking into the building. (PAUSE) Imagine reentering this very room and sitting down in the seat you are now in. (PAUSE) How did you feel as you first sat down, anticipating what was going to happen today? Think about how you feel now, as you sit comfortably, breathing easily and effortlessly, getting ready to learn. (PAUSE)

All of the body is in the mind, but sometimes all of the mind is not in the body. Take the time now to really focus in on your mind and body, as you sit comfortably in the seat you have chosen to be in. Gently think about the rest of the world for a moment, and let the thoughts go free. For now anyway, for you have chosen to be here. (PAUSE)

Focus your attention on your breathing now. Notice how easily and effortlessly you inhale through your nose and exhale through your mouth. Feel the life-giving sensation of the air you breathe in and out. Feel the cool and energizing air as you inhale and the moist warmth of the tension you are releasing. (PAUSE) Now focus your attention on the rest of your body, from the tips of your toes to the top of your head. You are really here, and for a purpose. Ask yourself now, "What is the purpose that I am here for? What is it that I want to accomplish by being here today? Why did I go through all of the preparations earlier to be here today?" (PAUSE)

You deserve to commit yourself fully to the purpose for being here today, to learn as much as you can, to fulfill your lifelong ambition of becoming a _____. Make that commitment to yourself now. (PAUSE) You can achieve anything that you commit yourself to. Now, at a rate that is comfortable for you, slowly become aware of your surroundings, open your eyes, and bring your mind and body back to this moment in time. You came here to learn.

Creative Thinking Exercise

This particular mind calm promotes greater awareness of the creative potential of the brain. It should be preceded by a breathing exercise and read with gentle, relaxing music playing in the background.

Script

Take a deep breath and hold it for a gentle moment, then slowly exhale and close your eyes. Think of the number three and repeat it to yourself in your mind. As you begin to relax, imagine a wave of relaxation flowing downward from your head to your toes. (PAUSE) This wave of relaxation blankets you with a warm and rich sensation of comfort and security. As this wave begins in your head, notice the muscles across your scalp beginning to relax. As the wave continues, you become aware of the relaxing sensations in your forehead, around your eyes, your cheeks, your nose, your mouth, and your jaw. (PAUSE)

While you bask in this feeling of comfort and security, feel the wave of relaxation gently flow down through your neck and shoulders, down your back and into your chest, down your arms, and through your fingers. Imagine this wave of relaxation washing all of the tension you have been storing in your upper body out through your fingertips. You smile as you notice a gentle tingling as the last bit of tension leaves your fingertips. (PAUSE) Imagine this wave of comfort relaxing your heart and your breathing muscles. Notice the rhythm of your heart and the gentle flow of your own breathing pattern as you continue to bask in this wave of comfort and security. (PAUSE)

Now that your upper body is relaxed, focus on this wave of relaxation flowing down into your abdomen and throughout your other life-sustaining organs. Imagine this flow gently moving down into your pelvis and hips, then continuing on down into your legs. Relax your muscles as this wave begins to gently caress your thighs, your calves, and your ankles. As you notice your heels and toes relaxing, imagine this wave of relaxation flowing right on out the soles of your feet, carrying with it all of the tensions you have been storing in your lower body. Your feet tingle with release as the tension continues to flow out of your lower body. (PAUSE)

You are in charge of your time, your life, and your destiny. Anytime you desire to relax as deeply or deeper than you are now, you can do so by focusing on this relaxation technique, the number three, and the word *relax*. You are in charge of your time, your life, and your destiny. (PAUSE)

Now take another breath, hold it gently, and slowly exhale, thinking of the number two and saying the word *relax* to yourself. Let go of all thoughts of the past or future, which intrude upon your relaxed mind. Let them go for now; you can deal with them later. Focus on the here and now. Imagine, with every exhalation, you are letting go of the fears, worries, and tensions that prevent you from achieving your goals. Smile as you blow them away. (PAUSE) With every inhalation, imagine you are breathing in serenity, tranquility, and calm energy that will help you achieve your goals. Smile as you become empowered with this realization. With every breath you take, you relax more and more, becoming more and more conscious of your own empowerment. You are in charge of your time, your life, and your destiny. (PAUSE)

Whenever you desire to relax even more deeply than you are relaxed now, you can do so by simply thinking of the number two and repeating the word *relax* to yourself.

Take another breath in and hold it for a moment; then slowly exhale and think of the number one as you repeat the word *relax* in your mind. Imagine a beautiful flower in your mind with all its natural beauty and vitality. Smell the fragrant aroma of the flower; feel its soft, smooth, cool petals. (PAUSE)

If you can see, smell, and feel this flower in your mind, you have reached the relaxed and resourceful learning state in your brain. You have unlimited creativity and potential in this state. Your inner mind is waiting for you to explore and grow. (PAUSE)

As you continue to contemplate the flower, bring yourself to a peaceful place in your mind. Broaden your awareness to other beautiful things in nature around you: the blue sky with billowy white clouds above you; the soft, plush green grass beneath your feet; the warm stimulating sunshine upon your skin. Relax and enjoy this peaceful, tranquil scene you have created. (PAUSE)

As you enjoy this creative state you have designed, become aware of the fact that you are a creative and willing learner, full of ambition and desire to learn. (PAUSE)

Your creative learning potential is limitless; it knows no bounds. You have all of the resources within you to accomplish any goal you set out for yourself. You are alert and ready to learn. You are in charge of your time, your life, and your destiny. (PAUSE)

When you are ready, bring yourself to conscious awareness by counting forward from one to five. With each number, imagine yourself entering this current learning environment fully aware of your own creative learning potential. As you now become more fully awake and conscious of the here and now, carry with you that peaceful, tranquil, comfortable feeling of security that you acquired in your relaxed and resourceful state. Open your eyes, smile, and know that you are in charge of your time, your life, and your destiny.

Sensory-Stimulating Mind Calm Exercise

When multiple sensory channels are stimulated, new information becomes more deeply rooted and easier to recall. This particular exercise encourages learners to become more aware of their present and past sensory experiences. When internal sensory awareness is expanded, the learner is more receptive to taking in and processing new information. For this particular exercise, the lights are left on and gentle music is played to ensure complete relaxation.

Script

Sit in a comfortable position with your feet on the floor and your hands resting comfortably in your lap, palms down and thumbs together. Straighten yourself so that your head, neck, and trunk are in alignment with each other. Choose a specific spot in the room to focus on, and every time you are asked to open your eyes, focus on that spot. (PAUSE)

(Continued)

(Sensory-Stimulating Mind Calm Exercise, continued)

Gazing comfortably at that spot now, become aware of three things you now see. (PAUSE) Close your eyes and go inside, becoming aware of three things you have seen in the past. (PAUSE) Open your eyes again and look at that spot. Become aware of three things you now hear. (PAUSE) Close your eyes and go inside, becoming aware of three things you have heard in the past. (PAUSE) Open your eyes and look at that spot again. Become aware of three things you now feel. (PAUSE) Close your eyes and go inside, becoming aware of three things you have felt in the past. (PAUSE)

Open your eyes now and look at that spot. Become aware of two things you now see. (PAUSE) Close your eyes and go inside, becoming aware of two things you have seen in the past. (PAUSE) Open your eyes again and look at that spot. Become aware of two things you now hear. (PAUSE) Close your eyes and go inside, becoming aware of two things you have heard in the past. (PAUSE) Open your eyes and look at that spot again. Become aware of two things you now feel. (PAUSE) Close your eyes and go inside, becoming aware of two things you have felt in the past. (PAUSE)

Open your eyes again and look at that spot. Become aware of one thing you now see. (PAUSE) Close your eyes and go inside, becoming aware of one thing you have seen in the past. (PAUSE) Open your eyes again and look at that spot. Become aware of one thing you now hear. (PAUSE) Close your eyes and go inside, becoming aware of one thing you have heard in the past. (PAUSE) Open your eyes and look at that spot again. Become aware of one thing you now feel. (PAUSE) Close your eyes and go inside, becoming aware of one thing you have felt in the past. (PAUSE)

Now, stay inside (PAUSE) and just become aware of your own awareness, this very experience you are having at this moment in time. (PAUSE) Enjoy this experience for a few moments, and when you are ready, open your eyes and bring your attention back to the purpose for which you came here today: to learn everything you can by activating your sensory memories of sight, hearing, and touch.

BALANCING THE BRAIN THROUGH MOVEMENT ACTIVITIES

Physical activity increases neuronal metabolism by increasing the amount of oxygen and glucose delivered to the brain. This increased metabolism stimulates the brain cells to connect and communicate with other brain cells and removes necrotic debris from brain cells. According to Dr. Dharma Singh Khalsa, who created the Brain Longevity program, physical exercise increases output of the brain-stimulating neurotransmitters norepinephrine and dopamine. Norepinephrine facilitates the transfer of short-term memories into long-term storage. Both of these neurotransmitters promote a stable and balanced mood as well (Khalsa, 1997).

Physical activity also reduces stress by decreasing cortisol output. In addition, physical activity lowers blood pressure and stabilizes blood sugar levels, thus promoting a balanced energy state. In his research on brain longevity in adults, Dr. Khalsa identifies nerve growth factor (NGF) and brain-derived neurotrophic factor (BDNF), chemicals that stimulate regeneration of the brain, as being most abundant in the hippocampus (the brain's memory center) of adults who are physically active.

Needless to say, a regular physical exercise program of at least 30 minutes every day is most ideal for maintaining optimal brain function. However, physical activity at the onset of a learning session can provide the same benefits for the purpose of that session. Laurie Glazener (2004) developed the Relax, Energize, Activate, and Lead into academic instruction (REAL) method for optimizing learning and increasing information processing. The Relax component focuses on mentally calming the mind to prepare, the Energize component focuses on hydration and on exercises that stimulate the delivery of oxygen to the brain, the Activate component focuses on balancing the two hemispheres of the brain through movement exercise, and the Lead component activates prior knowledge and warms up the sensory system.

Although Glazener's method was developed primarily for elementary school children, many of her techniques are quite adaptable to the adult learner as well. As previously mentioned, in working with adults, I also relax my students through mind calms, and I energize them with breathing exercises and encouragement to maintain an optimal state of hydration throughout the learning session. I strongly agree that balancing exercises help to activate both left and right hemispheres of the brain to engage whole-brain processing.

Carla Hannaford demonstrated that cross-lateral movements strengthen the corpus callosum, which is essential for smooth communication between hemispheres (Hannaford, 1995). According to educator Pat Wolfe (2001), the addition of movement exercises to the classroom adds one more component of sensory stimulation to the brain, thereby facilitating learning. I have developed a series of exercises designed to integrate and balance the right and left hemispheres of the brain as well as the brainstem and frontal lobes and the limbic system and cerebral cortex. In the following movement exercises, all parts of the brain work together for optimal processing of new information. I have broken up the exercises into three groups: those for movement, focusing, and centering.

• **Movement exercises:** Movement exercises ensure that information taken in through the senses can be processed smoothly and efficiently from right to left and left to right. In that way, the logical left hemisphere and the creative right hemisphere work in harmony to make sense out of incoming stimuli.

• **Focusing exercises:** Focusing exercises involve activation of the brainstem and frontal lobes, which are primarily involved in attending to and comprehending incoming information.

• **Centering exercises:** Centering exercises involve the limbic system and cerebral cortex, which promote a state of emotional balance. As you recall from Chapter 1, learning is promoted in a nonthreatening and emotionally pleasing environment. Once learners are emotionally balanced, they begin to attach meaning to what they are learning. When learners are emotionally imbalanced, they tend to downshift to the primitive brain state, where the focus is upon survival and self-preservation.

The following sections list exercises designed to promote learning in each of these three categories.

Movement Exercises

Cross Overs: Start by touching right hand to left shoulder and left hand to right shoulder, then right hand to left elbow and left hand to right elbow, right hand to left wrist and left hand to right wrist, and so on down to the feet. For fun, these can be done to music and with a bounce in the step!

Figure 8s: Draw a figure eight in the air (extending from shoulder to waist) with the right arm, then left arm, then both together. Keep eyes on the tips of fingers at all times while drawing.

Human Pretzel: Stand with feet crossed and extend arms out in front of you. Cross the right hand over the left and clasp hands together. Bring clasped hands in toward chest and tuck up under chin with head bowed down. Breathe easily in and out while holding this position for 15 seconds. This activity helps to increase oxygen flow to the brain. Reverse the process to unfold the pretzel going backwards.

Focusing Exercises

Stretch Ups: Bring arms outstretched above head while standing on tiptoes. Come down flat on feet, stretch arms out to sides, and point middle finger up toward ceiling. Bring arms back above head and stand on tiptoes again; then twist torso, stretch arms out front and back, and point fingers up toward ceiling.

Foot Flex: Sit in a chair with right ankle crossed over left lower leg. Close eyes and make circular movements with right foot: five times to left, then five times to right. Reverse position: Cross left ankle over right and repeat circling movements.

Chair Push: Stand and support self with hands on the back of a chair. Place left leg behind right leg and lean forward, flexing right leg while inhaling. Left leg should be straight with heel off the floor and full weight on right foot. Hold breath and shift weight to left leg, planting it firmly on the floor, and exhale slowly. Repeat three times; then shift to opposite leg and repeat three more times.

Centering Exercises

Neck Circles: Breathe in deeply while slowly circling the neck and the head forward and around, then backward and around, as if it were a heavy ball. Do with eyes closed, then with eyes open.

Energy Breathing: Sit at a table or desk with hands resting on top. While inhaling deeply, experience breath moving up from the seat like a burst of energy, lifting first forehead, then neck, then shoulders. Exhaling, curl head toward chest and bring forehead down to rest on the desk. Repeat three times.

Chair Flow: While sitting in a chair with the left foot crossed over the right, bend forward while exhaling, allowing upper body to flow as if being poured out of the chair, while hips and buttocks remain firmly seated. Reaching out in front, extend arms as far as possible for ten seconds; then slowly inhale while returning to sitting position. Repeat three times; then cross right foot over left and repeat three more times.

Repeat these centering cycles three to four times.

RECIPE FOR SUCCESS IN PROMOTING A RESOURCEFUL LEARNING STATE

Although you may feel awkward at first in implementing some of these strategies with your learners, give the activities a whirl, and gauge your effectiveness on learner feedback as well as learning outcomes. As previously mentioned, when learners understand the rationale behind these strategies, they are much more inclined to participate. I have used a few combinations that seem to be especially effective with adult learners. Figure 4.1 shows my recipe for success, which you can try out on your adult learners. The entire routine takes all of five minutes, and it can be repeated during the break period.

> "They who know enough know how to learn."
>
> —Henry Brooks Adams

Figure 4.1   Recipe for Successful Learning

Recipe for Successful Learning

1. Play baroque music softly as listeners enter the room.

2. Call learners together, and initiate deep diaphragmatic breathing for a cycle of three breaths (one minute).

3. Initiate ratio breathing, and lead learners into visualization for positive learning, energy, or creative thinking (two minutes).

4. Bring learners back, and have them participate in a combination of movement, focusing, and centering exercises (one minute).

5. End with a deep, cleansing breath and a full body stretch (one minute).

6. Continue playing baroque music at barely audible level during your presentation; then turn the music up to energize learners for group work.

7. Have a combination of aromas available in the room to stimulate creative thinking (if agreeable with all students—check for allergies).

Part 3

Active Learning Strategies

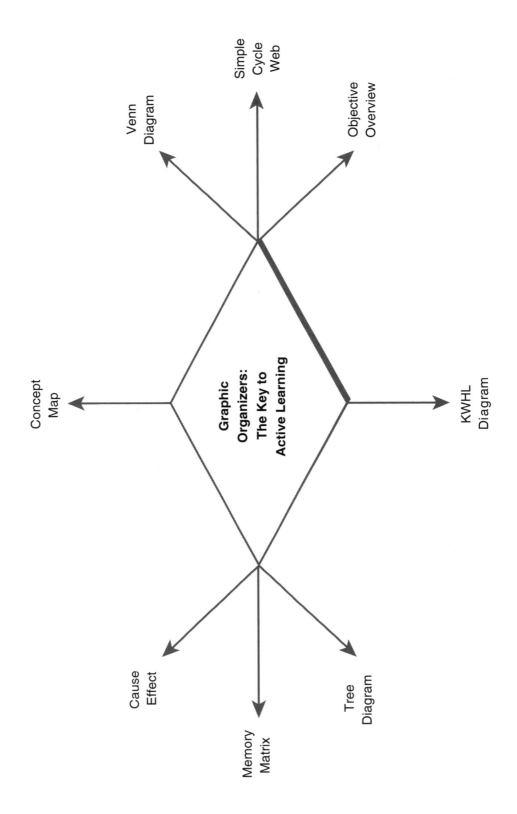

Simple
Cycle
Web

Venn
Diagram

Objective
Overview

Concept
Map

**Graphic
Organizers:
The Key to
Active Learning**

KWHL
Diagram

Cause
Effect

Memory
Matrix

Tree
Diagram

Key Metacognitive Learning Strategies

METACOGNITION AND THE ADULT BRAIN

From an educational perspective, true learning is looking beyond the superficial meaning of a concept and understanding the concept from multiple perspectives. Metacognition is the ability to understand your own thinking processes and to apply active learning strategies that will promote a sense of knowing—in other words, knowing what you know and knowing what you don't know as well as knowing those strategies to use to learn what you don't know!

Empowering Adult Learners

As you have learned from Chapters 1 and 2, the brain can process and integrate new knowledge in a very natural and effortless way when the information is processed through multiple memory pathways. Such multipathway processing makes the newly learned information more readily available in a variety of memory storage areas throughout the brain. Having conscious awareness of how the brain learns and knowing how to take full advantage of personal learning strengths is crucial in order for learners to become empowered and self-directed in applying personal learning strategies. Education is closely linked to cognitive sciences in that both study the relationship and interaction between the conscious mind (metacognition) and the brain (Damasio, 1999; Goldblum, 2001; LeDoux, 2002; Ornstein, 1991; Vedantum, 2002).

Brain Cells Need Active Engagement to Grow

Educator Robert Sylwester maintains that linear and passive learning activities are simply not compatible with the way the brain naturally learns (Sylwester, 1995). The brain cells need to be actively engaged in the process of learning in order for learners to gain knowledge from information taken in. Neural structures are grown from active involvement and application of concepts. During active engagement in learning, neurons begin growing new dendrites related to that specific learning. The axons of other neurons connect with these newly developed dendrites at the synapse. (Refer to Part 1 for a full discussion of how the brain learns.) According to numerous researchers (Bjorklund, 1988; Gopnik, Meltzoff, & Kuhl, 1999; Greenfield, 1997; Hart, 1999; Restak, 2003; Rose, 1992; Sylwester, 1995), the point at which this connection is made is when learning is said to occur. With the structural change in connections between dendrites, the learner turns raw information into knowledge by connecting and building upon previous memories already stored in the brain. Likewise, the brain eliminates unused connections as well, in a process referred to as pruning (Eriksson et al., 1998).

According to psychologist Leslie Hart, when learning activities are incorporated into prior knowledge bases, the speed of learning, or neural restructuring, is accelerated (Hart, 1999). Researchers studying rat brain cells, which bear a remarkable resemblance to human brain cells (Diamond, 1967, 1988; Greenough, Black, & Wallace, 1987; Renner & Rosenzweig, 1987), have found that stimulating and active learning environments enable learners to grow substantially greater neural connections than nonstimulating and inactive learning environments. Further research has validated that dendrite growth in human brain tissue proliferates in response to active and interactive involvement in novel and stimulating learning environments (Jacobs, Schall, & Schiebel, 1993).

Survival and Restructuring of Brain Cells

Educator Gerald Edelman suggests that the brain is genetically programmed to survive and evolve (Edelman, 1992). From this perspective, learning activities can be perceived as survival strategies. Adults, more so than children, are motivated to learn the necessary skills and knowledge in order to survive and flourish. The behaviorist orientation to teaching that centers upon a traditional and didactic philosophy of education is incongruent not only with learning but also with the brain's natural propensity to survive. The constructivist orientation to teaching is far more consistent with the brain's natural learning processes. New knowledge is constructed from existing knowledge banks as neural structures connect to and grow from preexisting cells (Goldblum, 2001).

Adult learners are self-directed and survival oriented. They understand how they learn best based upon past learning experiences. They insist upon being actively engaged in applying concepts as they learn. They want to draw upon personal experiences to enrich learning.

The fact that adult learners possess a lifetime of experiences to build upon makes active learning strategies even more brain-compatible. Having a firm knowledge base truly is the first step for constructing new knowledge. When the brain is able to integrate new learning with previously learned concepts, it constructs a new understanding, actually modifying or changing the neural pathways as it links new knowledge with existing knowledge.

Because of the amazing plasticity of the brain, adult learners' brains have been reorganized and rearranged many times over as a result of their extensive life experiences. According to neuroscientist John Ratey, the resultant pattern of neural connections guides the behavior of the learner, while the interactions within the learning environment continually modify the connections (Ratey, 2001). Adult learners have little patience or time for sitting passively in a traditional lecture-style classroom. They perceive education as an investment of their own time and energy as well as a vehicle to promote their careers. They desire to be active participants in rather than passive recipients of their own learning processes. These self-directed learners with strong metacognitive skills merely need to be guided through their own learning processes.

Multisensory Processing Abilities

Educator James Zull describes the process of learning as a cycle of gathering (information through the sensory cortex), analyzing (making meaning through the posterior integrative cortex), creating (new meaning through the front integrative cortex), and then acting (upon newly created ideas through the motor cortex) (Zull, 2003). In other words, learning is a dynamic and fluid process that involves the whole brain. When information is actively processed and organized in this manner, neural connections are strengthened, and overall recall and retention of information is enhanced (Robertson, 2000). The metacognitive learning strategies in this chapter promote the natural learning process by naturally engaging multiple areas of the brain to actively process new information, link this information to previously learned concepts, and modify connections so that a new understanding is created.

The Need for Mental Stimulation

Mental stimulation of the brain is the key to keeping the adult brain healthy and growing. According to educator Robert Kotulak, because of the plasticity of brain cells in adults, mental stimulation in the educational environment may be more essential to the adult brain than food. Stimulating learning activities produce significantly more connections between brain cells. Kotulak maintains that these connections increase memory and provide a healthy buffer against the neurological diseases that tend to impair memory in adults (Kotulak, 2004).

This intent of this chapter is to introduce adult educators to a variety of brain-energizing active learning strategies that can be utilized effectively to enhance adult learning in the formal academic setting as well as the informal workplace setting. The strategies in this chapter enhance metacognition by promoting knowledge acquisition, comprehension, and active learning. They have been developed from research on metacognition and the brain's natural ability to process information. The strategies include a variety of graphic organizers, study strategies, and discussion techniques that I have used to energize and stimulate adult learners in both academic and workplace settings. I have created a number of metacognitive strategies to facilitate active learning among adult students.

KNOWLEDGE ACQUISITION STRATEGIES

Knowledge acquisition strategies encourage learners to make knowledge their own instead of passively absorbing information. This includes activities that promote elaboration and organization of the material into a format that is more meaningful and easier for the learner to process and recall. Graphic organizers such as concept maps, Venn diagrams, cause-effect webs, simple cycle webs, tree diagrams, memory matrices, and objective overview diagrams are a few of the most effective strategies I have found to promote knowledge acquisition.

One of the most incredible abilities of the human brain is to absorb a variety of inputs and to reorganize them into a format consistent with the individual learner's knowledge base. So remarkable is this natural ability that the brain reassigns new information into specific categories or understandings based on previous memories, keeping the learner's perspective consistent and maintaining the status quo (Ramachandran & Blakeslee, 1998). But what about new information that cannot be easily categorized into previous knowledge? The brain strives to make sense of all incoming information and tends to either ignore or distort unfamiliar information to make it fit the learner's current belief system. Trivial information that cannot be linked eventually filters out altogether. Linking new information to existing knowledge reinforces the learner's belief system and strengthens the existing neural connections. When this happens, the new and existing knowledge become interconnected and are simultaneously recalled by the learner.

Graphic Organizers to Process and Integrate Knowledge

When graphic organizers are used, information is processed into patterns of association consistent with previous learning. The use of graphic organizers may also help learners to spot inconsistencies between new knowledge and previously learned information, thus promoting a change in neural patterns as more information is absorbed.

Reviewing information with graphic organizers reinforces knowledge acquisition by strengthening neural networks and influencing the processing of the next input, thus promoting a search for better interpretation of the sensory input (Ratey, 2001). As the brain forms new connections between synapses, learning occurs through a process of strengthening some synaptic connections while weakening others, thus having an overall effect on future learning (Ratey, 2001).

Best of all, graphic organizers encourage the adult learner's natural desire to be self-directed and autonomous. Self-directed learners are more likely to question what they already know as they process additional new information. Questioning information helps to reorder existing knowledge, literally forcing neurons to change connections, thereby contributing to new learning behaviors.

Promotion of Visual Processing

Graphic organizers are more novel and stimulating than traditional linear approaches to learning that most adults have been conditioned to. Since the brain's attention is selective, it tends to focus more on novelty, while ignoring the routine. This attentional specificity craves images and graphic representations (Ratey, 2001). The brain thinks in pictures, not in text; graphic organizers allow for this natural ability to process visually while learning and reorganizing patterns of association. Visually stimulating learning activities, such as graphic organizers, promote creative processing in the parietal lobes better than traditional learning activities, which focus on reading and writing activities that are processed primarily in the frontal cortex. Graphic organizers combine words with pictures, stimulating whole-brain processing, which has been found to increase recall, understanding, and retention of information (Markuson, 2003).

Graphic organizers naturally activate the visual processing areas of the brain as it seeks to understand complex information at a glance. Because it is easier for the brain to make meaning of complex information presented in a visual way, a picture is worth a thousand words!

Bridging the Gap From
Previous Learning to New Learning

Previous learning experiences also impact the ability of the learner to process and construct new knowledge. Long-term memories are stored by the hippocampus after it sifts through and sorts information into various parts of the brain (Ratey, 2001). However, not all long-term memories have been sifted and sorted correctly. Long-term memories are highly influenced by emotions and the environment at the time the memory was formed, and they can fade and change over time and with new experiences. Negative experiences can actually inhibit memory of previously learned material in a process called retroactive interference (Reeves & Nass, 1996). These interferences pose a challenge to the process of learning new information accurately. Graphic organizers actually refresh memories by connecting to previously learned concepts. Integrating core concepts from previous units into a graphic organizer can bridge the transition from previous learning to new learning.

It requires some preplanning on the educator's part to use graphic organizers in class. However, adult learners are generally extremely receptive and soon pick up on how to develop these strategies to use on their own. Using the computer to create graphic organizers is a stimulating activity that has positive implications, especially for adult learners.

TYPES OF GRAPHIC ORGANIZERS

There are a variety of brain-compatible learning strategies that can enhance the learner's ability to acquire knowledge in a more meaningful way. Many graphic organizers can be used in formal lecture as well as the informal workplace setting. Remember, using a combination of these active learning strategies will promote metacognitive skills in learners.

Graphic organizers are an excellent tool to use for organizing complex information into meaningful patterns of association. My own personal research with adult learners demonstrates that information processed graphically is much easier to recall than the same concepts processed in a linear fashion (Materna, 2000). Graphic organizers also engage the attention, getting learners actively involved in constructing knowledge. Better yet, graphic organizers reinforce concepts every time the learner reviews them. I have included in this chapter descriptions of a variety of graphic organizers that can be easily adapted to any field of study.

Concept Maps

Concept maps are not a new technique by any means. Educator David Ausubel first introduced concept mapping as a metacognitive strategy supporting assimilation theory (Ausubel, 1978). According to assimilation theory, learning is enhanced when behavioral learning strategies, such as rote memorization, are replaced with higher-level cognitive learning strategies, such as organizing and relating new concepts to existing concepts embedded within the learner's cognitive structure.

The essence of assimilation theory is the notion that new meaning is acquired as a result of the interactions of newly learned information with previously learned concepts. Consequently, new concepts are formed while existing concepts are continually modified and refined (Ausubel, 1978). Thus the potential for subsequent learning is strengthened considerably when learners develop the ability to assimilate newly learned concepts. Cognitive science supports Ausubel's theory that memory is strengthened when learners are mentally engaged by thinking about the meaning of what they are learning (Willingham, 2003). Concept maps enhance this process because they require learners to actively process the meaning of information.

Educator James Novak, who has further advocated the use of concept mapping in the sciences, maintains that information must be assimilated into existing knowledge structures for the learner to make meaningful connections out of the information (Novak, 1998). According to Novak, information taken in without assimilation is almost impossible to store and recall. Knowledge acquired in a meaningful way, such as through concept mapping, is retained much longer, enhances subsequent learning of related material, and can be applied to a wide variety of new problems or contexts, thus increasing transferability of knowledge (Novak, 1998). The ability to transfer concepts and learning further enhances higher levels of critical and creative thinking as well as meaningful learning.

Meaningful learning, according to Novak (1998), is an empowering process, whereby learners construct and exert control and ownership over the newly integrated knowledge. Using meaningful study aids such as concept mapping allow learners to create and construct knowledge in a personally meaningful way. They gain control of the incoming information by organizing and processing separate and unrelated facts, eventually turning this raw information into meaningful knowledge.

Likewise, concept mapping also visually demonstrates linkages and connections that are faulty, allowing learners the opportunity to rethink and correct misconceptions before building upon them (Novak & Gowin, 1984). Misconceptions in knowledge are more difficult for learners to see using traditional, linear methods of processing information and may not be recognized by the learner until years later. Adult learning principles (Apps, 1988; Knowles, 1980) are supported using metacognitive learning strategies such as concept mapping. Learners are free to relate new concepts to their prior knowledge and experiences, thus reinforcing and validating their own conceptual knowledge base. The very nature of concept mapping promotes active learning and higher-level cognitive skills, such as analysis, synthesis, and evaluation (Bloom, 1956).

Concept mapping is a metacognitive strategy that naturally provides students with the opportunity to visualize and integrate theory with professional practice. As critical thinking skills are essential for problem-solving, concept mapping can develop metacognitive abilities by promoting problem-solving and organizational skills. Figure 5.1 is itself a concept map that shows basic guidelines for building concept maps.

Use of Concept Maps in Higher Education

I have used concept mapping as a method for presenting new material by introducing a partially generated concept map of a theory at the beginning of a unit. Learners are given copies of the map and work along with me as I present new concepts and visually add them to the master map using a projector and screen. As concepts are introduced, I encourage learners to supply the rationale to support the relationships between concepts. They are encouraged to make their maps unique and to color-code the concepts and linkages in a way that will enhance their understanding. Because many learners feel more comfortable with the standardized outline version of presenting material, I provide the option of taking notes through concept mapping or outline format. With each exposure to concept mapping, however, I observe more and more learners participating in this strategy. I have successfully integrated theory concepts maps to introduce new concepts.

I have developed three examples of concept maps that could be used to introduce new concepts in an adult setting. The first example is a map used to introduce a unit on academic goal setting (see Figure 5.2). After they receive a general overview of types of goals set throughout an academic career, learners can begin setting personal academic goals and developing a strategic plan for how they will meet their goals. Learners may add concepts to this map to streamline their own goals. The next example (shown in Figure 5.3) is a concept map that can be used as a study guide to reinforce newly learned strategies of financial management. And finally, Figure 5.4 shows a brainstorming map that can be used to stimulate a discussion on effective study strategies. These maps were designed for a group of returning adult learners preparing to enter a degree program. When you develop your own maps, you can use color and graphics to greatly promote visual processing and recall of content each time the learner reviews the map.

Early in the semester, I empower learners by showing them how to use the Inspiration mapping software program as well as how to design tables

(Text continues on page 102)

Figure 5.1 Concept Map Guidelines

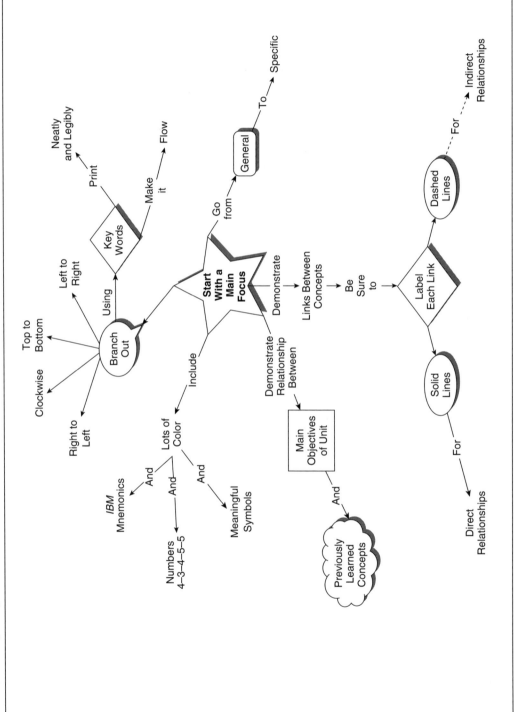

Figure 5.2   Academic Goal Setting

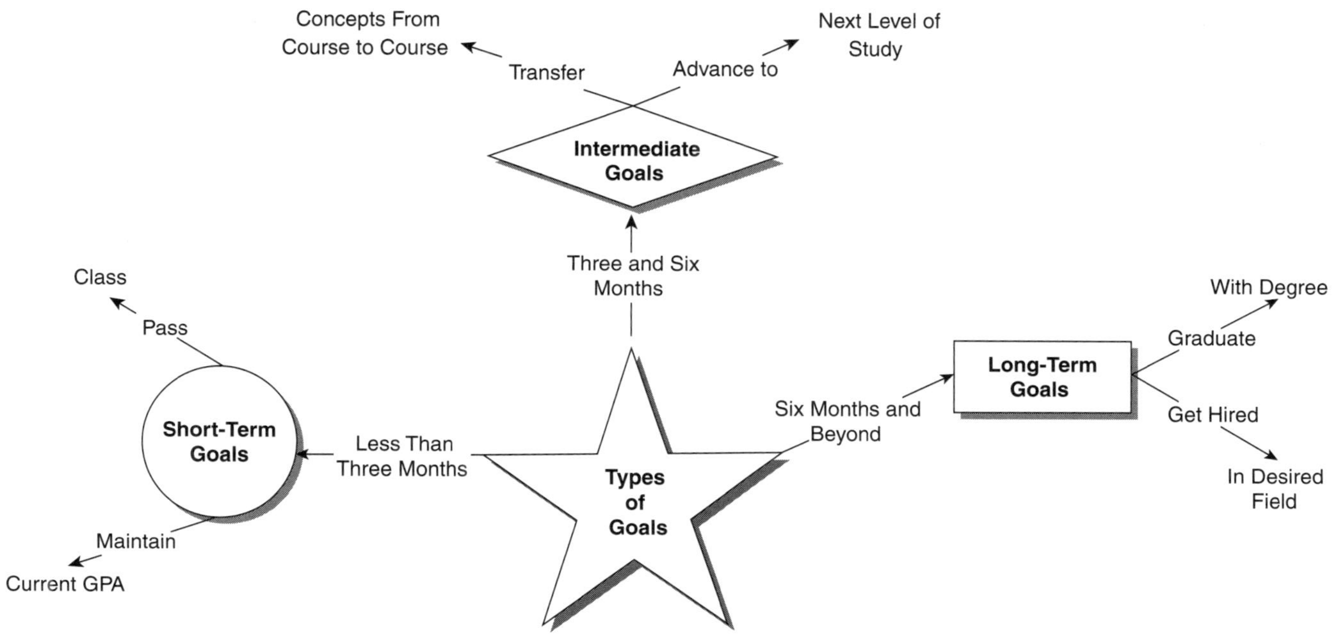

Types of Goals

Less Than Three Months → Short-Term Goals
- Pass → Class
- Maintain → Current GPA

Three and Six Months → Intermediate Goals
- Transfer → Concepts From Course to Course
- Advance to → Next Level of Study

Six Months and Beyond → Long-Term Goals
- Graduate → With Degree
- Get Hired → In Desired Field

100

Figure 5.3 Financial Management

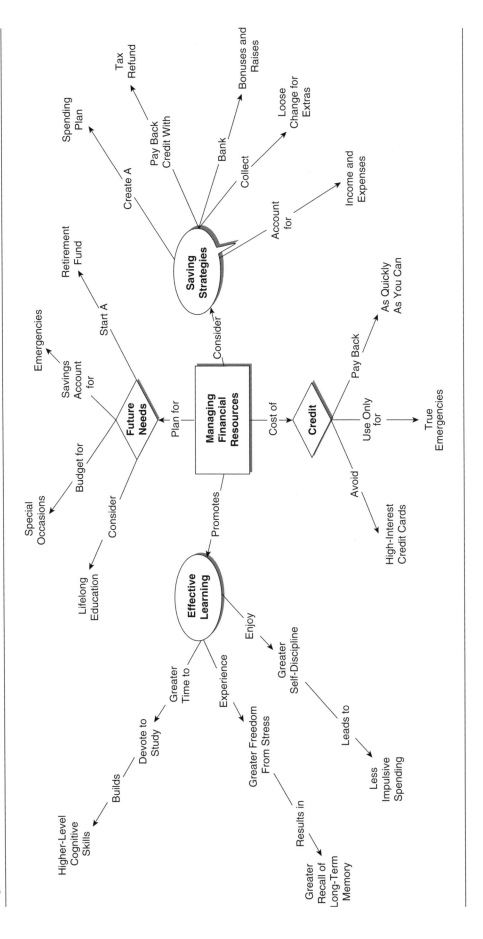

Figure 5.4 Effective Study Strategies

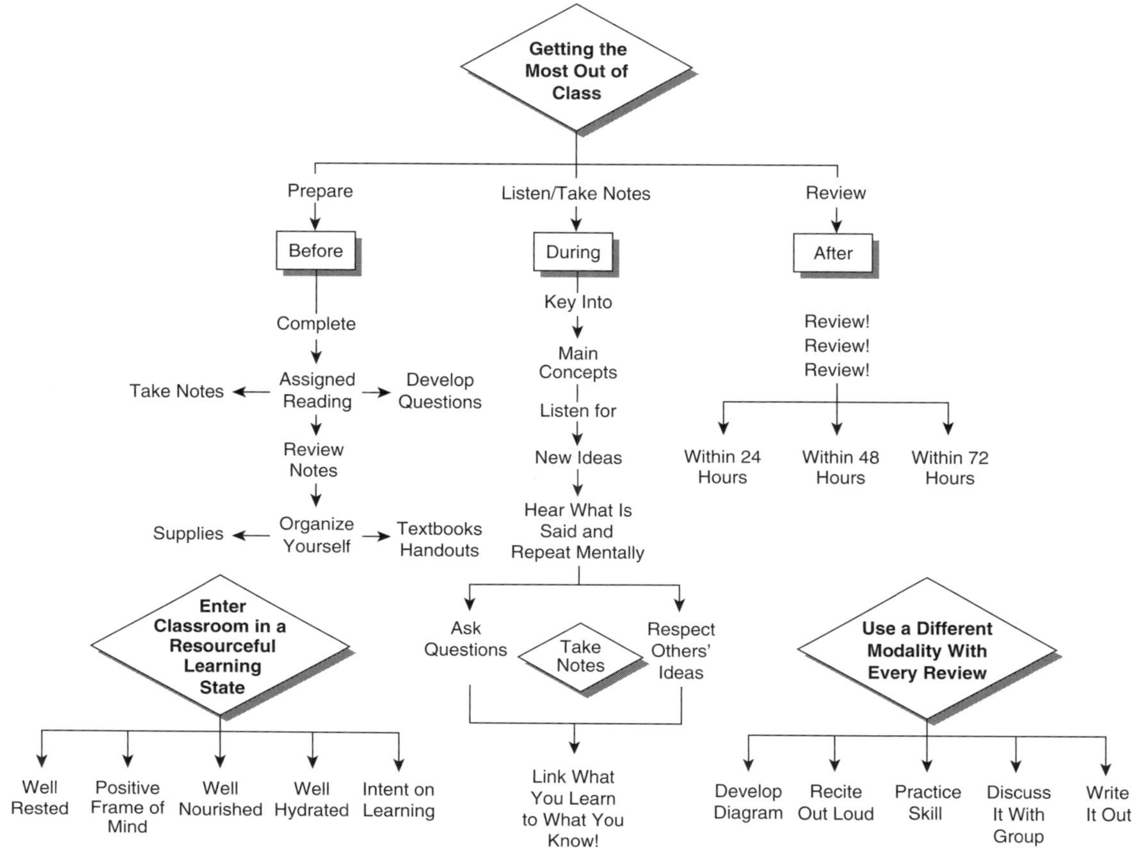

and graphs using Microsoft Word. Although I don't require it, I highly recommend that learners invest in some sort of mapping software and encourage them to use it to reorganize their notes into meaningful learning maps and study diagrams. The verbal feedback that I receive from learners is positive, and the academic feedback is phenomenal. When I see learners smiling from ear to ear as they tell me how excited they are about their improved test scores, I know that I have made an impact in the area of adult education!

Concept maps can be developed from almost any topic. Of course, the inclusion of color and graphics really makes the maps memorable and meaningful. You may also choose to use different symbols such as triangles, circles, clouds, etc. to differentiate and categorize concepts if color and graphics are not an option, as shown in Figures 5.5 and 5.6. Other sample templates can be found in the Resources at the end of this book.

Procedure Maps

Concept mapping also works well as a framework for presenting complex technical skills. I have found that when learners are required to demonstrate

Figure 5.5   Concept Map Patterns

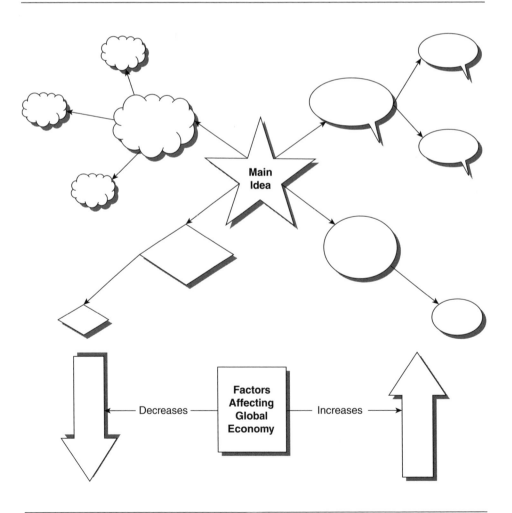

Figure 5.6   Basic Multibox Concept Maps

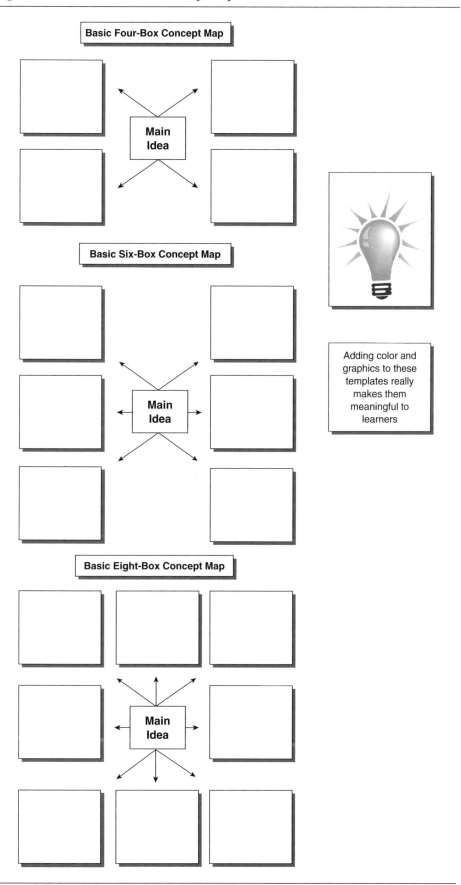

Basic Four-Box Concept Map

Main Idea

Basic Six-Box Concept Map

Main Idea

Basic Eight-Box Concept Map

Main Idea

Adding color and graphics to these templates really makes them meaningful to learners

competency in specific skills, their anxiety levels prevent them from learning complex skills effectively. As you recall from Part 1, increased anxiety interferes with learning and performing, as the brain downshifts under perceived threat. Concept map representations help to break down multiple steps into smaller chunks, which can be recalled easily through visual imagery.

Much of my teaching has been in the field of nursing, a vast field with many, many skills and procedures to learn and retain. I have observed that learners have traditionally tried to memorize all of the steps and variations of a procedure in order to demonstrate the skill in clinical lab. Naturally, when learners are anxious about learning, they tend to rely on rote memorization to learn. Unfortunately, this is an especially ineffective strategy to use, as the brain perceives threat and automatically downshifts to the survival mode.

Seeking a more brain-friendly way to get learners to master these essential skills, I began using procedure maps to teach required skills at the foundation level, such as oral medication administration. I actually began working with a handful of learners who were repeatedly failing the return demonstration. I explained how anxiety affects performance and demonstrated how effectively a procedure map could be used to visualize the steps in the procedure. Learners were encouraged to create their own procedure maps for subsequent procedures. After they created and utilized their procedure maps for practice demonstrations, they reported greater competence and less anxiety going into the clinical lab to demonstrate the skill. Consequently, learners were much better prepared to integrate the skill into the actual clinical environment.

Currently I work with students at all levels, as well as with practicing nurses, teaching how to create procedure maps to reinforce technical skills. Figure 5.7 shows a procedure map I have used to describe steps in completing a project.

Template for Developing a Procedure Map

Procedure maps are relatively easy to construct and can be applied to any field of study. Once learners know how to use procedure maps, they can easily develop their own maps, using the template as a guide. Remember, a learner-generated map is more empowering for the learner to use! Again, the inclusion of graphics, color, or symbols will make the procedure map more meaningful. Figure 5.8 shows a well-known acronym for fire emergencies that has been developed into a procedure map, and Figure 5.9 includes some generic procedure templates. Procedure maps work especially well in emergency situations when there is precious little time to read lengthy instructions!

Process Maps

Some of the most popular mapping strategies that I have developed so far have to be the maps used to teach nursing processes, care plans, and clinical preparation. These maps were designed to assist learners at the foundation level to understand nursing process in a more visual way. However, learners began sharing the maps and continued to use these maps as they progressed through the nursing curriculum. Interestingly, staff nurses at the clinical sites were intrigued with the nursing process maps as well. I have presented concepts maps

Figure 5.7   Procedure Map for Completing a Project

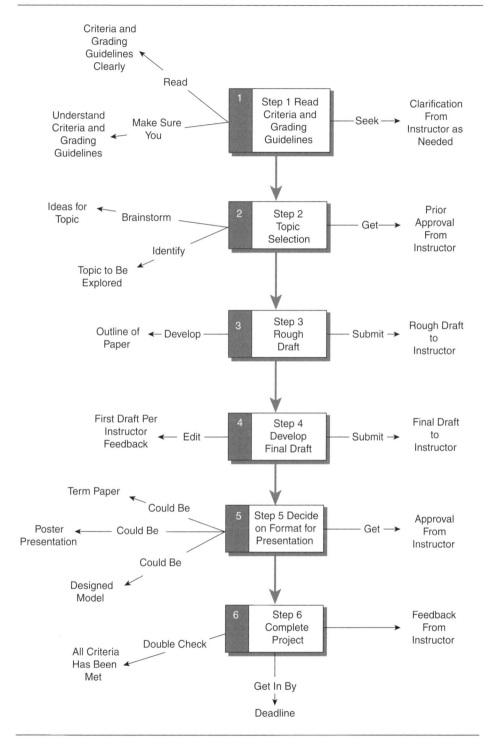

in nursing process and as a clinical preparation tool to countless nursing faculty at various levels of practice. The beauty is in the simplicity. Learners who are highly visual tend to enhance their maps with color-coding and diagrams. Further, learners are able to expand upon the structure of the map by drawing additional linkages to other areas of the map.

Figure 5.8   Procedure for Emergencies

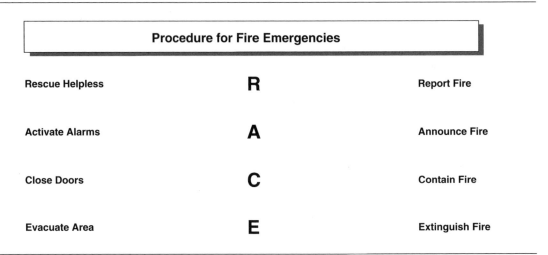

Figure 5.9   Procedure Templates

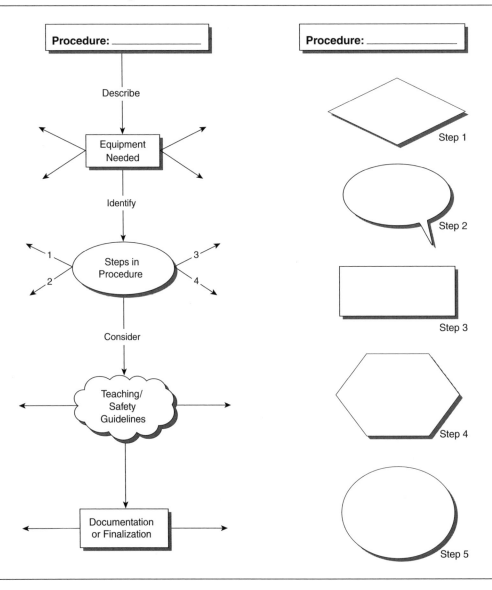

Creating a map to guide and direct adult learners with specific processes or protocols is a very empowering technique and can be used in any field of study. Use your imagination and brainstorm ideas on how your learners would benefit from these strategies. You will be impressed how the information just flows off the page. It definitely will make your job a lot easier! Figure 5.10 shows a process map for writing a resume, and Figure 5.11 is a template for making process maps. Process maps can be designed using a single level as well as multiple levels of processing. Related links can be drawn off any of the components of the process to build upon the process.

Cause and Effect Diagrams

Another type of graphic organizer that I have found to be helpful in understanding relationships between concepts is the cause and effect diagram. In this strategy, a situation or event and ensuing effects are drawn. The cause and effect diagram is especially useful as a review strategy to determine if your learners understand causes and effects of any given situation. Examination of cause and effect relationships can help learners construct logical arguments, examine life events, or analyze information for a more thorough understanding of concepts.

Cause and effect diagrams can be used to explain simple cause and effect relationships. The examples in Figure 5.12 are diagrams used in adult continuing education classes. The template in Figure 5.13 can be constructed to have one cause and one effect, one cause and multiple effects, or multiple causes and one effect.

Figure 5.10   Process Map for Writing a Resume

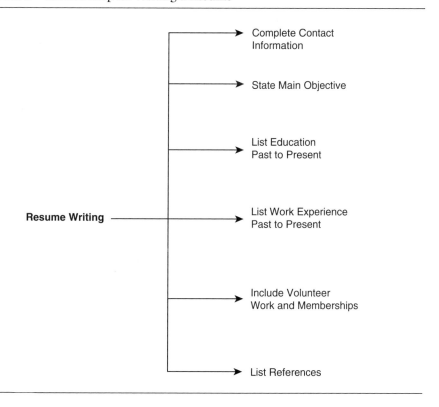

Figure 5.11 Process Map Template

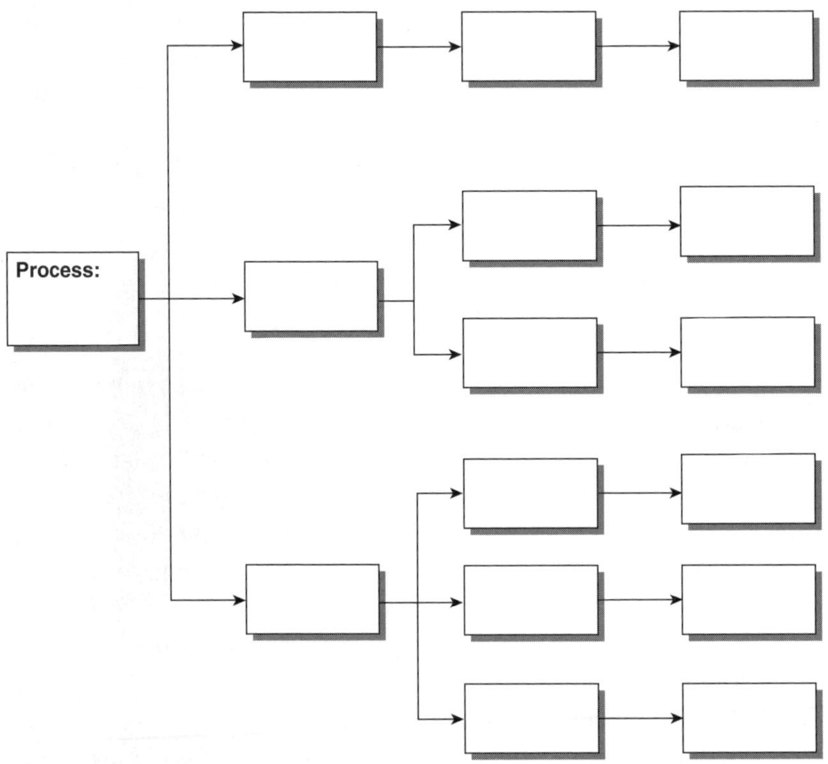

Venn Diagrams

A Venn diagram is another useful graphic organizer that I have used to illustrate comparisons and contrasts between two concepts or events. You can see at a glance the unique attributes that two events or concepts have in common as well as the unique attributes that set them apart. This strategy can be used for simple comparisons as well as for comparisons with much greater sophistication and complexity. For example, you might use a Venn diagram as a teaching strategy to compare the subtle similarities and differences between ethnic cultures, disease states, treatment options, and so forth. Figure 5.14 shows a Venn diagram comparing the differences between two potential job offers. A Venn diagram template is shown in Figure 5.15; there is another example in Resource E.

Simple Cycle Web

A simple cycle web is yet another handy graphic organizer that I have found valuable in demonstrating simple cycles and natural processes that are sequential in nature. In the field of science, for example, the developmental milestones of life generally follow a predictable cycle from infancy to the elderly years. A simple cycle web demonstrating this relationship is shown in Figure 5.16, and several other examples of templates are shown in Figure 5.17. With the simple cycle web, you or your learners can demonstrate other cyclical relationships among concepts, phases, or events.

Figure 5.12 Cause and Effect Diagrams

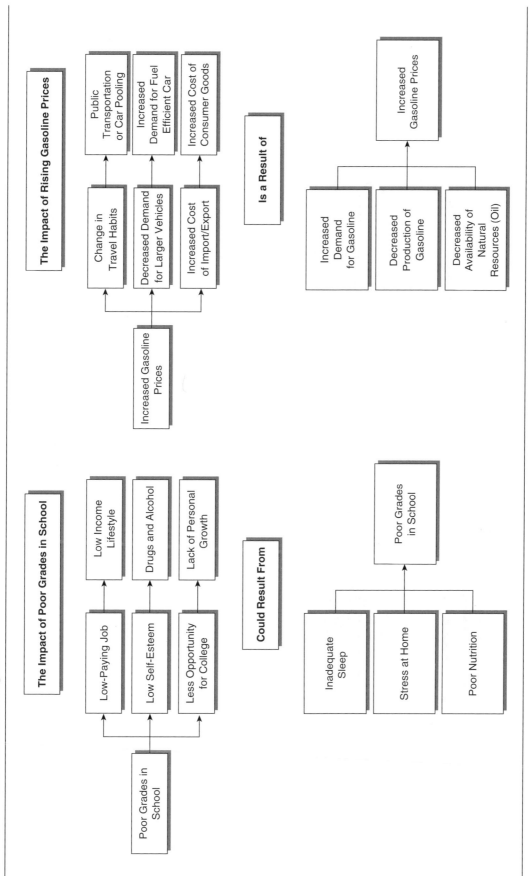

Figure 5.13 Cause and Effect Templates

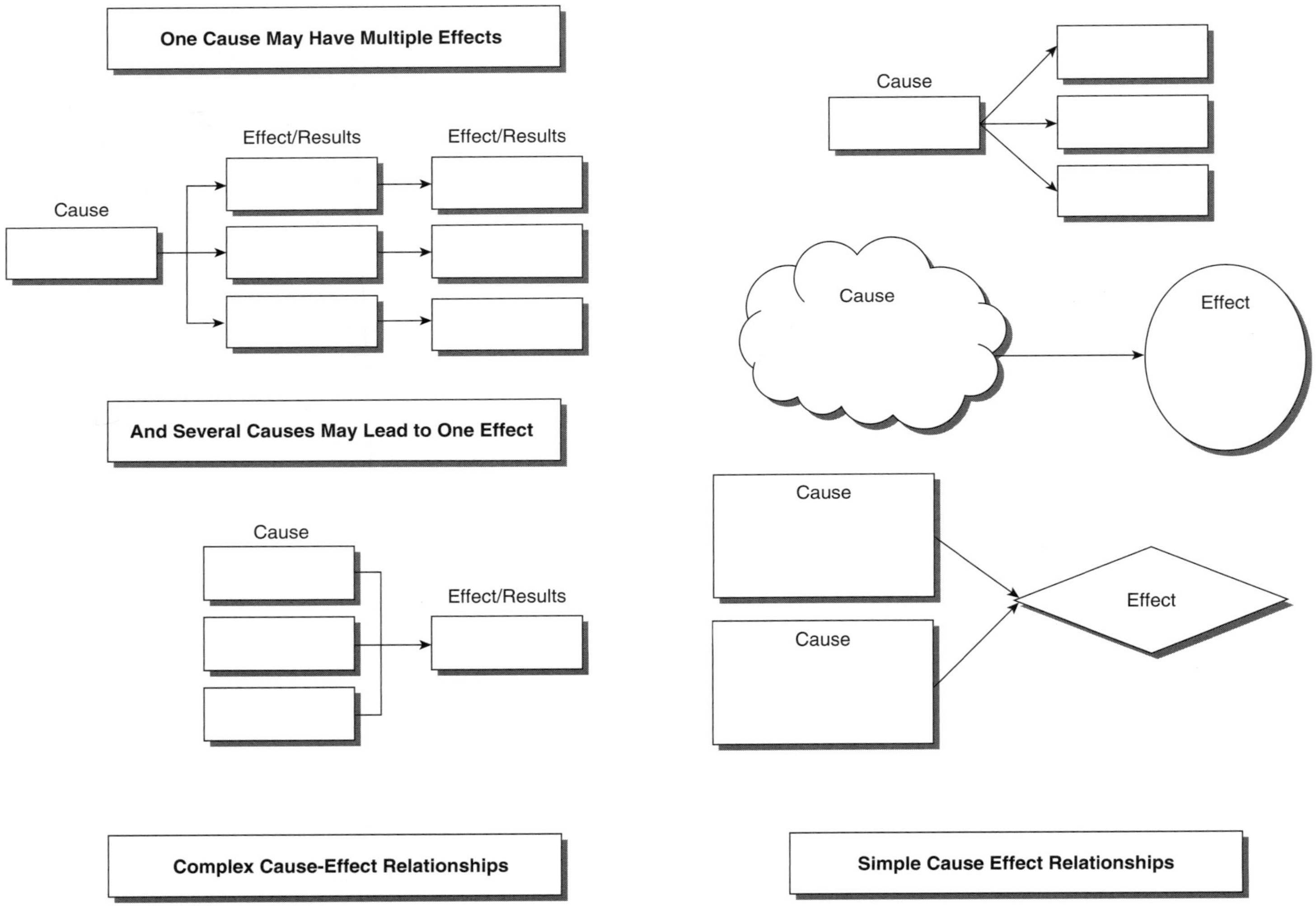

One Cause May Have Multiple Effects

Effect/Results

Effect/Results

Cause

And Several Causes May Lead to One Effect

Effect/Results

Cause

Complex Cause-Effect Relationships

Cause

Effect

Cause

Effect

Cause

Cause

Simple Cause Effect Relationships

Figure 5.14   Venn Diagram Comparing Differences Between Two Potential Job Offers

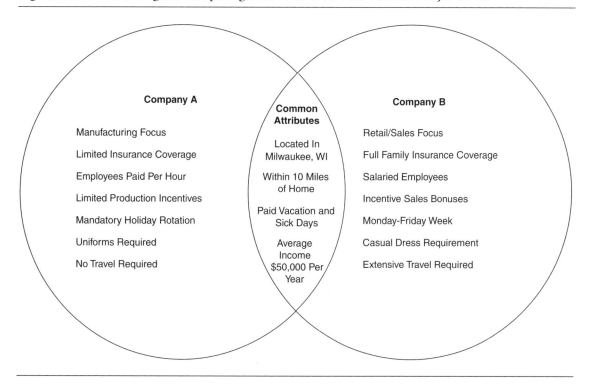

Figure 5.15   Venn Diagram Templates

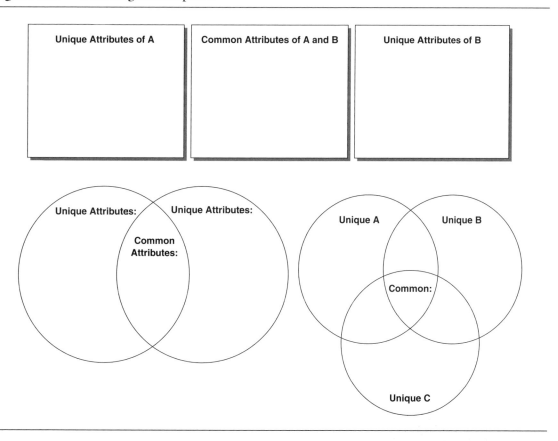

Figure 5.16   Cycle Web Examples

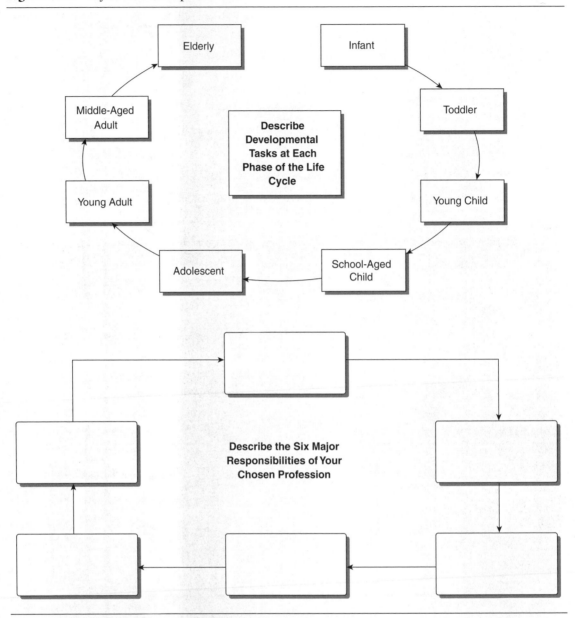

Objective Overview Diagram

Another graphic organizer that may appeal to you is the objective overview diagram. I have encouraged learners to review objectives prior to a lecture to make sure they understand the main idea of each objective. When learners understand the main idea of each objective and how it relates to the other objectives, they are generally better prepared to expand upon what they already know about the topic. The example in Figure 5.18 is an objective overview diagram for a unit on developing and implementing values. Notice the branching out from each objective to illustrate examples of the main ideas. Figure 5.19 includes several templates for objective overview diagrams.

Figure 5.17   Cycle Web Templates

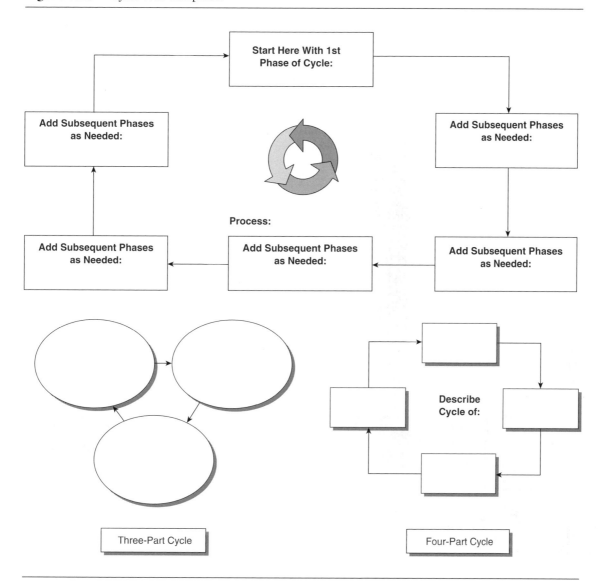

Have learners begin by writing out each objective and describing the main idea in their own words. Since these diagrams can become quite extensive, I recommend using four objectives per page. Color-coding and using symbols for related objectives will facilitate ease in reviewing the completed diagram. Encourage learners to write in examples to support the objectives and to link those examples that are also related to other objectives. The very act of creating a diagram like this and reviewing it at regular intervals is sure to reinforce learning.

Tree Diagram

Still another graphic organizer that works well to visually analyze concepts is the tree diagram (Figure 5.20). The tree diagram, commonly used to understand hierarchical relationships, can also help learners break down complex

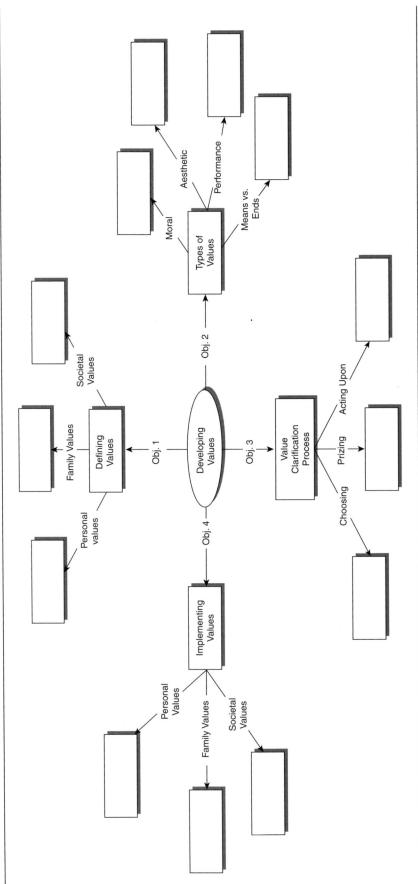

Figure 5.18   Objective Overview Diagram

Figure 5.19 Objective Overview Templates

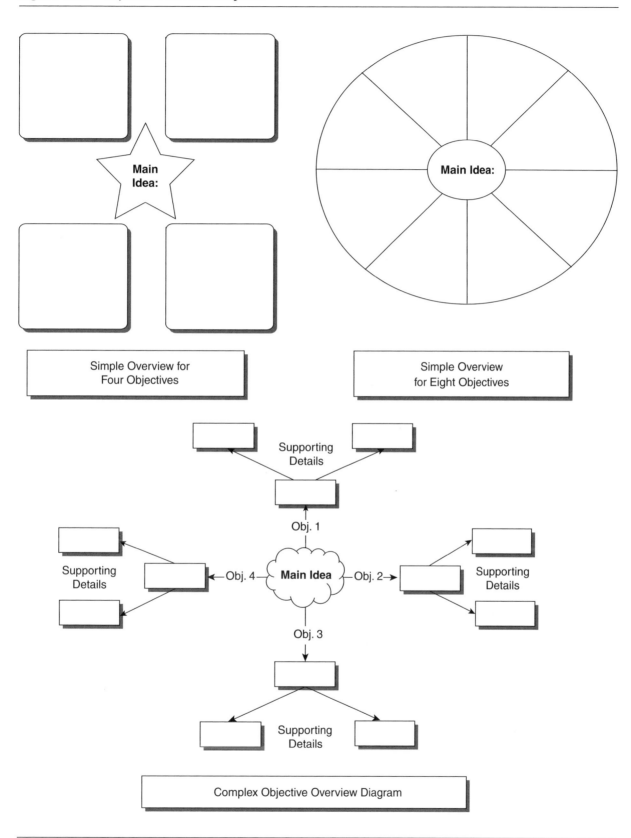

116

Figure 5.20 Research Design Tree

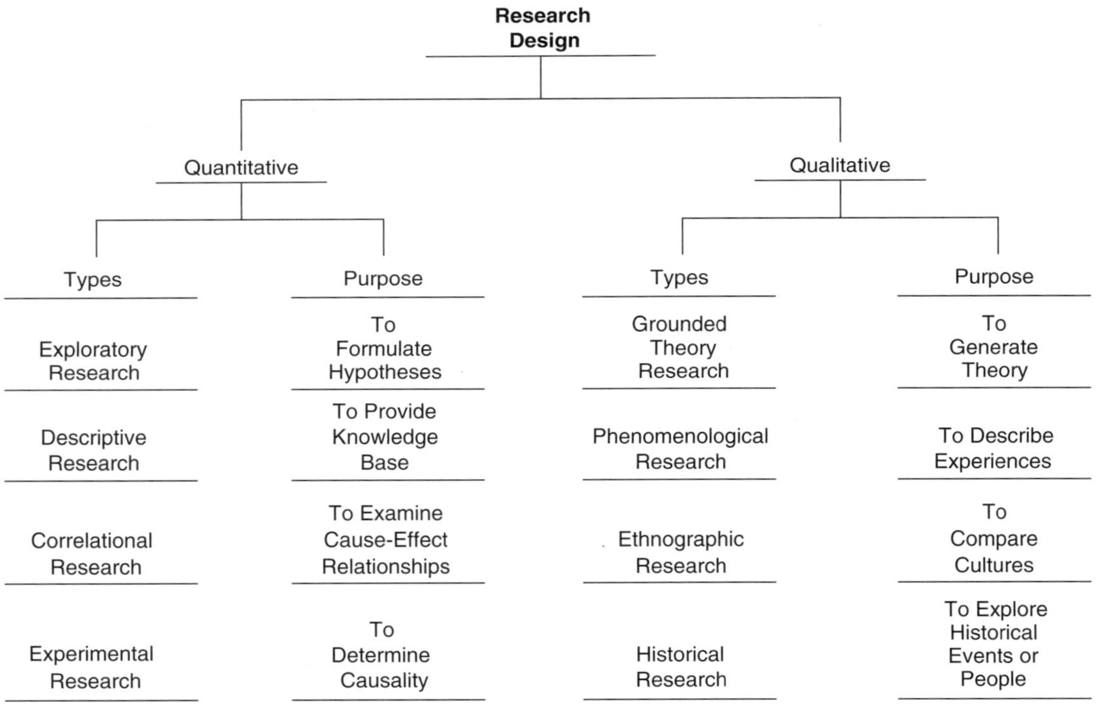

concepts into more manageable parts that are easier to understand. Although the brain strives to recognize the whole, when learners are unfamiliar with the components that make up the whole picture, it is most helpful to analyze the underlying components and understand how they fit into the larger whole. Tree diagrams can be constructed from top to bottom or right to left.

Memory Matrix

Educators Tom Angelo and Patricia Cross first introduced the idea of a memory matrix. The idea of the matrix is to provide students with a logical method for organizing information to increase comprehension and understanding (Angelo & Cross, 1993). Starting with a table format, a memory matrix can be designed as large or as small as the amount of content determines. Once the content is placed into the matrix format, students may color-code to further promote understanding at a glance.

One particularly useful memory matrix that I have used for clinical assignments is the medication matrix (Table 5.1). Using this strategy, learners are able to concisely summarize information related to the medications of assigned clients. They zero in on the most usual and typical side effects for that particular client. Once the table is completed, the student goes back and color-codes all cardiac side effects in pink, respiratory side effects in blue, gastrointestinal side effects in green, and so on. Using this strategy, I have noticed an increased competence and comprehension in learners with respect to their understanding of a client's medications.

Matrices can be developed from any theoretical or work-related content. Once learners are taught how to develop a matrix, they generally find a variety of ways to use it to organize study notes and learn new content. Tables 5.2 and 5.3 are memory matrixes from different adult continuing education classes.

Know, Want, How, Learn (KWHL) Diagram

Have you ever heard learners say that when they start to study a new unit, they are completely overwhelmed right from the beginning? A graphic organizer that can help learners streamline their study time is the KWHL diagram. The brain needs to have a reference point from which to start. KWHL diagrams assist learners not only in establishing that reference point but in finding the resources needed to actually learn about the topic. Figure 5.21 shows a KWHL diagram for a unit on Microsoft operating systems. Figure 5.22 is a KWHL template for you to use with students who need to get focused. Getting started is easy. Use the following instructions to direct learners:

- Select a topic, brainstorm what you already know about it, and write this in the first box (K).
- Next, brainstorm a list of things you want to know about the topic, and place this list in the W box.

Table 5.1   Medication Matrix

Medication/Dosage Classification	All Uses (star use for client)	How It Works (in your own words)	Side Effects and Contraindications	Nursing Implications/DX	Teach/Safety

Brainstorm! Color-code symptoms, implications, etc. to help spot patterns: pink = cardiac; blue = respiratory; green = gastrointestinal; yellow = skin; purple = neurological/peripheral vascular; underlined in red = life-threatening.

Table 5.2   Mineral Matrix

Group	Member	Formula	Description	Use
Silicates				
Carbonates				
Oxides				
Sulfides				
Sulfates				
Halides				

Table 5.3   Science Project Matrix

Scientific Investigation Project	
Steps in process	Describe specifics related to your project:
Statement of problem	
Information to gather	
Hypothesis formation	
Testing of hypothesis	
Conclusion	

Figure 5.21   KWHL Diagram for Computer Operating Systems

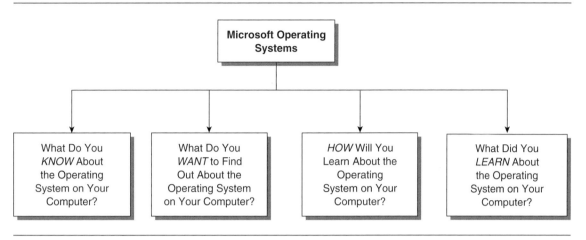

Figure 5.22   KWHL Template

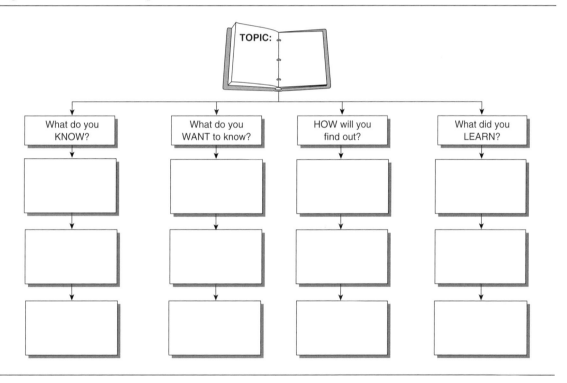

- Now, brainstorm ways of finding the answers to your questions, and list them in the H box. Think of all the resources available to you at school or at work. Now you are ready to tackle your resources!
- Finally, after you find the answers, jot them down in the L box.
- Don't forget: Add lots of color and symbols or graphics to your diagram to make it much more memorable. Have fun and make it your own!

STUDY STRATEGIES TO PROMOTE COMPREHENSION

Strategies to promote comprehension include any activity that increases personal understanding and comprehension of content. A few activities that I have used to promote comprehension include reading and note-taking techniques, mnemonics, and guided visual imagery. Using these strategies enhances self-directed learning by *actively* involving learners in higher-level thinking processes to assimilate and process the information. The activities in this section help students work with new concepts on their own, handling the information in such a way that the concepts become meaningful and personally relevant to them. When information is perceived by the learner to be relevant, the brain becomes excited and begins processing and linking the information, so that it forms connections and associations with the learner's knowledge base.

SQR3 Reading Strategy

SQR3 is an acronym for Survey, Question, Read, Recite, and Review. This method was first developed in 1941 by Francis Robinson (1970) and is still widely used today. When learners adopt the SQR3 reading strategy, they become actively involved in their reading and prepare their brains to learn the material more effectively. By following the five simple steps below, learners will begin thinking critically about what they are reading and associating it with what they already know. They will develop strategies to organize and link information before and after reading to improve long-term memory and retention. This makes SQR3 reading a perfect complement to other brain-based learning strategies.

Step 1: Survey. Browse through the chapter before you actually read it. Notice headings, bold print, tables, figures, graphs, pictures, diagrams, review questions, and anything else that stands out from the text. Identify the main ideas of the chapter. Scan the first and final paragraphs as well as the objectives at the beginning of the chapter.

Step 2: Question. Next, generate a few questions you may have thought of as you surveyed the chapter. Turn the headings and subheadings into questions. Ask yourself, "What is this chapter about? What do I already know about it? How does it relate to me?" By doing this, you will be actively thinking about what you will be reading.

Step 3: Read. Now, read the text actively in 15 minute segments. Your brain processes information more efficiently when you read in short segments. Seek out the answers to your questions. Read for meaning and understanding, stopping frequently to make sense out of the material to connect it to what you already know. Make notes in the margin and highlight key words only (never highlight what you already know).

Step 4: Recite. Teach yourself what you have just read by summarizing the main points out loud. You use a different brain pathway when you speak than when you think. Quiz yourself; add pictures and color; create a story from what you have read; get emotionally involved with what you have been reading. From a brain-based perspective, seeing, saying, and hearing will triple your learning power, while seeing, saying, hearing, and writing will quadruple your learning power!

Step 5: Review. The more you practice and review the information, the more easily you will be able to retrieve the information. Review out loud, to yourself, and in writing within 24 hours, within 48 hours, and within 72 hours after you have done the initial SQR3 reading.

In my experiences of using SQR3 reading strategy, learners cut their reading time in half! Once learners become empowered with this amazing reading method, they actually begin to enjoy reading. Recall of material is significantly improved, and learners' test grades improve as well.

Strategic Note Taking

Taking accurate notes can help learners transfer and recall information more efficiently. Long-term recall of information fades without regular practice and rehearsal. However, if learners adapt a note-taking system that is compatible with their learning style, they will find that a quick review of their notes, even after several months, will stimulate recall. Finding the right note-taking system is just as essential. Table 5.4 shows three systems for note-taking and a few general tips on taking notes in class and reviewing after class.

Guided Visual Imagery

Guided visual imagery is a valuable metacognitive strategy that actively engages learners in retrieving important concepts from memory. This technique naturally decreases the anxiety associated with trying to remember details and puts the learner in control of the recall. For example, before they perform a clinical skill for the first time on a client, I generally take learners to a quiet place and have them sit down, do relaxation breathing, and visually reconstruct the steps in the procedure just as they learned them in lab. I offer learners the option of verbalizing aloud while I guide them or visualizing privately and alone. For beginning learners, the guided imagery is usually most often requested. However, after learners know how to do this themselves, they can do it privately even more effectively.

I have also utilized group guided imagery to promote motivation and positive learner attitudes while facilitating study strategy courses and prior to presenting complex units of study. To promote relaxation, I start with breathing exercises, dim the lights, and play soft nature sounds. When I can see that

Table 5.4   Notes and Note-Taking Tips

Types of Notes	Description

Outline	I. Outline method
	   A. Provides a pattern to follow
	   B. Main points backed up by supporting points (indented)
	   C. Follows organized flow of thought
	   D. Best for formal lecture
	   E. Not necessary to follow formal rules of outlining

Block
  Narrative
  Separate main ideas
	Concentrate on getting down the main points and as many of the supporting details as you can in a **narrative** block format. **Separate** each **main idea** block by an open line. Go back and extract key words and place in recall column.

Mapping	Record notes on a chart or in graphic format: Use Symbols → Supporting Ideas → Provide Specific Examples Main Ideas → Provide Specific Examples
Note-taking tips for class	1. Use a full page of paper. 2. Write on one side only so that you can cut into flash cards. 3. Use a structure such as a box with recall column. 4. Always date notes; include topic and presenter. 5. Use a fine-tip marker or pen; pencils smear. 6. Use colored paper and markers if that appeals to you. 7. Use abbreviations and shorthand if you can. 8. Write in short phrases. Do not try to write down every word. 9. Do not jam notes together; separate main points by white space. 10. Use color-coding to organize main and subpoints. 11. Take down anything that is repeated, spelled out, or emphasized. 12. Copy down drawings, lists, and definitions given in class.
Note-taking tips for after class	1. Review notes for clarification after lecture. 2. Do not rewrite just to make notes neater, unless you are copying them to elaborate on the points. 3. Do not rely on hand-outs alone. 4. Edit notes after class: Fill in gaps and check for accuracy. 5. Add recall words and **BOLD HEADINGS**. 6. Highlight what you don't know. 7. Add questions in margin that are unanswered. 8. Find answers to questions in text.

learners' breathing patterns are consistent and relaxed, I begin the dialogue, which is often spontaneous. I allow learners to come out of the imagery at their own pace, and I end the session with a movement exercise to prepare learners for the session. Feedback has been encouraging, and many learners have asked me to prepare scripts so that they can use imagery as a study strategy to aid in personal comprehension of concepts.

Mnemonics

The use of mnemonics is a creative metacognitive strategy that helps learners encode and retrieve information more efficiently by reducing large numbers of data into smaller chunks or sets. I have utilized mnemonics myself to learn complex nursing theory and skills and have collected a large variety of learner-generated mnemonics over the years. Some of the mnemonics I have provided for learners include alphabet cues, first letter acronyms, and acrostics.

Alphabet cues use letters of the alphabet to trigger recall of associated information. Some examples are FBI (Federal Bureau of Investigation, CIA (Central Intelligence Agency), and DOT (Department of Transportation). Other examples include GPA (grade point average) and PIN (personal identification number).

Acronyms are probably the most common mnemonic used. Key words are identified, and the first letter of each key word is used to make another word. For example, RACE is a well-known fire safety acronym for Rescue, Activate alarm, Close doors, Evacuate area. PASS is an associated fire safety acronym for using a fire extinguisher (Pull pin, Aim hose, Squeeze handle, Sweep area).

Here are some other common acronyms:

- FACE: The musical notes represented by the spaces in the treble clef, bottom to top
- RAVEN: "Remember: Affect = verb, effect = noun"—appropriate use of the words *affect* and *effect*
- HOMES: The Great Lakes—Huron, Ontario, Michigan, Erie, and Superior

Acrostics are most helpful when information must be remembered in sequence. The first letter of each word in the sequence is used for the beginning of each word in a sentence you make up. For example, we probably all remembered the planets in order of distance from the sun as Mercury, Venus, Earth, Mars, Jupiter, Saturn, Uranus, Neptune, and Pluto. To remember this list in this order, I used the acrostic, My Very Energetic Mother Just Served Us Nine Pizzas (now that Pluto is no longer considered a planet, someone will have to come up with a new acrostic!). Here are some other handy acrostic examples to inspire you:

- Please Excuse My Dear Aunt Sally: order of algebraic calculations—parentheses, exponents, multiplication, division, addition, subtraction
- Lucky Cows Drink Milk: ascending order of Roman numerals—LCDM
- Kittens Prefer Cream Or Fish, Generally Speaking: Order of biological groupings— kingdom, phylum, class, order, family, genus, species

Mnemonics promote long-term retention and recall through George Miller's concept of "chunking information." Miller suggests that the human brain cannot retain in short-term memory more than seven chunks of information at any given time (Miller, 1956). However, the actual size of each chunk is determined by the amount of information each person stores in his or her long-term memory. Words can be stored as separate units or as chunks of phrases, such as mnemonics, as the learner increases baseline knowledge. As the learner gains more skill with chunking, the chunks increase in size to complete units of study. The more familiar the chunks are to the learner, the greater the recall. I encourage students to create their own mnemonics so that they will be more personally meaningful and therefore easier to recall.

Once a chunk of information is recalled by the learner, all the associated links are effortlessly pulled forth. As the learner links the chunked information to even greater past experiences and stored memories, the associated chunk grows larger and larger.

PROMOTING ACTIVE LEARNING

Active learning strategies help learners recognize how to discern the most important points in a lecture or unit of study in order to promote deep learning of relationships. Elements of active learning skills include talking and listening, writing, reading, and reflecting. Among a few of the techniques I have found to be helpful are reflective journaling, critical-thinking scenarios, concept essays, and key concept questions. These techniques can be used in conjunction with lectures, discussion, labs, and clinical settings. Once learners have been introduced to these types of activities, they can begin to utilize them independently to enhance personal study skills as well.

In contrast, traditional learning activities that are presented in a didactic, passive manner generally do not get the learners actively involved with the learning experience. The learners may perceive the information presented to be important, but without the active involvement, the learners generally do not learn the information at a deeper level. They often resort to trying to memorize the information (using rote rehearsal). Information that is leaned by rote is transferred to short-term memory but will not make it into the learner's long-term memory without active involvement on the part of the learner. Short-term memory may be sufficient for learners to recall information for a test, but when it comes time for the students to apply the information down the road, they may only be able to recall bits and pieces at best.

Concept Essay

The idea of a concept essay is to promote comprehension and understanding of critical concepts that learners must know for any given unit of study. The learner is given a list of concepts and is instructed to describe how the concepts are related to each other. The learner is encouraged to write a narrative essay but may draw a diagram or a map to illustrate understanding of the content instead. Figure 5.23 shows a few examples of concept essays on various topics.

Key Concept Questions

Prior to presenting new information on a specific unit, I develop key concept questions from the unit objectives. Part of my learners' preclass responsibility is to review assigned readings and unit objectives, and the key concept questions

Figure 5.23 Concept Worksheets

Concept Worksheet

Nutrition and Exercise

Using the ideas below, write a short story or draw a picture showing how you will eat better and exercise more. Include each idea at least once (cross each off as you use it)!

Water	Fruits	Breads and cereals
Exercise Fats	Vegetables	Meat Milk and dairy

Concept Worksheet

Handling Stress

Over the last two weeks, you have learned quite a bit about how your body reacts to stress. Using the terms below, develop a short paragraph describing how you will manage your stress in the future.

Stressor	Bad coping activities
Stress response	Good coping activities
Mental stress	Physical stress

Concept Worksheet

Personal Wellness Dimensions

Your personal level of wellness covers many dimensions of your life. Using the terms below, write a brief essay on how you plan to maintain wellness and balance in each of the following areas:

Physical health   Mental health   Spiritual health   Work/college
Financial health   Family relationships   Time management

provide focus and set the direction for the presentation. Sometimes the key concept questions are written on cards that are randomly distributed among groups of students. At other times, I will put the questions on overheads while learners are filing into the lecture hall. I set aside at least 15 minutes of a one-hour period and 30 minutes of a two-hour period for follow-up discussion on the questions. Learner participation is tremendous and builds a kind of anticipation and personal attachment for the upcoming presentation. Discussion on the key concept material can be both before and after the content presentation.

Key concept questions help learners make connections between theory and their understanding of newly learned concepts. It is also a wonderful way to draw learners into the unit of study and elicit personal interest in the unit objectives. I have found that when key concept questions are utilized, learners tend to score higher in areas related to the key concepts on tests. They actually look forward to using this strategy, which I use at least every other presentation. Another version of this strategy is to have learners develop key concept questions on their own and share them with a larger group. I have also collected learner-generated key concept questions for unit reviews at the end of the semester. This promotes a sense of ownership and respect for learner participation.

For example, key concept questions for a class on physics might include the following:

- Distinguish kinetic energy from potential energy and give three examples of each.
- Describe the three primary methods for transferring heat energy and give an example of each.

Reflective Journal Entries

The use of reflective journal entries is an excellent way to stimulate learner metacognitive awareness. I have used this strategy in a number of contexts, including clinical practice, small group discussion, and preunit presentation. As a clinical strategy, I allow 20 minutes of postclinical conference time for learners to gather their thoughts and reflect upon their clinical experiences for the week. I generally start them off with one of the following:

- My greatest fear preparing for clinical this week was. . . .
- If I could have changed something about this week, it would be. . . .
- The most admirable act of professional nursing that I observed this week was. . . .
- From this clinical week, the thing I will remember the most is. . . .
- My most effective nursing intervention this week was. . . .

Learners appreciate the opportunity to use clinical time to reflect upon their experiences and will often stay much longer than the 20 minutes allowed to finish up their thoughts. In the past, I have given the clinical journal as a take-home activity, but I found the responses to be rather brief and superficial. In contrast, the nature of the responses I have received when the journal is incorporated into the clinical week are profoundly rich and well thought-out. Although the journals are not graded, I give personal feedback and encourage students to share their insights during preconference time the following week. This provides an appropriate prologue for the next clinical week. Learners gain a great deal from each other by sharing feelings and experiences.

Just this last semester, I started writing my own journal to learners sharing my insights about their professional growth during the week. I keep the journal very objective and neutral, addressing the group as a whole. This strategy has increased my own metacognitive awareness of my personal expectations of the learners and my own attitudes toward their professional growth and development. The overwhelmingly positive feedback I have received from learners is all the incentive I need to continue with my reflective insights journal.

Critical Thinking Scenario

As a small group discussion activity, I may introduce a scenario for critical thinking to groups of four to five learners and ask them to individually respond to certain aspects of client care within it, such as legal or ethical concepts. Each group member is given an index card to record his or her thoughts. After 10 minutes, they share their responses and work together as a group to reply to the inquiries in the scenario. As there may be four or five small groups, I provide a different scenario for each group to respond to. In the end, each scenario is pulled together with the group input on specific areas of inquiry. This activity provides the opportunity for learners to learn the collaborative and networking skills that are so necessary for professional nurses.

Although many of the scenarios I have developed are related to nursing theory, I have included a few scenarios in the boxes that follow that are appropriate for general adult studies.

Scenario for Class on Organizational Behavior

Due to a significant decline in demand for steel production, Steel Company A and Steel Company B took measures to cut costs and minimize losses to their companies. Each company employed 2,000 workers and was not union-supported. Therefore, labor costs were controlled by management.

Company A's management team determined that only 50 percent of the workforce was required for current production needs. After a careful analysis of skills, performance reviews, and seniority status, 1,000 workers were given two weeks notice that they would be laid off and one week's vacation pay for each year of employment.

Company B's management team also determined that only 50 percent of their workforce was required for current production needs. However, the company maintained a serious commitment to a no-layoff policy. This company instituted an across the board cut in all 2,000 employees' hours. All employees were reduced to 20 hours per week. All

---

(Scenario for Class on Organizational Behavior, continued)

fringe benefits and sick days were maintained. Employees were encouraged to work outside the company to maintain their living standards but to be available for increased hours when production improved.

1. Which company would you have preferred to work for? Why?

2. How would each company's decision impact employees, their families, productivity, morale, and continued employment?

3. What would have happened if each company were unionized?

4. Think of another creative management strategy that could have been employed.

Scenario for Class on Interior Design

A new graduate in interior design has just become employed by a huge design showroom. After only a few weeks, she observes that the owner of the company is charging hefty fees for so-called designer originals that are on display in the showroom. However, when the artifacts are ordered, a knock-off version of inferior quality is substituted. The employee is paid extremely well and has very few other job options in her city.

1. How would you handle this dilemma?

2. Should past customers be notified of this fraud?

Scenario for Pain Management Discussion

As a preunit activity, I may simply put up a few thought-provoking reflections on overheads and have learners ponder these for five minutes or so before introducing new ideas. For example, prior to a unit on pain management, I have learners reflect upon the following:

The most intense pain I think a patient can experience is when. . . .

This strategy helps learners to link new theory related to pain with prior personal experiences in an extremely meaningful way, as pain is a very emotional as well as physiological experience. I notice that learners are much more interested in the content once they can relate it to their own lives. In addition to creating metacognitive awareness, this activity promotes empathy toward clients who may be experiencing pain.

All of these metacognitive strategies share common themes: promotion of comprehension, organization of ideas, self-regulation and control, active involvement in deep learning, greater transformation of information and acquisition of knowledge, elaboration and meaningful application of learning, and the promotion of effective study skills. Through these and other metacognitive and brain-based strategies, students learn to monitor and self-regulate their own learning processes to promote optimal learning at their own pace.

Considering the rapid technological advances of our current progressive, knowledge-based society, our educational system could serve all learners far better if a metacognitive framework were incorporated into educational design. However, metacognitive interventions or techniques become strategies only if learners have the knowledge of when, where, and how to use them. I strongly feel that the role of adult educators is to teach metacognitive skills, facilitate an awareness of underlying metacognitive knowledge, and to promote a variety of metacognitive strategies that learners can select from to develop their own metacognitive abilities for lifelong learning. When you teach learners to use their own metacognitive abilities for self-directed learning, they will be able to learn anywhere, anyplace, and anytime.

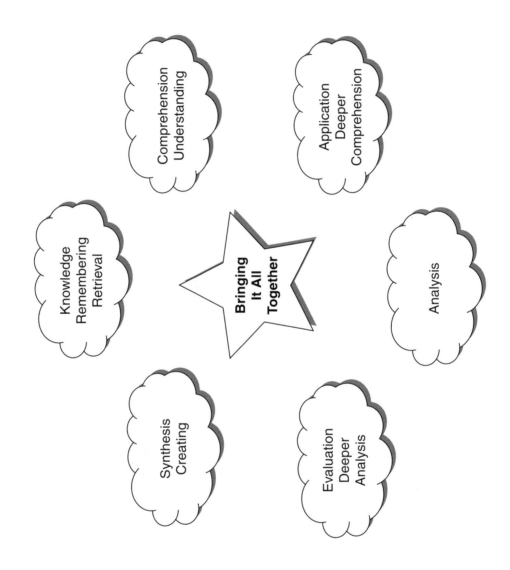

6

Blending
Taxonomies to
Bring the Learning
Process Full Cycle

Now that you have been introduced to several new teaching and learning strategies, you are probably wondering how to go about integrating them. This chapter will demonstrate how to effectively blend specific strategies with elements of brain-compatible instruction that can be used within the traditional classroom or workplace setting. But first, an appropriate taxonomy for understanding how adult learners process information must be discussed.

TAXONOMIES IN EDUCATION

I have always thought that metacognitive skills are closely related to the ability to process information, especially in adults, who bring a wealth of previous learning experiences and metacognitive skills to the classroom. Using the standard Bloom's taxonomy for curriculum development and assessment did not quite cover the complexities of teaching adults, and I was relieved to see that there have been other educators who grappled with that application, as well.

Bloom's Taxonomy Revisited

Until recently, educators have traditionally relied upon Bloom's taxonomy, an extensive framework developed in 1956, to classify learning in a hierarchal manner from knowledge levels through evaluation levels. Briefly, Bloom identified six specific levels of knowledge and skills and theorized that learners advance in a hierarchal ways from the lower levels (knowledge and comprehension) to the middle levels (application and analysis) to the highest levels (synthesis and evaluation). This taxonomy may have worked well over the past 50 years for organizing and evaluating instructional objectives and articulating program objectives and as a standard for assessing levels of knowledge. However, with the current shift over the last two decades toward brain-compatible instruction, Bloom's taxonomy, which focuses on levels of knowledge, does not provide educators with a plan for teaching learners how to learn. Although the taxonomy identifies the highest levels of learning (synthesis and evaluation), it does not directly address the necessary metacognitive skills required to process information at those highest levels. By far, the most common criticism of this taxonomy is that it is too simplistic a framework to explain the relationship between learning outcomes and how a person thinks, processes, transfers, stores, and retrieves information (Furst, 1994; Kreitzer & Madaus, 1994). Over the last decade, the inevitable need to revise Bloom's taxonomy has been addressed, most notably, by two groups of educators: Anderson and colleagues (2001) and Marzano and Kendall (2006).

Anderson and Colleagues' Update of Bloom's Taxonomy

In a recent attempt to update Bloom's taxonomy, Lorin Anderson, a former student of Benjamin Bloom, organized and worked with a group of cognitive psychologists to revise the one-dimensional taxonomy to address elements of cognitive psychology (Anderson et al., 2001). The revision involved development of two specific dimensions, the knowledge domain, and the cognitive process domain. The knowledge domain included basic factual, conceptual, procedural, and metacognitive knowledge. The cognitive process domain involved six dimensions of active thinking, including remembering, understanding, applying, analyzing, evaluating, and creating. By creating this two-dimensional approach, educational objectives could be addressed using elements from both dimensions.

Like Bloom's taxonomy, the categories were ordered in terms of complexity. Bloom's original knowledge level was renamed "remembering" to represent an actual form of thinking. The name of the original synthesis level was renamed "creating" and was exchanged with the former evaluation level, renamed "evaluating" under the new taxonomy. This change reflects the notion that creative thinking takes place at a much higher level than critical thinking. In other words, learners must go through the critical thinking steps of accepting or rejecting ideas before they can begin to judge a new idea and justify their choices.

My understanding of this two-dimensional framework, represented in Table 6.1, can be used by educators to plan educational objectives for a unit of study. Learning objectives are placed under one of the four knowledge categories on the vertical axis to align with the cognitive process on the horizontal axis that is being taught.

Table 6.1   Anderson and Colleagues' Model

Knowledge Dimension	Cognitive Process Dimension					
	Remember	*Understand*	*Apply*	*Analyze*	*Evaluate*	*Create*
Metacognitive						
Procedural						
Conceptual						
Factual						

SOURCE: Adapted from Anderson et al. (2001).

So, in planning objectives for a specific unit, the educator directs the cognitive learning activities to cover the relevant type of knowledge needed to ensure a successful outcome. As with Bloom's taxonomy, the implication is that learners advance from factual to metacognitive knowledge in varying degrees of complexity from remembering to creating.

Personal Reflections on Traditional Taxonomies

Although this framework advances Bloom's original work, it was still not a comfortable fit for me. The idea of metacognition being categorized as a type of knowledge (albeit high-level knowledge) goes against my personal experiences in teaching adult learners. To me, metacognition is a self-regulated process determined by the learner, not directed by the educator. This model may work well for primary educators; however, in terms of adult learners, neither the Bloom model nor the Anderson model addresses the complexities of the adult learner.

I have observed several times over my years of teaching that adult learners cannot be directed to attend to a new learning task if they are preoccupied with other dimensions of their lives. There have also been times when a self-directed and autonomous adult learner took the lead in a planned activity by sharing past experiences related to the topic at hand. If I had been tied down to a plan that directed me to cover objectives using a traditional taxonomy, I may have had a hard time redirecting my lesson plan. As a result of my observations with adult learners, I have learned to become flexible and creative in my approach to teaching.

I have also learned that the process of learning in adults always begins with the learner. If the learner is ready to learn, learning will progress at a natural pace. Adult learners have a wealth of personal experience to draw from and are quite capable of directing their own learning experiences. From my experiences in applying brain-compatible learning principles to the adult setting, I am also aware of the impact of emotions upon learning. If learners are negatively charged at the onset of learning, it is difficult for them to direct themselves into a productive learning state. That is why I place such emphasis on promoting the resourceful learning state (see Chapter 4). However, once learners redirect their energy into a positive mind set and make the conscious decision to attend to the learning task, they are able to tap into their own metacognitive reserves to set their own learning goals, and they activate their own success strategies to begin processing information. The processing begins with pulling information from their current knowledge pathways (transfer from long-term memory into working memory) and processing the old with the new (working memory). Then they restructure the new knowledge by laying down new connections that are eventually stored in long-term memory with practice and rehearsal.

This is indeed a very exciting process that requires minimal supervision for the extremely motivated and self-directed adult learner. That is why distance learning programs are becoming so successful today. The ability to set their own learning goals and direct their own learning objectives is an extremely attractive option for adult learners. Fortunately, the very process that I just described was revealed to me during the writing of this book. Robert Marzano and John

Kendall just recently wrote *The New Taxonomy of Educational Objectives* (2006). I was given a copy of this manuscript hot off the press and was delighted to see my own philosophy of teaching and learning validated.

Marzano and Kendall's New Taxonomy of Educational Objectives

This taxonomy, like Anderson's, includes a two-dimensional focus that includes types of knowledge and systems of mental processing. Knowledge is categorized into information, mental processes, and psychomotor processes. However, Marzano and Kendall do not order these categories as the previously discussed taxonomies do. The other dimension, systems of mental processing, is hierarchal and includes the self system, the metacognitive system, and the cognitive system. The cognitive system is further subdivided into retrieval, comprehension, analysis, and knowledge utilization. In this dimension, the hierarchal structure represents the natural flow of information processing. This taxonomy is illustrated in Table 6.2.

Using this model, the self system is the first step in the processing, with the learner taking the initiative to choose to learn or not. According to Marzano and Kendall, if a student is motivated to learn and determines the knowledge to be relevant, the metacognitive system is engaged. This system sets learning goals and determines the best way to meet the goals. The role of the cognitive system under this new taxonomy is to process information from simple retrieval to complex utilization of information. This system of mental operations can be applied to all three types of knowledge. Marzano and Kendall describe a wide variety of activities that can be used to promote cognitive processing that are consistent with a brain-compatible approach to adult learning.

Table 6.2   Marzano and Kendall's Objectives

Systems of Mental Processing From Highest to Lowest	Domains of Knowledge		
	Information	*Psychomotor Process*	*Mental Process*
6. Self-system			
5. Metacognitive system			
Cognitive system includes:			
4. Knowledge utilization			
3. Analysis			
2. Comprehension			
1. Retrieval			

SOURCE: Adapted from Marzano and Kendall (2006).

Personal Reflections on Marzano and Kendall's Taxonomy

I found this taxonomy to support many elements of brain-compatible instruction, in that it closely follows the information processing model (see Chapter 2). In theory, Marzano and Kendall's taxonomy validates many of the approaches to adult education that I espouse. However, I found their model to be linear and not quite representative of the dynamic interplay between the domains of knowledge and the levels of mental processing. As a visual processor myself, I took the main elements of their taxonomy and reorganized them into a pattern that made more sense to me (Figure 6.1). I will use this graphic to help my adult learners understand the dynamics of this new taxonomy.

THE MATERNA METHOD

Despite the emergence of these two new frameworks, Bloom's taxonomy remains the most widely recognized and utilized classification system among educators today. In my quest to teach both adult learners and educators of adult learners how to integrate principles of brain-compatible learning with the natural process of learning, I have developed a template that can be used as a facilitation guide. This guide, labeled "The Materna Method" and shown in Table 6.3, supports Bloom's taxonomy but integrates the active learning terminology and reordering advocated by Anderson and colleagues (2001). I have also pulled in aspects of Marzano and Kendall's model to reinforce the dynamic flow of information processing between the self system, the metacognitive system, and the cognitive system. Brain-compatible activities that I have developed over the years are backed up with a supportive rationale to promote an understanding of how the brain learns. A time frame is also included to help educators pace the class of one to two hours in length. This time frame includes the integration of the brain-compatible principles for promoting the resourceful learning state through movement exercises, breathing exercises, listening to music, and drinking water. These resourceful learning activities are utilized most effectively at the beginning of class and prior to the midpoint break. When these activities are used at the beginning of class, learners become actively engaged and involved in the learning process. It is at this point that the self system and metacognitive systems are activated and ready to learn. When the activities are used at the midpoint, they provide a much needed energy break. You may want to use only the ones you are most comfortable with at first. Refer to Part 2, Chapter 4 for a review of the resourceful learning activities.

I believe the integration of these three taxonomies with brain-compatible activities and rationales will help educators facilitate the natural evolution of learning in a more accelerated and brain-compatible manner. The Materna Method is a guide for educators designed to help in the process of selecting supplemental classroom activities to facilitate this natural flow of learning.

Several of these activities have already been described in the previous chapter, and in this chapter I will discuss a wide variety of additional teaching activities that can easily be blended into the traditional lecture hall or workplace setting.

Figure 6.1   Marzano and Kendall's Model

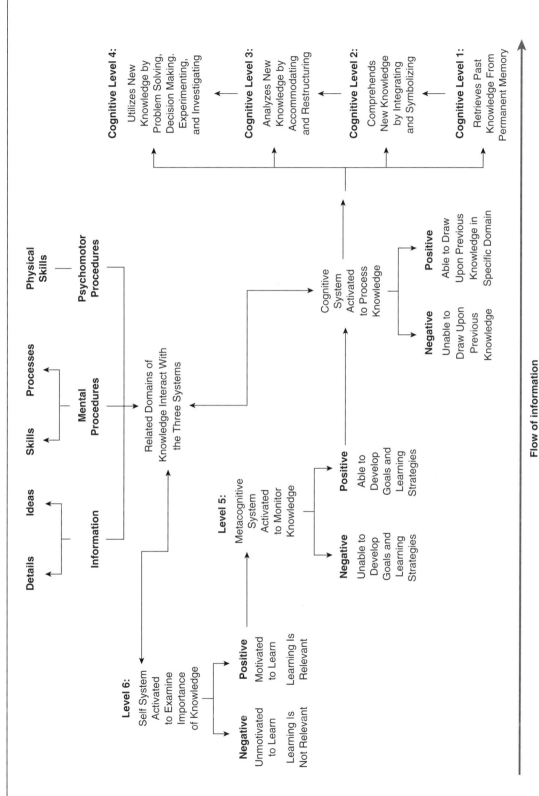

SOURCE: Marzano and Kendall (2006).

Table 6.3   The Materna Method: Brain-Compatible Learning Strategies for the Classroom

Preparation for Learning

- Begin with brain energizer/music/breathing/exercise to engage learners.
- Follow with activation of the self system; stress relevance of information and need to learn.
- Conclude by identifying learning goals and strategies to meet those goals.
- This set of activities should take 5–10 minutes.

Items From Blended Educational Taxonomies	Brain-Compatible Activities	Brain-Based Rationale	Time Frame and Learning Environment
Remembering and retrieving knowledge Basic recall of general concept from existing knowledge bases	• Show you know • Key concept review • Open-ended probe • KWHL strategy • Can be combined with brain stimulator • Play low volume baroque or classical music to stimulate recall	These strategies reinforce relevance for individuals and personal interest in the topic. They help learners key into what they do know and what they need to pay attention to, and they contribute toward the development of metacognitive awareness in the learner. Once learners know what they need to pay attention to, they become much more invested in learning the material.	• 5–10 minutes • Do at the start of class
Comprehension and understanding Demonstration of understanding through various activities meant to promote integration and symbolizing	• RSQC • Big picture overview • Memory matrix • Cause and effect web	These strategies give learners the opportunity to see the whole of what they will be learning before focusing on the parts. They put the learning experience into perspective and make it meaningful, so learners can connect to previous knowledge.	• 5–10 minutes • Do before getting into the specific content to be covered during the session
Application and deeper comprehension Abstract application of principles, theories, ideas, or concepts	• General/specific mini lectures • Concept map discussion • Tree diagram • Cycle web	These strategies allow learners to absorb, process, and apply new concepts to build upon previous knowledge. They engage learners' attention and allow time to handle and really work with the new concepts. Encourage learners to continue to handle the material and review at 24, 48, and 72 hours.	• 10–20 minutes of content overview • Follow with group or individual activities

Brain Break
- Do breathing and movement exercises; drink water; listen to music
- Reinforce activation of self system and metacognitive system
- These activities should take 5–10 minutes

Analysis Breaking down of principles, theories, ideas, or concepts into explicit relationships	• Application summary • Venn diagram analysis • Defining features grid • Analytic memo	These strategies provide an opportunity for learners to break apart their application and understanding of new concepts and to think critically about them. When these strategies are implemented just after the brain break, learners are energized and ready to shift up and examine their application at a much deeper and richer level.	• 10–20 minutes • Do after brain break, while learners are energized • Play upbeat music to stimulate energy and critical thinking
Evaluation and deeper analysis Appraising or making judgments of principles, theories, ideas, or concepts	• Critical consequences • Dynamic duos • One-sentence summary • Concept essay	These strategies promote understanding of the meaning and purpose that new concepts have in the real world. Open dialogue promotes learner collaboration and social interaction. Community brainstorming stimulates critical thinking.	• 10–20 minutes • Play low-volume baroque or classical music during dialogues
Synthesis: creating and utilizing knowledge Bringing principles, theories, ideas, or concepts back together into a new order or structure	• Concept map review • Concert review • Reflective journal • Wrap-up quiz and evaluation of presentation	These strategies allow learners the opportunity to generate new meaning and create new ideas. They support and validate the relevance and importance of concepts presented and ensure that learners have "got it" by allowing for review of main points. They also provide an opportunity for evaluation of the presentation.	• 10–20 minutes • Provide overview or summary activity before presenting quiz or evaluation

SOURCE: Anderson et al. (2001), Bloom (1956), and Marzano and Kendall (2006).

The various activities listed in each row with each taxonomy label provide an explanation of the brain-compatible principle they support as well as a suggested time frame. Following this guide, a one- to two-hour class can easily be accommodated. If you have classes longer than this, you may want to consider giving a second brain break and increasing the interactive component in application, analysis, or synthesis. Notice that the content delivery, or didactic portion, of the Materna Method is only 10–20 minutes long. If additional lecture time is needed, I recommend dividing the content up into two 10–20 minute sections with a brain break and a variety of interactive brain-based learning strategies sandwiched between.

Remember, this is only a guide; please feel free to modify it to suit your unique teaching situation. Start by selecting one or two new activities each week. Get learners invested in this process by explaining that you are trying something new to promote learning. They may be somewhat uncomfortable at first, since most learners have been conditioned over the years by the passive style of learning. However, when they understand that they are indeed active members of this process and their feedback is an essential component as well, they will relax and enjoy this very natural and brain-compatible learning process.

Strategies for Remembering and Retrieving Knowledge

The intent of this level of processing is to stimulate basic recall of general concepts—to recognize and retrieve information from long-term memory (Anderson et al., 2001; Bloom, 1956; Marzano & Kendall, 2006). Since new learning is meant to build upon previous learning, it is absolutely critical to take the time to show students what they know and what they need to know or learn. When learners connect with what they already know about a topic, the learning experience becomes personally meaningful and relevant. This insight alone will promote an appreciation of the importance of building upon previous knowledge. Knowledge strategies promote an understanding of what is most important and help the learners focus on just that. Once learners know what to pay attention to, they are more invested and interested in learning. This step also promotes learner recognition of strengths and areas to develop, which enhances metacognition. The more familiar and competent learners are with the content, the less time is spent at this level.

Spend at least five to ten minutes exploring what learners already know. Ideally, this is done immediately following a five-minute brain stimulator activity. A brain stimulator is a word or number puzzle that can be placed on the overhead or included in the handouts for the unit. The idea of the brain stimulator is to get learners to think outside the box. I have included a variety of brain stimulator puzzles in Resource A. Try them out and have fun with them. Try to tie them into the unit of study by modifying the content. Some of the best word puzzles that I have found have come from the backs of paper menus in family-style restaurants. Keep your eyes open and start your own collection!

As you can see from Figures 6.2 and 6.3, show-you-know strategies can easily be adapted to any unit of study. The examples in these figures are from the field of nursing.

Figure 6.2   Show-You-Know Diagram

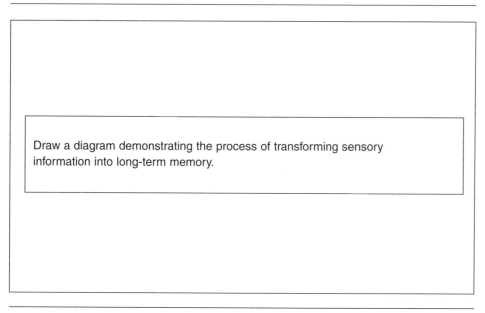

Open-Ended Probe

The open-ended probe is a technique that I use to assess general baseline knowledge and previous experience with concepts prior to a new unit of study. Unlike the Key Concept Quiz or Show-You-Know, it is not meant to reflect on what learners read in preparation for the lecture. Rather, it is meant to get them to reflect upon their own personal experiences with the concepts to be discussed. Learners are instructed to answer the probes in no more than two concise sentences. The following probe is to get returning adult students to think about their own educational experiences throughout their lives.

- My first memory of being a student is. . . .
- I will stop learning when. . . .
- As a high school student, I was. . . .
- The most important aspect of learning is. . . .
- My most successful learning experience was. . . .

KWHL Strategy

The KWHL strategy, introduced in the previous chapter, can be used to promote study skills among learners or as a knowledge booster at the beginning of class. See Figure 6.4 for a KWHL developed for a learning strategies seminar for returning adult learners.

Learners can complete the first three sections before the unit of study, and then complete the last section to review what they just learned. In this way, the KWHL can be used for both knowledge and evaluation. Many learners will ask for the empty template after class so that they can use this strategy to prepare them for other units. This activity becomes an empowering metacognitive skill that students can use independently.

Figure 6.3   Show-You-Know Worksheet

1. Describe several physical and psychological indicators of stress.

Physical Indicators	Psychological Indicators

2. Define stress according to the following indicators.

Stimulus	Response	Transaction

3. Differentiate between mild, moderate and severe anxiety in terms of the following signs.

	Mild	Moderate	Severe
Physical signs			
Behavioral signs			

(Continued)

Figure 6.3 (Continued)

4. Differentiate between the NANDA labels of fear and anxiety.

NANDA Label	Definition
Fear	
Anxiety	

5. How would the nurse assess for each of the following factors influencing stress in a client?

Factor	Interview Question
Nature	
Perception	
Duration	
Experience	
Support	

6. According to Hans Seyle's general adaptation syndrome, a person responds to stress in a very predictable way, progressing through three distinct stages in efforts to adapt. Think of an example of a noxious stimulus that could create this reaction in a client, identify each stage, and describe and what happens to the body, using the boxes below.

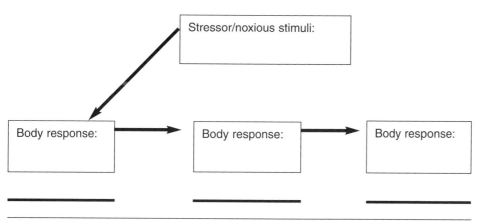

Figure 6.4   Learning Strategy KWHL

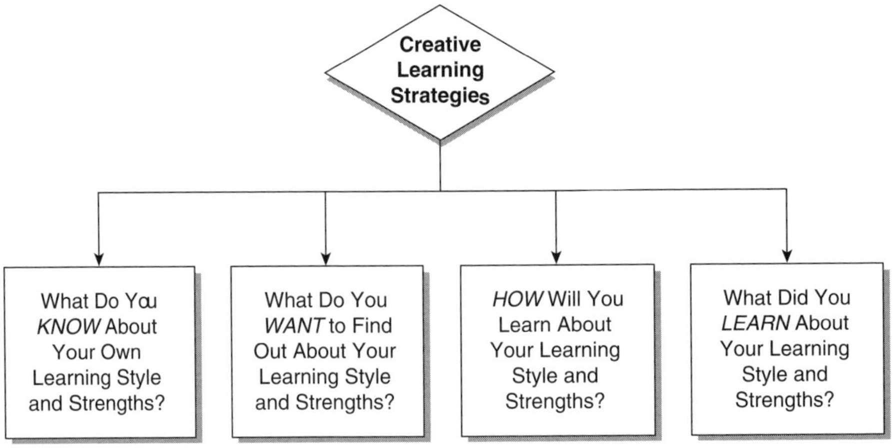

Strategies for Comprehension and Understanding

At this level of processing, new knowledge is encoded, integrated, exemplified and interpreted (Anderson et al., 2001; Bloom, 1956; Marzano & Kendall, 2006) into the learner's current knowledge base. From a brain-based learning perspective, once learners see the whole of what they will be learning, they can begin to focus on the parts. Learners need to understand where they will be going before they can comprehend where they are in their knowledge of a topic—it puts the learning experience into perspective and provides a much more meaningful foundation from which learners connect to previous knowledge and understandings.

Strategies for comprehension and understanding can be easily implemented at the same time as those for remembering and retrieving knowledge or immediately following. Plan to spend five to ten minutes on this activity before moving into the presentation of new material. For classes that meet once a week, the RSQC activity is most beneficial. Following are examples of activities that can be used to stimulate comprehension.

RSQC Strategy

The Recall, Summarize, Question, Connect (RSQC) strategy is modified from a classroom assessment technique introduced by Thomas Angelo and Patricia Cross (1993). Through RSQC, learners are prompted to remember the most important and meaningful aspects of the previous week's content. Learners get a kick-start into the new week by focusing their attention on newly learned material before expanding on the content. Use the template in Figure 6.5 to help your learners get focused on the new unit of study.

Big Picture Overview

Using the big picture overview on the topic of test taking strategies (Figure 6.6), learners know right from the start (the center shape and the four shapes

Figure 6.5   RSQC Grid

RSQC STRATEGY
RECALL: List words or phrases of most meaningful points from the last class. Underline the most important concept you gained from participating in the class.
SUMMARIZE: Write one sentence to summarize the essence of the previous class in terms of you personally.
QUESTION: Jot down one or two questions that you still may have about the content from the previous class.
CONNECT: Identify the connection between the concepts learned in the previous class and the goals and abilities of this course.

Figure 6.6 Big Picture Overview: Test Taking

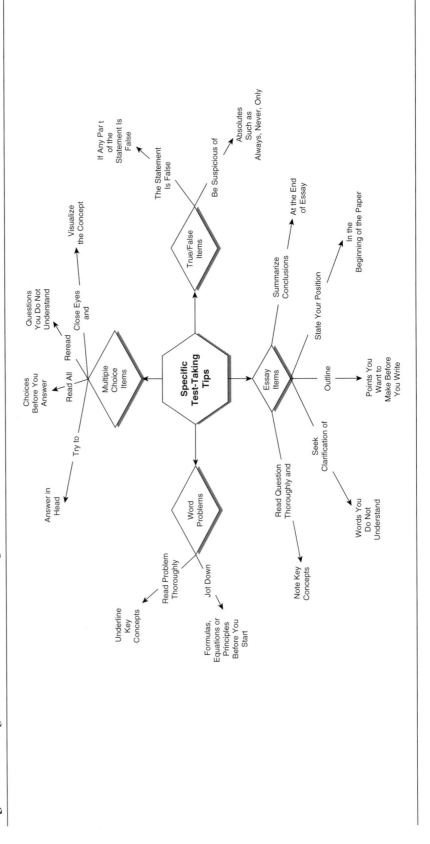

around it) that a variety of strategies for specific test types will be explored. Each of the main shapes can then be broken down and discussed more thoroughly through a concept map presentation, examples, or traditional outline format. The advantage of using a big picture overview up front is that learners know the direction the instructor is taking and are less anxious trying to keep up.

Memory Matrix

The memory matrix strategy, discussed in the previous chapter, is a graphic organizer that can be used at any level of the Materna Method. It is easy to construct and implement, and virtually any topic can be integrated. I especially like to use this technique to introduce complex topics that require focused attention and understanding. The example in Table 6.4 is a memory matrix that could be used to explore the cells of the human body. Learners know at a glance that I will be stressing structure and function as well as examples of each of the cells.

I introduce the concepts and point out a few examples of what I want learners to key into. As the material is presented, students have the empty matrices to complete in the application phase. This same matrix can be used during the analysis and synthesis phases to promote a deeper level of understanding as students work collaboratively. I may use this strategy in the evaluation phase as well to review what they hopefully have picked up as the most essential parts. The memory matrix is a truly universal tool!

A matrix for a class on research design (Table 6.5) is a handy tool for understanding and comparing research methods. Still another matrix, designed for a business class, might look like the one in Table 6.6.

Strategies for Application and Deep Comprehension

Reflecting upon all three taxonomies, this level of processing knowledge is where learners come to a greater depth of understanding by directly applying new knowledge, thinking abstractly (Bloom, 1956), implementing, executing (Anderson et al., 2001) and problem-solving using the new knowledge (Marzano & Kendall, 2006). The following activities are designed primarily to provide learners with the opportunity to work with the newly presented concepts. This can be considered the lecture portion of the presentation. Once the content is presented, learners need time to handle the information through some form of interactive work. They best absorb new and complex material when it is provided in a presentation of 10-20 minutes in length followed by application activities.

The activities described in this section can be done by individuals or groups. Angelo and Cross (1993) suggest the use of 10- to 30-minute punctuated lectures. The purpose of such an approach is to allow opportunities for learners to reflect and apply information shortly after they receive it. A punctuated lecture is a condensed overview that gets right to the point of the main concepts traditionally covered in far greater depth within the typical one- to two-hour lecture. The content is interrupted by two to three breakout sessions in which learners are able to actively discuss and apply concepts they are learning. It is much more suited to adult education than a traditional lecture.

Table 6.4   Biology Matrix

Types of Cells in the Human Body			
Cell Type	Structure	Function	Example
Nerve cell			
Muscle cell			
Bone cell			
Blood cell			
Reproductive cell			
Gland cell			

Table 6.5   Research Matrix

Qualitative Research Design					
Design	Purpose	Methods	Literature Review	Analysis	Outcomes
Phenomenological					
Grounded theory					
Historical					
Ethnographic					

Table 6.6   Business Matrix

Business Structures					
Type of Business	*Purpose*	*Structure*	*Legal Issues*	*Tax Breaks*	*Officers*
Sole proprietor					
Partnership					
Limited liability					
Corporation					

In addition to facilitating brain processing, exercises for application and deep comprehension reinforce the self system as well as the metacognitive system (Marzano & Kendall, 2006), as learners tend to pay greater attention to the presentation when they realize they will be expected to apply the concepts in class. I have included a few examples of activities that are designed to promote application of learning.

General/Specific Overview

Working in pairs, students are instructed to give a five- to ten-minute overview of the material presented to each other. Give learners five minutes to record their ideas before presenting. Instruct learners to go from general to specific concepts in presenting their overviews. It is truly amazing how much information can be recorded within a short period of time. The nice thing about having learners work in pairs, however, is that if one learner has an inaccurate appraisal of the content, the other one picks up on it. I generally walk around the classroom listening to various conversations and correct misconceptions that learners may have as well.

The act of teaching newly learned information reinforces learning. If learners use their general/specific overviews to review after they leave class, they are doubly reinforcing their learning. Promote the use of personal learning styles by encouraging visual learners to color-code, auditory learners to recite out loud, and kinesthetic-tactile learners to demonstrate or role-play concepts while reviewing the information.

Concept Map Discussion

The use of the concept map to gather and organize information is another powerful way to have learners apply concepts and connect them with what they already know. Have learners select a main focus of the material just presented and draw a map demonstrating relationships between what was just presented and what the learner already knows. See the previous chapter for a handy guide to concept maps.

Tree Diagram and Cycle Webs

Tree diagrams and cycle webs work well for information that occurs in stages or has a hierarchical arrangement. For example, a class on organizational behavior may benefit by having the structure of an organization presented using a tree diagram. This same class may come to a greater understanding of the stages of forming a solid organization by developing a cycle web in a small group.

A class on computer programming could easily apply tree diagrams to examine various computer operating systems. Likewise, a cycle web in this same class could be developed to illustrate the evolution of various operating systems used today.

A top-down tree makes an excellent tool for planning when working in a collaborative group setting. For example, learners may use the tree diagram shown in Figure 6.7 to identify traits and study strategies of sensory learning styles. A follow-up cycle web that could be developed to discuss phases in one specific study strategy—the SQR3 method (Survey, Question, Read, Recite, Review)—is shown in the example in Figure 6.8. This method allows the group to visually see the project as it is evolving.

Figure 6.7 Tree Diagram

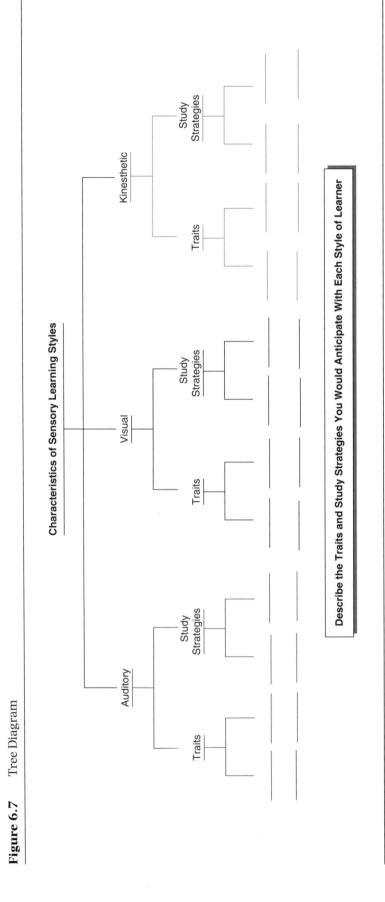

Characteristics of Sensory Learning Styles

Auditory

Traits

Study
Strategies

Visual

Traits

Study
Strategies

Kinesthetic

Traits

Study
Strategies

Describe the Traits and Study Strategies You Would Anticipate With Each Style of Learner

Figure 6.8   Cycle Web

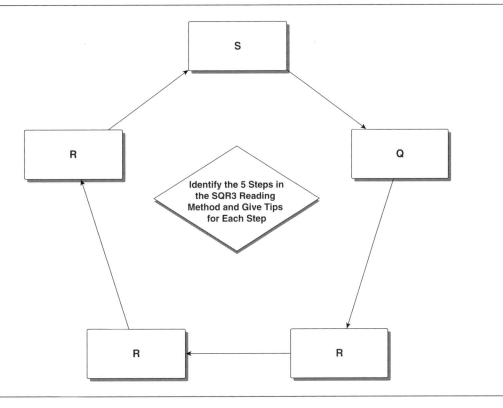

Strategies for Analysis

Analysis strategies provide the opportunity for learners to break apart, organize, classify, and think critically about how they applied the new concepts and how their understanding and comprehension have developed as a result. In the analysis phase, the learner can explore relationships (Bloom, 1956), differentiate and organize (Anderson et al., 2001), and specify, generalize, and classify concepts (Anderson et al., 2001; Bloom, 1956; Marzano & Kendall, 2006).The best time to implement analysis activities is after a brain break, when students are energized both physically and mentally. Reinforcement of the self system and the metacognitive system can be articulated by the educator to help keep learners focused on learning goals and objectives as well as on the relevance of the topic. Analysis activities naturally flow from and build upon application activities to further enhance meaningful learning. Here are a few suggestions for you to consider using.

General/Specific Analysis

After learners have worked in pairs applying newly learned concepts in the general/specific overviews, instruct them to go back and analyze each other's responses in terms of quality of the content, relationship to the objectives of the unit, and finally relationship to the topic in general. Analyzing in pairs promotes critical thinking and problem-solving at a much higher level than that achieved when learners do this activity individually. The template in Table 6.7 can be used to guide learners in this process.

Table 6.7   General/Specific Analysis

Quality of Content:
   Accuracy
   Completeness
   Organization (general
      to specific)
	Relationship to Objectives
	and Unit:
	   Identify objectives
	   Explain relationship
		Relevance to Nursing:
		   Purpose for learning
		   How you will use
		      concepts

Venn Diagram Analysis

The Venn diagram, presented in the previous chapter, is another technique that can be used by learners either individually or in small groups to analyze concepts according to common and unique attributes. Graphic organizers like the Venn diagram allow students to see a visual representation of information they may have recorded in linear fashion in their notes. By restructuring information into a graphic format, new relationships and patterns emerge that may not have been explicit to the student before.

Defining Features Grid

Angelo and Cross (1993) have another suggestion for promoting analysis of new information: the defining features grid. This activity is unique in that it requires the learner to differentiate and categorize concepts according to the presence or absence of important, preselected defining features. The activity helps learners to identify explicit and critical distinctions as they analyze complex comparisons into meaningful and manageable chunks of information. Table 6.8 shows such a grid designed for a biology class on the topic of recessive

Table 6.8   Defining Features Grid

Defining Features Grid *Inherited Traits*		
Trait	*Recessive*	*Dominant*
Red hair	X	
Attached ear lobe	X	
Night blindness	X	
Blue eyes	X	
Brown eyes		X
Thin lips	X	
Full lips		X
Tongue roller		X
Freckles		X
Dimples in cheeks		X
Flat feet	X	
High arches		X
Farsightedness		X
Astigmatism	X	

versus dominant inherited traits. Responses can range from a simple checkoff indicating presence or absence of a feature (as shown) to a short description by the learner of distinguishing characteristics of the variables on the grid. When using this technique, keep in mind that the simpler the grid, the more striking the features become. In other words, limit the comparison to two or three concepts and the defining features to no more than ten.

A defining features grid could be developed for a psychology class to examine the distinguishing features between two or three personality types. Likewise, a political science instructor may develop a grid to characterize the differences between two or three governmental structures.

Pro/Con Grid

The pro/con grid (Angelo & Cross, 1993) promotes analysis of the pros and cons of a specific topic or policy. I have found that this technique works well when content is covered that requires students to distinguish advantages and disadvantages of select topics or events. A pro/con grid can help students analyze potential costs and benefits and alternative solutions to a problem. Table 6.9 shows a grid to establish the pros and cons of popular Internet search engines.

Strategies for Evaluation and Deeper Analysis

After coming to terms with the new knowledge and initiating analysis activities, learners have had the opportunity to handle the knowledge and become familiar with it. At this point, they are ready to critique the knowledge, detect inconsistencies and appropriateness (Anderson et al., 2001), form judgments and opinions of the topic (Bloom, 1956), and determine errors (Marzano & Kendall, 2006).

Interestingly, Anderson and colleagues (2001) have reordered this level of processing to follow analysis and precede Bloom's synthesis level, which they renamed *creating.* I heartily agree with this reordering and renaming! In my experiences, I have observed adult learners being unable to generate new ideas from the content until they have checked them against their own personal beliefs and values and have accepted them as truly valid. I also agree that creativity and synthesis are synonymous terms. I have always been an excellent synthesizer, and as a result, I have been able to develop new and creative ideas for my learners quite naturally!

By evaluating new ideas, learners begin to bring the new concepts back together into a meaningful structure. Information becomes knowledge when learners actively summarize and integrate new information. Checking and critiquing activities allow students to distinguish key concepts from supporting data and compose the big picture. Getting learners involved in group evaluation promotes learner collaboration, social interaction, and professional networking skills as well. Consider the following activities that naturally promote critical thinking.

Critical Consequences

Have students pair up or form into small groups, and give them a scenario that pulls together integral and key points. Have them discuss the consequences

Table 6.9   Pro/Con Grid

Pro/Con Grid *Internet Search Engines*		
Search Engine	*Pro*	*Con*
Google		
Yahoo!		
Dogpile search		
Meta search		

of not fully understanding or implementing key concepts you have covered. Provide five minutes for them to read the scenario and five minutes for them to respond; if they're working in teams or small groups, allow an extra five minutes for them to discuss their responses. Randomly select teams or groups to share their response with the group. This activity stimulates critical thinking and leads to a dynamic discussion on the consequences and implications of not following protocol.

Dynamic Debates

Assign learners opposing perspectives on certain issues, ethical controversies, legal issues, or policies related to the content covered during the lecture. Allow five minutes for groups to come up with arguments for or against the issue. Assign a moderator to each group, and give them ten minutes to debate their assigned perspectives. Randomly select teams to share their viewpoints with the rest of the class. To promote even greater critical thinking, assign students to debate the issue from two different viewpoints, such as those of a policy maker, consumer, lawyer, or client.

One-Sentence Summary

After doing an analysis activity, have learners come up with a one-sentence summary of the content presented. You may offer prompts, such as, "The most important thing I learned about _____ is. . . ." This technique also works well in reverse to help students identify vague areas that they need clarified. You may offer a prompt such as, "One thing that I still do not understand about _____ is. . . ." Have learners respond to both these prompts. Collect the responses and address the issues they bring up at the next class session before moving onto new content.

Concept Essay

Give learners a list of the most important concepts covered during a presentation. Instruct them to describe how the concepts relate to each other and to the unit of study. If time allows, have learners write a narrative or formulate a diagram or map to visually demonstrate their understanding of the concepts. Keep the number of concepts to no more than 15. The concepts can be broken down into clusters of three to five, so learners can use the clusters together in a sentence or two to really fine-tune their ability to evaluate.

Strategies for Synthesizing, Creating, and Using Knowledge

After evaluating new concepts, principles, or theories, learners are ready to generate and produce new ideas (Anderson et al., 2001), experiment and use higher-level thinking skills such as problem solving and decision making (Marzano & Kendall, 2006), and bring concepts back into a whole as new knowledge structures are created (Bloom, 1956). I have found that the ideas that learners generate after applying, analyzing, and evaluating the material are well thought-out, validated by supporting evidence, and relevant as well as accurate. Having spent a considerate amount of time handling the information and investing personal energy in the classroom activities, learners have developed a much deeper and broader understanding of the concepts. In other words, they have internalized them and have made them part of their knowledge structures. They are now ready to use the knowledge at a more efficient level (Marzano & Kendall, 2006). The activities in this section support this process.

Concept Map Review

In this activity, learners validate the concepts they have applied, analyzed, and evaluated by developing their own concept map review of what they have learned. Using the objectives of the unit as a foundation, instruct learners to link the unit objectives to the evidence and supporting details they have gathered during analyzing and evaluating activities to come up with the big picture for the unit. This strategy works well if learners use their concept map discussions from the application activities as a springboard for the concluding overview. Visual learners can enhance their maps with color and symbols.

What's Your Concept? Review

Have learners form into small groups or pairs, and give each learner at least five concepts or principles that have been covered during the presentation. Allow ten minutes for learners to write an example or clues related to the assigned concepts. Learners then quiz each other by reading only the example or clue. Have each group select the most accurate and concise descriptions to share with the rest of the class.

Reflective Journal

This creating strategy promotes metacognitive awareness of what has been learned. Instruct learners to prioritize three to five of the most important things that they got out of the lecture and to write in their journals about these things. I have found that when learners have had the opportunity to apply, analyze, and evaluate information, they are much more connected with what they have learned. They are more likely to discern the key elements of the discussion from less relevant information. Although this is an individual activity, it is helpful, if time permits, to have learners volunteer their reflections to the class. This is also an easy way to gather information on how learners perceived the presentation.

Wrap-Up Quiz

Finally, a wrap-up quiz that focuses on the most salient points of the lecture/discussion makes a superb creating activity. You can even use the same key concept review that was used at the start of class as a kind of pretest/posttest strategy. Be sure to supply the answers after learners complete the quiz, so that they can validate their learning. I have also had learners create their own test questions on specific content. To take that idea one step further, assign a group of five learners one or two concepts and have them develop a series of questions.

This is an exciting and refreshing activity for learners, and I have actually collected a few really great test questions this way!

Personal Reflections on the Integrated Taxonomy

Although I had been fairly comfortable with Bloom's (1956) taxonomy, after integrating the basic elements from Anderson and colleagues (2001) and Marzano and Kendall (2006), the overall structure was much more comprehensive and representative of how I have observed adult learners process information.

Anderson and colleagues (2001) validated many of the brain-compatible activities I had been using for years and contributed greatly to my understanding of the relationship between synthesis and creativity. This understanding has allowed me to empower my adult learners even more to spread their wings and fly! They have reinforced Bloom's taxonomy and supported the concept of learning from simple to complex, or general to specific. However, the idea of categorizing metacognition as a type of knowledge rather than a mental process made me quite uncomfortable, since I tend to promote metacognitive skills concurrently with instruction.

I was more comfortable with the model developed by Marzano and Kendall (2006). It made sense to me to order the mental processes starting with the self system. It certainly supports my understanding of self-directed, autonomous adult learners. They do exert control over their own learning, starting with their own personal acceptance of the knowledge and followed by self-determination of their own learning goals (the metacognitive system). Once those systems are flowing in a positive direction, the cognitive system is ready to process new knowledge.

From Marzano and Kendall (2006), the brain-compatible principle of linking personal relevance to learning was greatly enforced through my understanding of the self-system. I now articulate that relationship clearly to my students at the beginning of each learning session as well as at the midpoint, and I pair this articulation with activities to promote the resourceful learning state. In addition, Marzano and Kendall's promotion of symbolizing at the comprehension level validates my understanding of the visual processing capabilities of the brain. I have observed adult learners go from puzzlement to competence when I use visual graphic organizers to present complex concepts. My philosophy of promoting metacognition among adult learners was also validated after reviewing Marzano and Kendall's taxonomy. Although I have always addressed this during teaching activities, I now have a clearer understanding of how the flow of processing has to activate the self and metacognitive systems before new knowledge can be processed!

> "The man who is too old to learn was probably always too old to learn."
>
> —Henry S. Haskins

APPLICATION OF BRAIN-COMPATIBLE PRINCIPLES IN THE ADULT CLASSROOM

As I discussed in Part 2, dramatic developments in brain research and technology are rapidly advancing our understanding and utilization of the human brain. Geoffrey and Renate Nummela Caine (1994) have synthesized much of the research by postulating a list of 12 brain-mind principles. Several educators have adapted the Caine principles in whole or in part to promote learning within various groups of learners (Allen, 2002; Jensen, 2000; Kovalik, 1997; Sousa, 2001; Sprenger, 2002; Tate, 2003, 2004; Wolfe, 2001). While these principles have become well regarded and are often cited within the K–12 educational community, there are few applications that address the adult learner.

I have worked with the Caines' principles over the years, tweaking them and massaging them to come to a better understanding of just how they can be applied to the adult setting. As a result, I have synthesized and modified the original 12 to create a new and improved collection of 7 adult learning principles that are supported by recent findings among neuroscientists.

However, please understand that these principles are merely my personal interpretation of how brain research can be applied to the adult setting. Because every learning environment is unique, you may want to use this list as a starting point and continue to modify these principles to link the underlying brain research into your particular setting.

Principle 1

Learning is collaborative and influenced by interactions with others.

Interaction of the brain with the environment and with other learners has been proven to net a more enriched brain. According to Ronald Kotulak (2004), an enriched environment can yield up to a 25 percent increase in neural connections at any age. In other words, developing interpersonal relationships and interacting with others strengthens the brain's ability to process information.

Application of Principle 1

This principle is addressed by allowing learners to select their own seating as well as the other members of groups they will work with during collaborative learning activities. I suggest that learners move their seating into comfortable arrangements, such as a circle or semicircle, when interacting with other learners. I have observed a greater willingness to be flexible and to consider other perspectives when adults can see and interact with other learners. To get learners engaged in a topic, I may pair learners up and send them out for a "walk and talk" brain break. Group warm-up and review activities just prior to starting a new unit of learning also provide enrichment for the brain and activate links to previous learning.

Principle 2

The adult brain creates meaning by linking past to present into familiar patterns.

Through brain research, we know that the brain strives to make meaning out of incoming sensory information by creating patterns or associations to link with previous learning (Pribram, 1971). Because of this natural affinity for making sense out of information, the brain organizes and discriminates bits and pieces until a logical whole is created. I have observed, over and over, adult learners challenging and debating information, dissecting it and putting it back together until it makes sense to them. Once the data are accepted, they are connected to existing neural networks. The new knowledge then becomes integrated into the learner's existing knowledge database.

Every event is processed in the brain as a complex experience consisting of many parts embedded within a larger whole. In this way, the brain perceives separateness and interconnectedness simultaneously. We know through neuroscientific research (Gazzaniga, 1998; Sperry, 1966) that the brain processes information sequentially and holistically through communication between hemispheres as the entire brain interacts as a dynamic whole. This is liberating information for educators who have been conditioned to think that all information must be made explicit in order for learners to come away with an accurate understanding.

Application of Principle 2

To promote meaning, I encourage my learners to question their own assumptions as well as their understanding of the concepts we are working with. When introducing new ideas, I frequently do a comprehension check: "Does this make sense to you?" If the answer is no, we discuss the concept until it does make sense. The excellent reading comprehension strategy SQR3 (Survey, Question, Read, Recite, Review; see Chapter 5) prompts learners to write out questions and turn headings and subheadings into questions after surveying and before reading. When they actually begin the reading, the brain automatically seeks out the answers to the questions.

To encourage pattern-making, I use a variety of graphic organizers when presenting new information and urge learners to reorganize their study material into patterns that make more sense to them. In that way, learners are formulating their own meaningful patterns of understanding and reconfiguring their internal maps both mentally and physically. An excellent software program for teaching learners to develop their own graphic organizers is Inspiration, a mind-mapping program. I actually developed an elective study strategy course where I have learners redesign study notes into meaningful patterns and diagrams using Inspiration.

Finally, to promote whole-brain learning, I use the big picture overview to present unit objectives, and then I demonstrate the relationships among the objectives before breaking them down into component parts for discussion. At the end of the period, I summarize by bringing them back together again as a whole. It may sound simplistic, but it definitely facilitates learning! Using the objective overview map to introduce a new unit of study promotes an understanding of broad study objectives to focus on.

Principle 3

Emotions and stress can adversely impact learning.

The brain is heavily influenced by emotional stimuli. The brain makes greater connections between neurons when it is appropriately challenged in the learning environment. However, under stressful and threatening circumstances, the brain tends to shift down to the primitive region, where survival is the main focus. Brain research has confirmed that emotions are critically linked to learning and promote recall of memories. On a biological level, emotions are originated within the limbic structures. Incoming sensory information is relayed to the thalamus, which in turn relays information to the various sensory cortices. When sensory information reaches the amygdala (the emotional clearinghouse), it is registered as an emotionally pleasing or stimulating event or an emotionally charged threat. If the information is perceived as threatening, the fight or flight response kicks in as the body naturally responds to this threat in the learning environment. Chemical messengers, called neurotransmitters, flood the endocrine system, interacting within the synapses to consciously process the situation within the frontal cortex.

Positive emotions generate positive memory retention. Removing the threat from the learning environment promotes positive emotions. Negative emotions in the learning environment are linked to the memories they create and surface consciously as information is recalled, stimulating the stress response again. Because emotions and thoughts are so closely linked, it is impossible to separate them from learning experiences. Almost every thought is accompanied by an emotion.

As a result, learners are less likely to tap into their higher-order thinking and creativity when negative emotions surface. An emotionally negative threat perceived by the learner is immobilizing, while the occasional anxiety related to new learning is actually beneficial. Either way, positive as well as negative emotions will affect the way a person learns. Positive emotions promote shifting up to higher-level thinking, while negative emotions cause the brain to downshift to the primal survival state discussed earlier. Educators can promote learning by promoting self-efficacy and creating an environment of relaxed alertness, which involves low threat and high challenge.

Application of Principle 3

When my learners arrive, I greet them at the door and welcome them by name. Throughout the class period, I invite dialogue and sharing of ideas related to the topic. Making learners aware of how they feel about what they are learning promotes affective processing of ideas and encourages learners to understand issues from other perspectives as well as their own. I make my learners aware of the importance of maintaining a positive emotional state while learning and studying. By simply investing five minutes at the start of every class with baroque music, breathing exercises, education kinesiology exercises, and a visualization of the objectives for the class, I make this principle part of the classroom environment. During breaks, I invite learners to join in on brain breaks of deep breathing and visualization exercises along with a brief interlude to discuss learning with peers. This seems to keep stress levels down and to promote an open, receptive state of mind (see Chapter 4). Students report feeling centered, focused, and ready to learn following these brief exercises. Using a round table or circular seat setting can promote a more open learning environment as well.

Principle 4

Adults learn through both conscious focused attention and unconscious peripheral processing.

The brain takes in so much more than the topic at hand. It is totally immersed in the learning environment, absorbing and selecting a continuous flow of sensations, input, and images. Peripheral signals from the instructor, learning peers, and the environment may have a tremendous impact upon learning outcomes. Much of learning is processed at a subconscious level. Learners may not even be aware that their brains continue to process information outside of the classroom, awake and asleep, until it becomes meaningful to the brain. Making learners aware of how they actually process information throughout the day and even while they sleep promotes autonomy. The educator who recognizes this principle will make efforts to have students reflect upon what they have learned and to creatively elaborate on their reflections, ideas, and experiences to make the learning more meaningful.

While educators have no control of internal stimuli, they can reduce external stimuli, such as noise and their own gestures as well as other nonverbal behavioral cues that may get in the way of focusing on the lesson. The brain also needs frequent breaks from direct focused attention to process information in a more effective manner. A nonstop flow of information, such as in the traditional lecture, may actually be counterproductive to the natural way the brain learns.

Application of Principle 4

By placing student-generated learning aids—such as posters, maps, and diagrams constructed during collaborative group work—on the walls of the classroom, this principle becomes reality. In this way, the learning aids become part of the periphery. Learners who begin to drift away are immediately drawn back to the topic at hand. Interestingly, although the learning aids are removed prior to testing, learners tend to turn to the spots where they were posted and visualize what was on each poster as they recall concepts that are being evaluated.

I also use classical or baroque music to stimulate the alpha brain state, which promotes focused attention, throughout the learning sessions. Although the music is noticeable while learners are first coming into the classroom and during the opening comments, I turn the volume down so that it does not become a distraction during the learning session. However, the learners continue to respond to the vibrations, maintaining the optimal brain wave state for learning. To keep learners focused and attentive to the topic at hand, I also punctuate learning sessions with brain breaks every 20–30 minutes. During a brain break, the music is turned up, learners are invited to participate in a breathing exercise and a movement exercise, and they are given the opportunity to discuss what they learned with each other. By the end of the 5–10 minute break, they are refreshed and ready to focus their attention once more on the learning objectives.

I also apply this principle by encouraging learners to review newly presented information within 24 hours of class, then again within 48 hours, and again within 72 hours. Each review session, learners are encouraged to process information using a different modality. For example, during the first review, information may be mapped out; during the next review, the student may use flashcards or develop a game with the content; and during the next review, the learner may teach the content to a learner peer or family member. This intense level of focused attention as well as frequent rehearsal and repetition of concepts promotes processing at both the conscious and subconscious levels, because the learner is turning the information over and over as it is transferred into long-term memory knowledge banks.

Principle 5

Adult learners process information through multiple memory pathways.

There are two primary memory systems that operate throughout the learning process—nondeclarative (implicit) memory and declarative (explicit) memory. Nondeclarative memory is described as a system for storing and categorizing memories learned by rote, such as facts, skills, and procedures as well as emotional responses. Declarative memory, which is spatially oriented, allows for instant recall of personal events and experiences. Declarative memories are memories of events that occur in relationship to each other, and they are called up simultaneously as we experience those events or interactions with others.

This dynamic memory system takes time to develop and is continuously being updated as events of the day unfold. It is the declarative memory that pulls up the stored nondeclarative memories. With repeated rehearsal, learners can store files of unrelated information in nondeclarative memory, which can be accessed and integrated into declarative memory as needed. The most distinguishing difference between the two memory systems is the fact that declarative memory is recalled as a spatial map of relationships, whereas nondeclarative memory may be recalled as parts of the map. Educators can promote more effective use of declarative memory by presenting information as it relates to familiar concepts and by promoting rehearsal of nondeclarative memory through active learning strategies.

Application of Principle 5

By encouraging learners to integrate what they are learning into their own personal life experiences, I am promoting the use of both memory systems. When paying attention to how facts, skills, and procedures relate to the adult learner's developing profession or job description, taxon memory merges with locale memory systems as learners apply the concepts to real life. The use of mnemonics and memory pegs also helps learners to link memory systems for easier recall. Again, the use of the 24-48-72–hour review activity strengthens the natural link between the memory systems.

This principle can also be applied by encouraging learners to relate new concepts to past experiences and prerequisite knowledge. The RSQC (Recall, Summarize, Question, Connect) strategy prompts adult learners to recall concepts from a past class or from work experience, summarize the most important points and how they apply to new learning, question what is not understood, and finally connect the new learning to the past in order to reconstruct the learner's internal mental map. Another strategy that addresses this principle is the KWHL (Know, Want, How, Learn) template. This strategy assists learners in brainstorming everything they already know about a topic, focusing on what they want to learn, identifying resources to facilitate learning, and finally evaluating what they have actually learned about the topic. This is a strategy that learners can use autonomously in almost any type of learning environment.

Principle 6

The adult brain is uniquely organized and never stops learning.

Every learner entering the classroom has her or his own unique combination of learning styles and strengths. Adult learners have a diversity of learning strengths and experiences that they bring into the learning environment. The educator who appreciates the uniqueness of all learners ensures that a variety of teaching modalities are used to meet the needs of as many learners as possible. All brains are not alike, and learners need to become aware of how they learn best and how they can improve in areas in which they are less proficient.

Along the same line, life experiences have the potential for physically modifying the learner's neural connections. Current research on plasticity supports the idea that new neural pathways are created every time we challenge our brains. Growth and development continue throughout life, barring physical brain damage, building on what has been learned before. Educators who understand this principle understand that adults can learn throughout their lifetimes as long as they are adequately challenged and have the opportunity to make the most of their natural learning strengths.

Application of Principle 6

From day one, I make an effort to recognize the uniqueness of each of my adult learners and help them to understand that their ability to learn is heavily influenced by personal experiences as well as concerns that they may carry with them into the classroom. I have learners complete a learning style inventory and discuss strategies to promote learning strengths to build upon learning deficits. See Chapter 3 for a sample learning style inventory and a multiple intelligence survey. Learners express a sense of empowerment and autonomy when they understand how to work with their own unique blend of learning styles and talents.

I also incorporate teaching techniques to appeal to auditory, visual, and kinesthetic learners throughout my presentations. For example, I may present a diagram (visual), have learners discuss how the diagram applies to the current topic (auditory), and engage learners in an activity of redesigning the diagram to incorporate additional concepts (kinesthetic). Another example would be to show a short video clip or movie of a procedure (visual), assign pairs of learners to design a poster board highlighting key concepts or certain steps in the procedure (kinesthetic), and have the learners present their assigned portion of the procedure to the group (auditory).

Principle 7

A healthy lifestyle contributes to optimal learning.

A healthy lifestyle can promote mental sharpness as adults age. Balanced nutrition, especially, promotes optimal functioning of brain cells. Dr. Dharma Singh Khalsa, creator of the Brain Longevity program, maintains that dietary deficiencies reduce cognition as a person ages (1997). Deficiencies in folic acid, Vitamin B6, Vitamin B12, iron, and zinc have been linked to memory loss and to reduced visual perception, spatial reasoning, and concentration. The brain requires a steady blood glucose level to function most efficiently. Ideally, complex carbohydrates, fruits, vegetables, and whole grain products are the healthiest choices. In addition, controlling blood pressure, getting regular exercise and adequate sleep, keeping alcohol intake moderate, and managing stress are among the lifestyle behaviors that Dr. Khalsa has linked to optimal brain functioning.

Application of Principle 7

Recognition and adaptation of these lifestyle behaviors is paramount for adult learners who want to stay on the cutting edge of their own learning potential. I like to promote this principle through role modeling above all else. I talk openly with my adult learners about the importance of integrating wellness behaviors into their daily routines. I begin every class with a visualization exercise to promote a healthy and productive state for learning. Throughout the class, I use positive affirmations to maintain this focus on learning. Additionally, learners need to understand how their personal physiology impacts their learning. I use a holistic framework of health and wellness to guide learners in making lifestyle choices to promote wellness. Nutrition, sleep, exercise, stress management, and time management are among the wellness values that I advocate. Once learners understand the relationship between their own brain physiology and their learning, they are much more committed to adapting the healthy lifestyle behaviors that optimize learning.

These adult learning principles reinforce what has been discovered about how the brain learns and reacts within the traditional learning environment. Feel free to modify them and apply them to your own unique learning environment. It is important to develop a working comfort with using these principles. They are not one-size-fits-all principles! Some may be more relevant to your situation than others. The important thing is to make them your own!

The new biologically based brain theories suggest that current time-honored, traditional beliefs about instruction, learning, and memory are simply erroneous. Robert Sylwester suggests that assessment policies and teaching practices currently used in schools, which merely reflect society's beliefs about what is educationally important, are inadequate because they were developed before we clearly understood the complexity of the brain systems (Sylwester, 1995).

No matter which theoretical framework an educator champions, the bottom line is that learning is a complex and dynamic process, and that students learn in different ways. Terry O'Banion refers to the old way of learning as analogous to the factory model of production: Students move through the line at the same rate and are imprinted with only the knowledge that the school deems important (O'Banion, 1997). Educators who understand new learning perspectives and acknowledge and respond to unique differences in learning styles will facilitate success in learning. Application of the theories of multiple intelligences, learning styles, and brain-compatible education offer greater numbers of students the opportunity to succeed by focusing directly upon how they learn.

Proponents of brain-compatible learning theory (Edelman, 1992; Gazzaniga, 1992) suggest that the brain has an infinite and genetically predetermined ability to learn but is foremost prewired to survive before responding to formal instruction. In other words, the brain is programmed to naturally unfold and learn in the right environment, providing that survival needs have been met. Neuroscientist Richard Restak maintains that the brain is programmed to make order and sense out of learning experiences (Restak, 1995).

From an educational perspective, this means that all learners have unlimited potential to develop their genetically preprogrammed brains and to integrate their learning experiences into their personal realities. However, the environment must be perceived as safe and secure for this natural process to occur. It also means that educators may have been underestimating the capability of learners and actually impeding their natural learning processes by not validating that learning has occurred among those who demonstrate less than the desired behavioral outcomes.

> "True education is to learn how to think . . . not what to think."
>
> —*Krishnamurti*

FREE YOUR CREATIVE SPIRIT!

Brain-compatible approaches provide a very exciting and creative way to teach and learn. I hope I have jump-started your own creative juices and given you some innovative ideas on how to apply brain-compatible learning principles in the adult learning environment! It is my sincere desire that the strategies and activities in this book will help you gain confidence in your own creative potential as an adult educator. By the time you have read this far, you should have acquired a new perspective and fresh insight on teaching and learning.

The strategies presented in this book are available for you to use directly or adapt to your unique adult population. Take these strategies and run with them—create fun and exciting lesson plans. Learning does not have to be the same old same old! Now that you have become aware of just how beneficial brain-compatible techniques are with adult learners, the possibilities are infinite.

Science has taken us far into understanding the intricacies of the brain and the amazing learning potential we are all born with. It is now up to us, as educators and adult learners, to revitalize, rejuvenate, and reenergize the current educational system. When you begin using creative learning strategies such as the ones offered in this book, you begin unleashing your own creative spirit. Creative people not only think of new ways to do things, they put those creative ideas into action! By putting your creative ideas into action, you will become inspired to become even more creative, fertilizing new ideas and coming up with inventive solutions to the many challenges you may face as an educator.

Resource A

Brain Warm-Ups

Here are a few brain warm-ups to use at the start of class. Simply put two or three up on an overhead or whiteboard while students are entering the room. I give students three to five minutes to ponder these while I take attendance. It really helps to get them to think outside the box. The answers are in italics.

1 AT 3:46PM *One at a time*	**13579 AZ** *Odds and ends*	**2um** **+ 2um** *Forum*
ECNALG *Backward glance*	**NAFISH** **NAFISH** *Tuna fish*	**ONE** **ONE** *One on one*
BJAOCKX *Jack in the box*	**_____IT** *Blanket*	**HE'S/HIMSELF** *He's beside himself*
HIJKLMNO H_2O	**LAL** *All mixed up*	**DOCTOR** **DOCTOR** *Paradox*

(Continued)

(Continued)

TIMING **TIM ING** *Split second timing*	**ME QUIT** *Quit following me*	**+ +** *Double cross*
WHEATHER *Bad spell of weather*	**II II** **O O** *Circles under the eyes*	**COPI COPPY** **COPY** *Copyright*
ME NT *Apartment*	**SEA SON** *Open season*	**LEAN** **REVO** *Lean over backwards*
GESG *Scrambled eggs*	**$$ ⫫T** *Money market*	**ON** **THOUGHT THOUGHT** *On second thought*
BALLO 𝕋 *Absentee ballot*	**COME CO** *More to come*	**+ER SCHOOL** *Summer school*
PERFORMANCE **× 2** *Repeat performance*	**COLOWME** *Low income*	**DICE** **DICE** *Paradise*

CLOSE **CLOSE** **CLOSE** **CLOSE** *Foreclose*	**<u>0</u>** **MD** **PhD** **LLD** *Three degrees below zero*	**ONE ANOTHER** **ONE ANOTHER** **ONE ANOTHER** **ONE ANOTHER** **ONE ANOTHER** **ONE ANOTHER** *Six of one, half dozen of another*
THHAENGRE *Hang in there*	**H/E/A/D** *Headquarters*	**W,I** *I'm upset*
<u>HEAD</u> **LHEOEVLSE** *Head over heels in love*	**NIRENDEZVOUSGHT** *Midnight rendezvous*	**E A T** **R ST URAN** *Eat out restaurant*
+ OR − *More or less*	**THER** *Almost there*	**LILATEFE** *Late in life*
<u>13579R</u> **WHELMING** *Odds are overwhelming*	**<u>STAND</u>** **I** *I understand*	**SYMPHON** *Unfinished symphony*
MIND **MATTER** *Mind over matter*	**BJEOTBWJEOEBN** *Between jobs*	**FEET GOING IN** *Going in feet first*

(Continued)

(Continued)

<u>LOYAL</u> TIES *Split loyalties*	EYE E SEE EXCEPT *I before E except after C*	<u>GI</u> CCC CC C *GI overseas*
GRAPH **GRAPH** *Paragraph*	**RASINGINGIN** *Singing in the rain*	**FORGOTTE** *Almost forgotten*
DEATH/LIFE *Life after death*	**R/E/A/D** *Read between the lines*	**KNEE** **LIGHTS** *Neon lights*
<u>WEAR</u> LONG *Long underwear*	**STANDING** MISS *A little misunderstanding*	**HO** *Half an hour*
XQQQME *Excuse me*	**WEEKKKKKK** *Long weekend*	**YUO'ER** *You're confused*
S B M U H T *Thumbs up*	K C E H C *Check up*	ISSUE ISSUE ISSUE ISSUE ISSUE ISSUE ISSUE ISSUE ISSUE ISSUE *Tennis shoes*

Resource B

*Active Learning
Strategies for Knowledge,
Remembering, and Retrieval*

Show You Know for Physical Assessment Unit

Draw a Diagram Depicting the Flow of Cardiac Blood Through the Arteries
in Red and the Veins in Blue.

Open-Ended Probe for Unit on Elderly Issues

1. What do you think of when you think of the elderly?

2. How do you picture yourself when you are elderly?

3. What would be your three most essential **physical concerns?**

4. What would be your three most essential **psychosocial concerns?**

KWHL Diagram for Unit on Alterations in the GI System

...

What do I KNOW?	What do I WANT to Know?	HOW will I Find out?	What did I LEARN?
Structures of Upper GI:	Dysfunctions of Upper GI:		
Structures of Lower GI:	Dysfunctions of Lower GI:		
Process of Digestion:	Diversions/ Treatments for Alterations in Digestion:		

Key Concept Review for a Unit on Stress

Identify several physical and psychological stress reactions.

Physical	Psychological

Resource C

*Active Learning Strategies
for Comprehension and Understanding*

RSQC Strategy Template

Recall: List words or phrases of most meaningful points from the last class. Underline the most important concept you gained from participating in the class.

Summarize: Write one sentence to summarize the essence of the previous class in terms of you personally.

Question: Jot down one or two questions that you still may have about the content from the previous class.

Connect: Identify the connection between the concepts learned in the previous class and the goals of and skills to be learned in this course.

Describe the multiple effects of prolonged anxiety.

Level of Anxiety	Physiological Effects	Emotional Effects	Cognitive Effects
Mild			
Moderate			
Severe			

Cause-Effect Diagram for a Unit on Anxiety Disorders

183

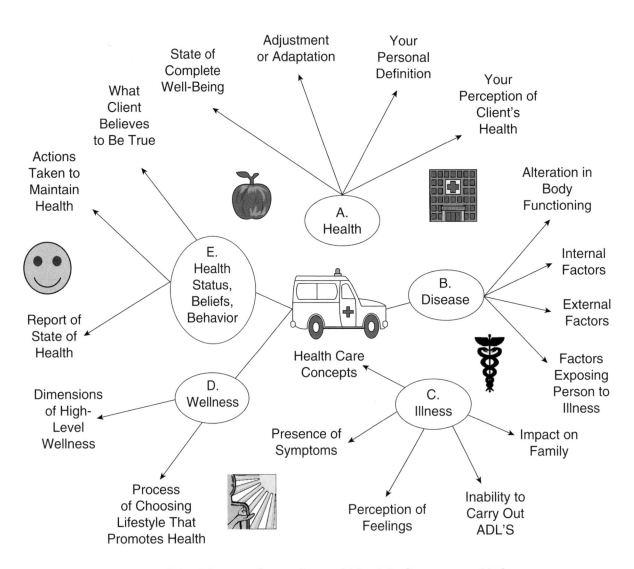

State of
Complete
Well-Being

Adjustment
or Adaptation

Your
Personal
Definition

What
Client
Believes
to Be True

Your
Perception of
Client's
Health

Actions
Taken to
Maintain
Health

A.
Health

Alteration in
Body
Functioning

E.
Health
Status,
Beliefs,
Behavior

Internal
Factors

B.
Disease

External
Factors

Report of
State of
Health

Factors
Exposing
Person to
Illness

Health Care
Concepts

Dimensions
of High-
Level
Wellness

D.
Wellness

C.
Illness

Impact on
Family

Presence of
Symptoms

Process
of Choosing
Lifestyle That
Promotes Health

Perception of
Feelings

Inability to
Carry Out
ADL'S

Big Picture Overview of Health Concepts Unit

Medication Matrix

Med Category Generic/Trade	How It Works	Major Side Effects	Interactions Safety	Nursing Implications

Resource D

*Active Learning Strategies for
Application and Deeper Comprehension*

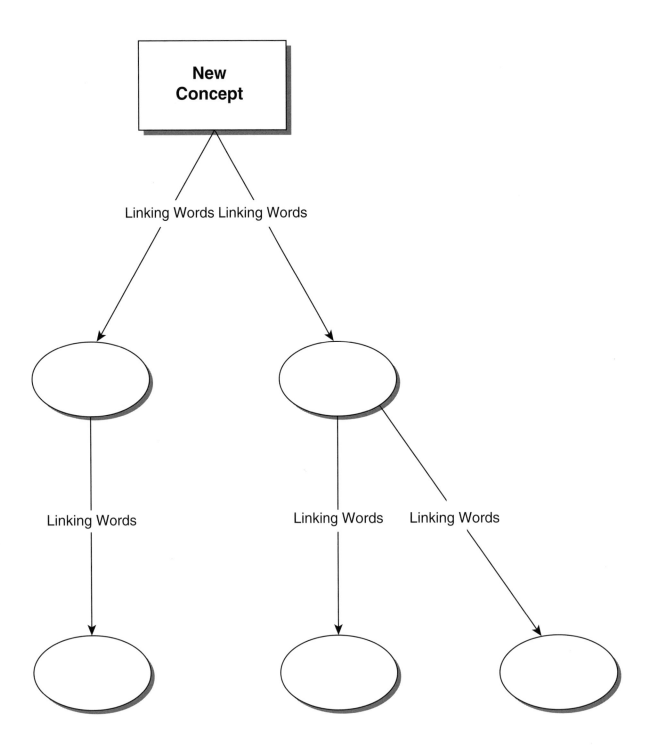

Concept map: To demonstrate relationship between ideas to help analyze information, chain of events, or systems.

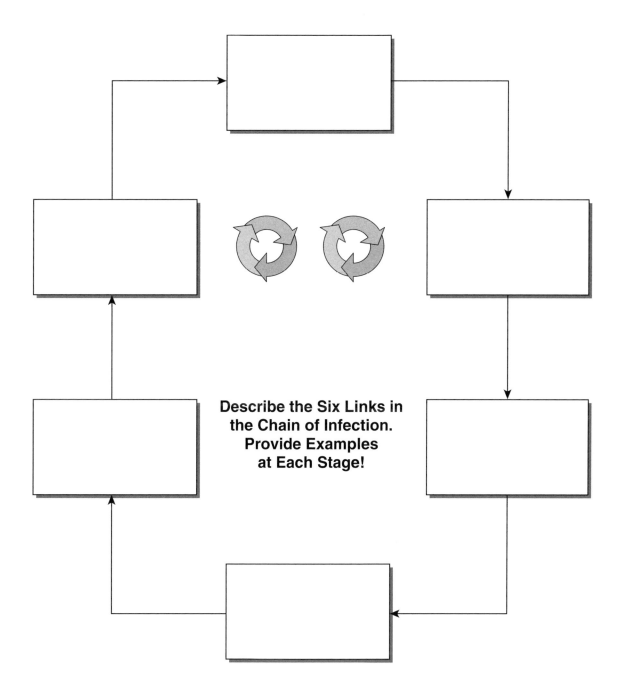

Describe the Six Links in
the Chain of Infection.
Provide Examples
at Each Stage!

Simple cycle web: To demonstrate understanding of cycles and processes
at a simple level before introducing more complex information

General/Specific Overview of Objectives

With a partner, discuss each of the following
objectives from general terms to specific applications

General ➡️ **Specific**

Obj. 1

Obj. 2

Obj. 3

Obj. 4

Main Idea:

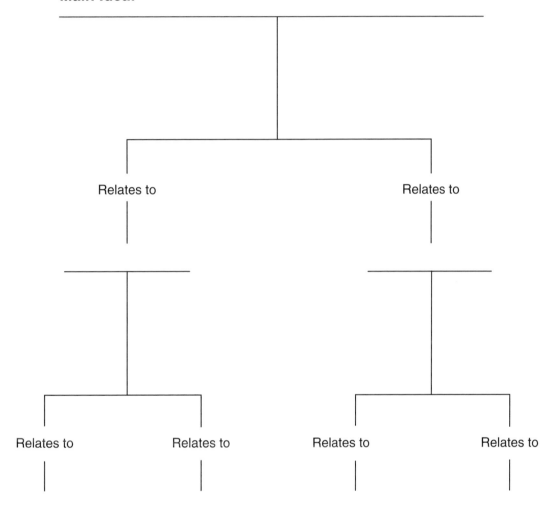

Relates to

Relates to

Relates to

Relates to

Relates to

Relates to

Tree diagram: To demonstrate the breaking down of complex ideas into component parts and to allow student to explore relationship between a whole and its parts

Resource E

Active Learning Strategies for Analysis

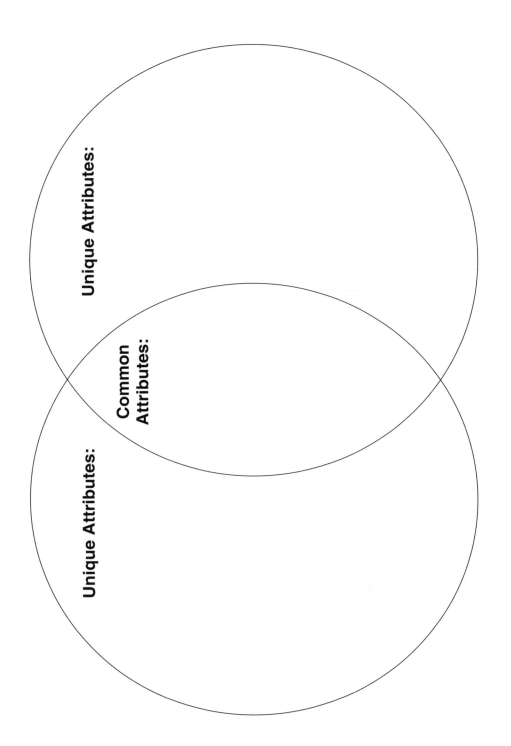

Unique Attributes:

Common
Attributes:

Unique Attributes:

Venn Diagram: To Demonstrate Ability to Compare and Contrast

General/Specific Analysis Worksheet			
	Quality of Content: *Accuracy* *Completeness* *Organization*	**Relationship to Objectives:** *Identify Objectives* *Explain Relationship*	**Relevance to Nursing:** *Purpose for Learning How You Will Use Concepts*
General ↓ Specific			

General/Specific Analysis for Any Unit of Study: Students analyze each other's responses to general/specific overview of objectives according to above criteria

Defining Features: Chronic Bronchitis, Emphysema, and Asthma

	Age of Onset	Smoking History	Type of Cough	Body Build	Lung Sounds
Chronic Bronchitis					
Emphysema					
Asthma					

Defining Features Grid for Unit on Respiratory Disorders

Pro/Con Grid: Surgical Options		
Options	Pro	Con
Inpatient Surgery		
Outpatient Surgery		

**Pro/Con Grid for Unit on
Pre- and Postoperative Procedures**

References

Allen, R. H. (2002). *Impact teaching: Ideas and strategies for teachers to maximize student learning.* Boston, MA: Allyn & Bacon.

Anderson, L. W., Krathwohl, D. R., Airasian, P. W., Cruikshank, K. A., Mayer, R. E., Pintrich, P. R., et al. (Eds.) (2001). *A taxonomy for learning, teaching, and assessing: A revision of Bloom's taxonomy of educational objectives.* New York: Longman.

Anderson, O., Marsh, M., & Harvey, A. (1999). *Learn with the classics: Using music to study smart at any age.* San Francisco: Lind Institute.

Angelo, T. A., & Cross, K. P. (1993). *Classroom assessment techniques: A handbook for college teachers* (2nd ed.). San Francisco: Jossey-Bass.

Apps, J. W. (1988). *Higher education in a learning society: Meeting new demands for education and training.* San Francisco: Jossey-Bass.

Ausubel, D. R. (1978). *Educational psychology: A cognitive view.* New York: Holt, Rinehart, and Winston.

Baddeley, A., Hitch, G., & Andrade, J. (2002). *Working memory in perspective.* New York: Taylor and Francis.

Bandler, R. (1988). *Learning strategies: Acquisition and conviction.* Boulder, CO: NLP Comprehensive.

Benedetti, A., Charil, A., Rovaris, M., Judica, E., Valsasina, P., Sormani, M. P., et al. (2006). Influence of aging on brain gray and white matter changes assessed by conventional, MT, and DT MRI. *Neurology, 66*(4), 535–539.

Benson, H., Malhotra, M. S., Goldman, R. F., Jacobs, G. D., & Hopkins, P. J. (1990). Three case reports of the metabolic and electroencephalographic changes during advanced Buddhist meditation techniques. *Behavioral Medicine, 16*(2), 90–95.

Bjorklund, D. F. (1988). *Children's thinking: Developmental function and individual differences* (3rd ed.). Belmont, CA: Wadsworth/Thomson.

Bloom, B. S. (Ed.). (1956). *Taxonomy of educational objectives: Vol. 1. Cognitive domain.* New York: McKay.

Broadbent, D. E. (1971). *Decision and stress.* London: Academic Press.

Brookfield, S. D., & Preskill, S. (1999). *Discussion as a way of teaching: Tools and techniques for a democratic classroom.* San Francisco: Jossey-Bass.

Caine, R. N., & Caine, G. (1994). *Making connections: Teaching and the human brain.* New York: Addison-Wesley.

Caine R. N., Caine, G., & Crowell, S. (1999). *Mindshifts: A brain-compatible process for professional development and the renewal of education.* Tucson, AZ: Zephyr Press.

Canli, T., Zhao, Z., Brewer, J., Gabrieli, J. D. E., & Cahill, L. (2000). Event-related activation in the human amygdala associates with later memory for individual emotional experience. *Journal of Neuroscience, 20,* 1–5.

Canli, T., Zhao, Z., Desmond, J. E., Kang, E., Gross, J., & Gabrieli, J. D. E. (2001). An fMRI study of personality differences on brain reactivity to emotional stimuli. *Behavioral Neuroscience, 115*(1), 33–42.

Carter, R. (1998). *Mapping the mind.* Berkeley: University of California Press.

Clore, G. (2000). *Theories of mood and cognition: A user's guidebook.* Mahwah, NJ: Erlbaum.

Corby, J. C., Roth, W. T., & Zarcone, V. T. (1978). Psychophysiological correlates of the practice of tantric yoga meditation. *Archives of General Psychiatry, 35*(5), 571–577.

Cornett, C. E. (1983). *What you should know about teaching learning styles.* Bloomington, IN: Phi Delta Kappa.

Courtney, S. M., Ungerleider, L. G., Keil, K., & Haxby, J. V. (1996). Object and spatial visual working memory activate separate neural systems in human cortex. *Cerebral Cortex, 6*(2), 39–49.

Cowan, N. (2005). Working memory capacity limits in a theoretical context. In C. Izawa & N. Ohta (Eds.), *Human learning and memory: Advances in theory and application: The 4th Tsukuba International Conference on Memory* (pp. 155–175). Mahwah, NJ: Erlbaum.

Crane, L. D. (1989). *The alert scale of cognitive style.* Kalamazoo: Western Michigan University.

Csikszentmihalyi, M. (1990). *Flow: The psychology of optimal experience* (1st ed.). New York: Harper & Row.

Damasio, A. R. (1994). *Descartes' Error: Emotion, reason, and the human brain.* New York: Avon Books.

Damasio, A. R. (1999). *The feeling of what happens: Body and emotion in the making of consciousness.* Philadelphia: Harcourt-Brace.

Delmont, M. M. (1984). Physiological responses during meditation and rest. *Biofeedback Self Regulation, 9*(2), 181–200.

Demb, J. B., Desmond, J. E., Wagner, A. D., Viadya, C. J. , Glover, G. H., & Gabrieli, J. D. E. (1995). Semantic encoding and retrieval in the left inferior prefrontal cortex: A functional MRI study of task difficulty and process specificity. *Journal of Neuroscience, 15,* 5870–5878.

Diamond, M. (1967). Extensive cortical depth measurements and neuron size increases in the cortex of environmentally enriched rats. *Journal of Comparative Neurology, 131,* 357–364.

Diamond, M. (1988). *Enriching heredity.* New York: Free Press.

Dillbeck, M. C., & Vesely, S. A. (1986). Participation in the transcendental meditation program and frontal EEG coherence during concept learning. *International Journal of Neuroscience, 29*(1–2), 45–55.

Dolan, R. J. (2002). Emotion, cognition, and behavior. *Science, 298,* 1191–1194.

Doyan, J., Song, A. W., Karni, A., Lalonde, F., Adams, M. M., & Ungerleider, L. G. (2002). Experience-dependent changes in cerebellar contributions to motor sequence learning. *Proceedings of the National Academy of Science, 99*(2), 1017–1022.

Dunn, K., & Dunn, R. (1992). *Bringing out the giftedness in your child.* New York: John Wiley.

Dunn, R. (1988). Teaching students through their perceptual strengths or preferences. *Journal of Reading, 31,* 304–308.

Echenhofer, F. G., & Coombs, M. M. (1987). A brief review of research and controversies in EEG biofeedback and meditation. *The Journal of Transpersonal Psychology, 19*(2), 161–171.

Edelman, G. M. (1992). *Bright air, brilliant fire: On the matter of the mind.* New York: Basic Books.

Eriksson, P. S., Perfilieva, E., Bjork-Eriksson, T., Alborn, A. M., Nordborg, C., Peterson, D. A., et al. (1998). Neurogenesis in the adult human hippocampus. *Nature Medicine, 4*(11), 1313–1317.

Eysenck, H. J. (1982). Introduction. In H. J. Eysenck (Ed.), *A model for intelligence* (pp. 1–10). New York: Springer-Verlag.

Funahashi, S., Bruce, C. J., & Goldman-Rakic, P. S. (1989). Mnemonic coding of visual space in the monkey's dorsolateral prefrontal cortex. *Journal of Neurophysiology, 61*(2), 331–349.

Furst, E. J. (1994). *Bloom's taxonomy: A forty-year retrospective: Ninety-third yearbook of the National Society for the Study of Education* (pp. 28–48). Chicago, IL: University of Chicago Press.

Gardner, H. (1983). *Frames of mind.* New York: Basic Books.

Gardner, H. (1999). *Intelligence reframed: Multiple intelligences for the 21st century.* New York: Basic Books.

Gardner, H., & Hatch, T. (1989). Multiple intelligences go to school: Educational implications of the theory of multiple intelligences. *Educational Researcher, 15*(8), 4–9.

Gazzaniga, M. S. (1992). *Mind matters: How mind and brain interact to create our conscious lives.* Boston: Houghton Mifflin.

Gazzaniga, M. S. (1998). *The mind's past.* Berkeley, CA: University of California Press.

Glazener, L. (2004). *Sensorcises: Active enrichment for the out-of-step learner.* Thousand Oaks, CA: Corwin Press.

Goldberg, E. (2001). *The executive brain: Frontal lobes and the civilized mind.* New York: Oxford University Press.

Goldberg, E., & Costa, L. D. (1981). Hemisphere differences in the acquisition and use of adaptive systems. *Brain Language, 14*(1), 144–173.

Goldblum, N. (2001). *The brain-shaped mind: What the brain can tell us about the mind.* Cambridge, UK: Cambridge University Press.

Goleman, D. (1995). *Emotional intelligence: Why it can matter more than IQ.* New York: Bantam Books.

Gopnik, A., Meltzoff, A. N., & Kuhl, P. K. (1999). *The scientist in the crib: Minds, brains, and how children learn.* New York: William Morrow.

Gould, E., Beylin, A., Tanapat, A., & Shors, T. J. (1999). Learning enhances adult neurogenesis in the hippocampal formation. *Nature Neuroscience, 2*(3), 260–265.

Gould, E., Reeves, A. J., Graziano, M. S., & Gross, C. G. (1998). Neurogenesis in the neocortex of adult primates. *Science, 286,* 548–552.

Gould, E., Tanapat, P., McEwen, B. S., Fluge, G., & Fuchs, E. (1998). Proliferation of granule cell precursors in the dentate gyrus of adult monkeys is diminished by stress. *Proceedings of the National Academy of Science 95*(6), 3168–3171.

Graziano, A. B., Peterson, M., & Shaw, G. L. (1999). Enhanced learning of proportional math through music training and spatial-temporal training. *Neurological Research, 21,* 139–152.

Gredler, M. E. (2001). *Learning and instruction: Theory into practice* (4th ed.). Upper Saddle River: NJ: Prentice-Hall.

Greene, J. D., Sommerville, R. B., Nystrom, L. E., Darley, J. M., & Cohen, J. D. (2001). An fMRI investigation of emotional engagement in moral judgment. *Science, 293,* 2105–2108.

Greenfield, S. A. (1997). *The human brain: A guided tour.* New York: Basic Books.

Greenough, W. T., Black, J. E., & Wallace, C. S. (1987). Experience and brain development. *Child Development, 58,* 539–559.

Hannaford, C. (1995). *Smart moves: Why learning is not all in your head.* Arlington, VA: Great Ocean Publishers.

Hariri, A. R., Bookheimer, S. Y., & Mazziotta, J. C. (2000). Modulating emotional responses: Effects of a neocortical network on the limbic system. *Neuroreport, 11,* 43–48.

Hariri, A. R., Mattay, V. S., Tessitore, A., Francesco, F., & Weinberger, D. R. (2003). Neocortical modulation of the amygdala response to fearful stimuli. *Biological Psychiatry, 53,* 494–501.

Hart, L. A. (1983). *Human brain and human learning.* New York: Longman.

Hart, L. A. (1999). *Human brain and human learning* (5th ed.). Kent, WA: Books for Educators.

Herrmann, N. (1989). *The creative brain.* Lake Lure, NC: Brain Books.

Herzog, H., Lele, V. R., Kuwert, T., Langen, K. J., Kops, E. R., & Feinendegen, L. E. (1991). Changed pattern of regional glucose metabolism during yoga meditative relaxation. *Neuropsychobiology, 23*(4), 182–187.

Heuberger, E. (2001). Effects of chiral fragrances on human autonomic nervous system parameters and self-evaluation. *Chemical Senses, 26,* 281–292.

Higley, C., & Higley, A. (1998). Reference guide for essential oils. *Abundant Health, 19*(1), 35–45.

Hyerle, D. (Ed.) (with Alper, L., & Curtis, S.). (2004). *Student success with thinking maps.*

Jacobs, B., Schall, M., & Schiebel, A. B. (1993). A quantitative dendritic analysis of Werniecke's area in humans, II: Gender hemispheric and environmental factors. *Journal of Comparative Neurology, 327,* 98–111.

Jensen, A. R. (1993). Why is reaction time correlated with psychometric g? *Current Directions in Psychological Science, 2,* 53–56.

Jensen, A. R. (1997). The psychometrics of intelligence. In H. Nyborg (Ed.), *The scientific study of human nature: Tribute to Hans Eysenck at eighty* (pp. 221–239). New York: Elsevier.

Jensen, E. (2000). *Brain-based learning: The new science of teaching and training.* Thousand Oaks, CA: Corwin Press.

Johnson, J. K., Cotman, C. W., Tasaki, C. S., & Shaw, G. L. (1998). Enhancement of spatial-temporal reasoning after a Mozart listening condition in Alzheimer's disease: A case study. *Neurological Research, 20,* 666–672.

Johnson, R. C., & Brown, C. (1988). Cognizers: *Neural networks and machine that think.* New York: Wiley Science Editions.

Joyce, B. R., & Showers, B. (2002). *Student achievement through staff development* (3rd ed.). Alexandria, VA: Association for Supervision and Curriculum Development.

Karni, A., Meyer, G. Jezzard, P., Adams, M. M., Turner, R. & Ungerleider, L. G. (1995). Functional MRI evidence for adult motor cortex plasticity during motor skill learning. *Nature, 377,* 155–158.

Kegan, R. (2000). What form transforms? A constructive-developmental approach to transformative learning. In J. Mezirow (Ed.), *Learning as transformation* (pp. 35–71). San Francisco: Jossey-Bass.

Khalsa, D. S. (1997). *Brain longevity: the breakthrough medical program that improves your mind and memory.* New York: Warner Books.

Klingberg, T., Fernell, E., Olesen, P. J., Johnson, M., Gustafsson, P., & Dahlstrom, K. (2005). Computerized training of working memory in children with ADHD: A randomized, controlled trial. *Journal of the American Academy of Child and Adolescent Psychiatry, 44*(2), 177–186.

Knowles, M. (1980). *The modern practice of adult education* (Rev. ed.). Chicago: Follet.

Kolb, D. A. (1981). Learning styles and disciplinary differences. In A. W. Chickering and Associates (Eds.), *The modern American college* (pp. 232–255). San Francisco: Jossey-Bass.

Kolb, D. A. (1984). *Experiential learning: Experience as the source of learning and development.* Englewood Cliffs, NJ: Prentice-Hall.

Kotulak, R. (2004). Scientists offer hope for poor readers. *The Dan Foundation's Brain in the News, 11*(5), 1–2.

Kovalik, S. J. (with Olsen, K.). (1997). *ITI: The model: Integrated thematic instruction* (3rd ed.). Kent, WA: Susan Kovalik & Associates.

Kreitzer, A. E., & Madaus, G. F. (1994). Empirical investigations of the hierarchical structure of the taxonomy. In L. W. Anderson & L. A. Sosniak (Eds.), *Yearbook of the National Society for the Study of Education.* (pp. 64–81). Chicago, IL: University of Chicago Press.

LeDoux, J. (1996). *The emotional brain: The mysterious underpinnings of emotional life.* New York: Simon and Schuster.

LeDoux, J. (2002). *A mind at a time.* New York: Simon and Schuster.

Leiner, H. C., & Leiner, A. L. (1997). How fibers subserve computing capabilities: The similarities between brains and machines. In J. D. Schmahmann (Ed.), *International Review of Neurobiology, Vol. 41: The Cerebellum and Cognition* (pp. 535–553). San Diego, CA, Academic Press.

Letteri, C. A. (1980). Cognitive profile: Basic determinant of academic achievement. *The Journal of Educational Research, 73*(4), 195–198.

Levinthal, C. (1988). *Messengers of paradise: Opiates and the brain.* New York: Doubleday.

Liberzon, I., Phan, K. L., Docker, L. R., & Taylor, S. F. (2003). Extended amygdala and emotional salience: A PET activation study of positive and negative affect. *Neuropsychopharmacology, 28, 726–733.*

Lyubimov, N. N. (1992, May). *Mobilization of the hidden areas of the brain.* Paper presented at the Second Russian-Swedish Symposium on New Research in Neurobiology, Moscow, Russia.

MacLean, P. D. (1978). A mind of three minds: Educating the triune brain. In J. Chall & A. Mirsky (Eds.), *Education and the brain* (pp. 308–342). Chicago, IL: University of Chicago Press.

Markuson, D. (2003). *Manufacturing knowledge.* Seattle, WA: New Horizons for Learning.

Martinussen, R., Hayden, J., Hogg-Johnson, S., & Tannock, R. (2005). A meta-analysis of working memory components in children with attention-deficit/hyperactivity disorder. *Journal of the American Academy of Child and Adolescent Psychiatry, 44*(4), 377–384.

Marzano, R. J., & Kendall, J. S. (2006). *The new taxonomy of educational objectives.* Thousand Oaks, CA: Corwin Press.

Marzano, R. J., Pickering, D., & Pollock, J. (2002). *Classroom instruction that works.* Alexandria, VA: Association for Supervision and Curriculum Development.

Materna, L. (2000). *The impact of concept mapping upon meaningful learning and metacognition of foundation-level nursing students.* Unpublished doctoral dissertation, Capella University, St. Paul, MN.

Matteris, M., Silvestrini, M., Troisi, E., Cupini, L. M., & Caltagirone, C. (1997). Transcranial Doppler assessment of cerebral flow velocity during perception and recognition of melodies. *Journal of the Neurological Sciences, 149, 57–61.*

McCarthy, B. (1987). *The 4Mat system: Teaching to learning styles with right/left mode techniques.* Barrington, IL: Excel.

Mentkowski and Associates. (2000). *Learning that lasts: Integrating learning, development, and performance in college and beyond.* San Francisco: Jossey-Bass.

Miller, G. A. (1956). The magical number seven, plus or minus two: Some limits in our capacity to process information. *Psychological Review, 63, 81–97.*

Mills, R. C. (1987, November). *Relationship between school motivational climate, presenter attitudes, student mental health, school failure and health damaging behavior.* Paper presented at the annual conference of the American Educational Research Association, Washington, DC.

Milner, P. M. (1999). *The autonomous brain: A neural theory of attention and learning.* Mahwah, NJ: Erlbaum.

Myers, I. B. (1962). *The Myers-Briggs type indicator.* Palo Alto, CA: Consulting Psychologists Press.

Novak, J. D. (1998). *Learning, creating, and using knowledge.* Mahwah, NJ: Erlbaum.

Novak, J. D., & Gowin, D. B. (1984). *Learning how to learn.* New York: Cambridge University Press.

O'Banion, T. (1997). *A learning college for the 21st century.* Phoenix, AZ: Onyx Press.

Ornstein, R. (1991). *The psychology of consciousness: The origins of the way we think.* New York: Prentice Hall.

Peper, E., & Ancoli, S. (1979). The two end points of an EEG continuum of meditation: Alpha/theta and fast beta. In E. Peper, S. Ancoli, & M. Quinn (Eds.), *Mind/body integrations: Essential readings in biofeedback* (pp. 289–290). New York: Plenum.

Perkins, D. (1995). *Smart schools: From training memories to educating minds.* New York: Free Press.

Pernille, J. O., Westerberg, H., & Klingberg, T. (2004). Increased prefrontal and parietal activity after training in working memory. *Nature Neuroscience, 7*(1), 75–79.

Pert, C. B. (1997). *Molecules of emotions: Why you feel the way you do.* New York: Scribner.

Pfurtscheller, G., & Berghold, A. (1989). Patterns of cortical activation during planning of voluntary movement. *Electroencephalography and Clinical Neurophysiology, 72,* 250–258.

Poldrack, R. A., Desmond, J. E., Glover, G. H., & Gabridi, J. D. E. (1998). The neural basis of visual skill learning an fMRI study of mirror reading. *Cerebral Cortex, 8,* 1–10.

Pribram, K. (1971). *Languages of the brain: Experimental paradoxes and principles in neuropsychology.* New York: Prentice-Hall.

Ramachandran, V. S., & Blakeslee, S. (1998). *Phantoms in the brain.* New York: William Morrow.

Ratey, J. J. (2001). *A user's guide to the brain.* New York: Pantheon Books.

Reeves, B., & Nass, C. (1996). *The media equation.* Cambridge, UK: Cambridge University Press.

Reid, J. (1998). *Understanding learning styles in the second language classroom.* New York: Prentice-Hall.

Renner, M., & Rosenzweig, M. (1987). *Enriched and impoverished environments: Effects on brain and behavior.* New York: Springer Verlag.

Restak, R. M. (1995). *Brainscapes.* New York: Hyperion.

Restak, R. M. (2003). *The new brain: How the modern age is rewiring your mind.* New York: Rodale Press.

Roberts, R. W. (1977). *Vocational and practical arts education.* New York: Harper & Row.

Robertson, I. (2000). *Mind sculpture: Unlocking your brain's untapped potential.* New York: Fromm International.

Robin, D. E., & Shortridge, R. T. (1979). Lateralization of tumors of the nasal cavity and paranasal sinuses in relation to aeriology. *Lancet, 8118,* 695–696.

Robinson, F. (1970). *Effective study* (4th ed.). New York: Harper & Row.

Rose, C. (1995). *Accelerated learning action guide.* Aylesbury, Buckinghamshire, UK: Accelerated Learning Systems.

Rose, S. (1992). *The making of memory: From molecules to mind.* New York: Doubleday.

Russell, P. (1979). *The brain book.* New York: E. P. Dutton.

Schacter, D. L. (1996). *Searching for memory: The brain, the mind, and the past.* New York: Basic Books.

Schacter, D. L. (2001). *The seven sins of memory: How the mind forgets and remembers.* New York: Houghton Mifflin.

Seger, C. A., Poldrack, R. A., Prabhakaran, V., Zhao. M., Glover, G. H., & Gabrieli, J. D. E. (2000). Hemispheric asymmetries and individual differences in visual concept learning as measured by functional MRI. *Neurophyhologia, 38,* 1316–1324.

Silver, H. F., & Hanson, J. R. (1998). *Learning styles and strategies* (3rd ed.). Woodbridge, NJ: The Thoughtful Education Press.

Silver, H. F., Strong, R. W., & Perini, M. J. (2000). *So each may learn: Integrating learning styles and multiple intelligences.* Alexandria, VA: Association for Supervision and Curriculum Development.

Sousa, D. (2001). *How the brain learns: A classroom teacher's guide* (2nd ed.). Thousand Oaks, CA: Corwin Press.

Sousa, D. (2003). *How the gifted brain learns: A classroom teacher's guide* (2nd ed.). Thousand Oaks, CA: Corwin Press.

Spearman, C. (1904). General intelligence objectively determined and measured. *American Journal of Psychology, 15,* 201–293.

Sperling, G. (1960). The information available in brief visual presentations. *Psychological Monographs: General and Applied, 74*(11), 1–30.

Sperry, R. W. (1966). The great cerebral commissure. In S. Coppersmith (Ed.), *Frontiers of psychological research* (pp. 60–70). San Francisco: W. H. Freeman.

Spiker, T. (2003). The brain. *Fortune, 148*(7), 117.

Sprenger, M. (1999). *Learning and memory: The brain in action.* Alexandria, VA: Association for Supervision and Curriculum Development.

Sprenger, M. (2002). *Becoming a "wiz" at brain-based teaching.* Thousand Oaks, CA: Corwin Press.

Squire, L. R., & Kandel, E. R. (1999). *Memory: From mind to molecules.* New York: W. H. Freeman.

Steinberg, R. J. (1990). Thinking styles: Keys to understanding student performance. *Phi Delta Kappan, 71*(5), 366–371.

Sternberg, R. J. (1977). *Intelligence, information processing, and analogical reasoning: The componential analysis of human abilities.* Hillsdale, NJ: Erlbaum.

Sternberg, R. J. (1988). *Beyond IQ: A triarchic theory of human intelligence.* New York: Cambridge University Press.

Sullivan, E. V., Adalsteinsson, E., & Pfefferbaum, A. (2006). Selective age-related degradation of anterior collosal fiber bundles quantified in vivo with fiber tracking. *Cerebral Cortex, 16*(7), 1130–1139.

Svinicki, M., & Dixon, N. M. (1988). The Kolb model modified for classroom activities. *College Teaching, 35*(4), 141–146.

Swiegers, D. J., & Louw, D. A. (1982). Intelligensie. In D. A. Louw (Ed.), *Inleiding tot die psigologic* (2nd ed.; p. 145). Johannesburg: McGraw Hill.

Sylwester, R. (1995). *A celebration of neurons.* Alexandria, VA: Association for Supervision and Curriculum Development.

Tate, M. L. (2003). *Worksheets don't grow dendrites: 20 instructional strategies that engage the brain.* Thousand Oaks, CA: Corwin Press.

Tate, M. L. (2004). *Sit and get won't grow dendrites.* Thousand Oaks, CA: Corwin Press.

Taylor, K., Marienau, C., & Fiddler, M. (2000). *Developing adult learners: Strategies for teachers and trainers.* San Francisco: Jossey-Bass.

Thomas, L., Ratcliffe, M., Woodbury, J., & Jarman, E. (2002). *Learning styles and performance in the introductory programming sequence.* New York: ACM Press.

Trayer, M. (1991). Learning styles differences: Gifted vs. regular language students. *Foreign Language Annals, 24,* 419–425.

Vedantum, S. (2002, May 20). A new thinking emerges about consciousness: Descartes notwithstanding, some neuroscientists find the answer in chemistry, not philosophy. *The Washington Post,* p. A9.

Volkow, N. D., Wang, G. J., Fowler, J. S., Ding, Y. S., Gur, R. C., Gatley, J., et al. (1998). Parallel loss of presynaptic and postsynaptic dopamine markers in normal aging. *Annals of Neurology, 44*(1), 143–147.

West, M. A. (1980). Meditation and the EEG. *Psychological Medicine, 10*(2), 369–375.

Willingham, D. T. (2003, Summer). Students remember what they think about. *American Educator,* pp. 37–41.

Wolfe, P. (2001). *Brain matters: Translating research into classroom practice.* Alexandria, VA: Association for Supervision and Curriculum Development.

Woodbury, M. A. (2004). Build a better memory. *Health, 18*(2), 93.

Wurtman, J. (1988). *Managing your mind and mood through food.* New York: HarperCollins.

Wyman, P. (2001). *Three keys to self-understanding: An innovative and effective combination of the Myers-Briggs type indicator assessment tool, the enneagram, and inner-child healing.* Gainesville: FL: Center for Application of Psychological Type.

Zeineh, M. M., Engel, S. A., Thompson, P. M., & Bookheimer, S. Y. (2003). Dynamics of the hippocampus during encoding and retrieval of face-name pairs. *Science, 299,* 577–580.

Zull, J. (2003). *The art of changing the brain.* Retrieved June 13, 2004, from http://www.newhorizons.org/neuro/neu_review_zull.htm

Index

*Accelerated Learning Action
    Guide* (Rose), 27, 37
Accelerated Learning Techniques, 72
Acetylcholine, 40
Acronyms, 125
Acrostics, 125
Active learning strategies, 126–131
    for analysis, 194–197
    for application and deeper
        comprehension, 188–191
    for comprehension and understanding,
        182–185
    for knowledge, remembering, and
        retrieval, 176–179
Adams, Henry Brooks, 87
Adult brain, the
    age-related memory loss in, 38–39
    brain-compatible learning for, 41–43
    effects of aging on, 39–41
Aging
    effects on the brain, 39–41, 169–170
    -related memory loss, 38–39
Alphabet cues and mnemonics, 125
Alternate nostril breathing, 74
Amygdala
    aging and, 40
    memory and, 8–9, 31, 33
Analysis strategies, 155–158, 193–197
Analytical intelligence, 59
Anderson, Lorin, 134–137, 158, 162
Anderson, Ole, 78, 79
Angelo, Thomas, 117, 146, 157
Anterior cingulated cortex, 7
Aromas used to promote learning, 75–76
Assimilation theory, 96
Auditory cortex, 78
Auditory learners, 51
Auditory memories, 27
Ausubel, David, 96

Baddeley, Alan, 32
Bandler, Richard, 29
Berghold, Andrea, 22
Big picture overview, 146, 148,
        149, 164, 184

Binet, Alfred, 56
Bloom, Benjamin, 23, 133–134
Bloom's taxonomy, 162
    Anderson and colleagues'
        update of, 134–137
    basic framework, 133–134
Bodily-kinesthetic intelligence profile
        learners, 61
Boorstin, Daniel, 53
Brain
    adult, 38–43, 169–170
    balance through movement
        activities, 84–87
    breathing exercises and, 72–74
    cell decay, 24
    cerebellum, 5–6
    circuitry and transmission
        of thought, 23–25
    dominance, 14–16
    downshifting, 4, 11
    effect of aging on, 39–41
    hemispheres, 13–16
    lower, 3–7
    major areas, 4
    middle, 7–12
    multisensory processing abilities, 93
    need for mental stimulation of, 93–94
    stem, 4–5
    synergy, 25
    upper, 13–16
    warm-ups, 171–174
Brain Book, The (Russell), 32
Brain-compatible learning for adults, 41–43
    application in the classroom, 162–170
    creativity in, 170
    See also Materna Method, the
Brain Longevity program, 84, 169
Breathing exercises, 72–74
Broadbent, D. E., 31
Brookfield, Stephen, 42

Caine, Geoffrey, 163
Caine, Renate Nummela, 163
Calming visualization, 80
Caltagirone, C., 78

Canli, Turhan, 9
Carter, Rita, 24
Cause and effect diagrams, 107,
    109–111, 183
Cells, brain
    active engagement and growth, 92
    survival and restructuring of, 92–93
Centering exercises, 81, 85, 86–87
Cerebellum, 5–6, 27
Cerebral cortex, 22
Cerebrum, 5, 13
Chunking information, 125–126
Circuitry, brain, 23–25
Clore, Gerald, 10
Cognitive exercises, 25
Collaborative learning, 163
Combination learners/educators, 51–52
Componential intelligence, 59
Comprehension
    application and deep, 149, 153,
        154, 188–191
    study strategies, 122–126
    and understanding strategies, 146–149,
        182–185
Concept essays, 126, 160
Concept maps, 96–102, 153, 188
    reviews, 161, 179
Concept questions, 126–128
Conscious and unconscious thought, 22
Consolidation, 29
Contextual intelligence, 59
Costa, L. D., 14
Creation and storage of
    memories, 27–29
Creative intelligence, 59
Creative thinking exercises, 82–83
Creative visualizations, 79–84
Creativity visualization, 80
Critical thinking scenarios, 129–131,
    158, 160
Cross, Patricia, 117, 146, 157
Csikszentmihalyi, Mihaly, 4–5, 72
Cupini, L. M., 78
Cycle of learning theory, 52–53
Cycle web diagrams, 108, 112–113,
    153, 155, 189

Damasio, Antonio, 10
Defining features grids, 157–158, 196
Dendrites, 24
Dewey, G. A., 7
Diaphragmatic breathing, 73
Dietary fat, 77
Dixon, Nancy, 53
Dolan, Raymond, 10
Dominance, brain, 14–16
Downshifting, 4, 11, 19, 21
Dunn, Kenneth, 48
Dunn, Rita, 48
Dynamic debates, 160

Echoic memory, 29–31
Edelman, Gerald, 92
Einstein, Albert, 43, 80
Elaborative rehearsal, 36–37
Emotional intelligence, 10
Emotional pathway, 33–34
Emotional processing and the amygdala, 8–9
Emotions
    learning and, 10–11, 71–72, 164–165
    memory and, 9, 164–165
Encoding, 28
Energizing visualization, 80
Episodic pathways, 32–33
Essays, concept, 126, 160
Evaluation and deeper analysis strategies,
    158–160
Experiential intelligence, 59
Eysenck, Hans, 57

Fat, dietary, 77
Fight or flight response, 4
Floral scents, 75
Flow state in learning, 5, 19, 21, 72
Focusing exercises, 85, 86
Friedman, Bonnie, 72

Gallagher, Michela, 39
Gardner, Howard, 57, 58, 59, 60
General/specific analysis worksheets, 195
Giardino, Karen, 74
Glazener, Laurie, 85
Goldberg, Elkhonon
    on Alzheimer patients, 40
    on cognitive exercises, 25
    on the frontal cortex and working
        memory, 32
    on learning styles, 48
    on left and right hemispheres, 14, 15
Goleman, Daniel, 10
Graphic organizers
    big picture overviews, 146, 148,
        149, 164, 184
    bridging the gap from previous to new
        learning, 95, 164
    cause and effect diagrams, 107,
        109–111, 183
    concept maps, 96–102, 153, 161,
        179, 188
    defining features grids, 157–158, 196
    Know, Want, How, Learn (KWHL)
        diagrams, 117, 121, 143, 146, 178
    memory matrix, 117, 118–120, 149,
        150–152, 185
    objective overview diagrams, 112–113,
        114–115
    procedure maps, 102–104, 105–106
    to process and integrate knowledge, 94
    process maps, 104–107, 108
    pro/con grids, 158, 159, 197
    promotion of visual processing, 95

Show-You-Know diagrams, 142, 143–145, 176
simple cycle web, 108, 112–113, 153, 155, 189
tree diagrams, 113, 116, 117, 153, 154, 191
types of, 95–121
Venn diagram, 108, 111, 157, 194
Guided visual imagery, 123–125

Hannaford, Carla, 85
Hanson, J. Robert, 54, 55
Hariri, Ahmad, 8
Hart, Leslie, 4, 92
Harvey, Arthur, 79
Haskins, Henry S., 162
Hayes, Ron, 39
Hemispheres of the brain, 13–16
Herrmann, Ned, 15
Hippocampus
    aging and, 40
    memory and, 8, 31, 32–33
Hitch, Graham, 32
Hypothalamus, 75

Iconic memory, 29–31
Imagery, guided visual, 123–125
Implicit memory pathway, 34
Information chunking, 125–126
Intelligence
    active learning strategies to
        expand, 66–67
    emotional, 10
    learnable, 59
    personal profiles, 62, 63–65
    theories of, 56–59
    theory application to adult
        education, 60–69
Interpersonal intelligence profile learners, 61
Intrapersonal intelligence profile learners, 61
Inventory, learning styles, 50–51

Jackson, Laura Riding, 33
Jensen, Arthur, 57
Jensen, Eric, 6, 33
Journals, reflective, 128–129, 161
Jung, Carl, 54

Kandel, Eric, 8
Karni, A., 6
Kegan, Robert, 42
Kendall, John, 136–138, 139, 162
Khalsa, Dharma Singh, 84, 169
Kinesthetic memory, 27, 31
    aging and, 40–41
Kinesthetic-tactile learners, 52
Know, Want, How, Learn (KWHL) diagrams, 117, 121, 143, 146, 178
Knowledge acquisition strategies, 94–95
Kolb, David, 48, 52–53, 55–56

Kotulak, Robert, 93–94, 163
Krishnamurti, 170

Lavender aroma, 75
Learnable intelligence, 59
Learners, adult
    application of brain-compatible principles
        for, 162–170
    auditory, 51
    combination, 51
    empowering, 91
    kinesthetic-tactile, 52
    left-brain versus right brain, 15–16
    personal application of intelligence
        theory to, 60–69
    personal application of learning
        styles theory to, 54–56
    visual, 51, 55
    See also Teaching
Learning
    active, 126–131
    attitudes toward, 47–48
    brain-compatible, 41–43
    breathing exercises to promote
        better, 72–74
    bridging the gap from previous
        to new, 95, 163–164
    as collaborative, 163
    creative visualizations and mind
        calms for, 79–84
    cycle of, 52–53
    emotional balance and the middle brain,
        11–12
    emotions and, 10–11, 71–72, 164–165
    flow state in, 5, 19, 21, 72
    knowledge acquisition strategies, 94–95
    movement and, 7, 84–87
    multisensory processing abilities and, 93
    music and, 78–79
    nutrition and, 76–78
    peripherals used in, 74–75, 166–167
    promoting combination, 52
    resourceful state for, 72
    rituals and the lower brain, 6–7
    styles, 27–28
    transformative, 42
    and the upper brain, 23
    use of aromas to promote, 75–76
    whole-brain, 16–19
Learning styles
    inventory, 50, 50–51
    personality preferences and, 53–54
    preferred, 48–52
    theory application to adult education,
        54–56, 168
Learn with the Classics (Anderson, Marsh, &
    Harvey), 79
LeDoux, Joseph, 10, 34
Left-brain teachers, 15
Left-brain thinkers, 15

Left hemisphere of the upper brain, 13–14
Leiner, Alan, 5
Leiner, Henrietta, 5
Linguistic intelligence profile learners, 60
Logical-mathematical profile learners, 60
Long-term memory
    pathways, 32–34
    processing in the brain, *30*
    retention of, 35–37
Long-term potentiation (LTP), 28
Lorde, Audrie, *12*
Lower brain, 3–7
Lubbock, John, 69

MacLean, Paul, 10–11
Managing Your Mind and Mood through Food
    (Wurtman), 76
Mapping the Mind (Carter), 24
Maps
    concept, 96–102, 153, 161, 179, 188
    procedure, 102–104, 105–106
    process, 104–107, 108
Markuson, Donnalee, 41
Marsh, Marcy, 79
Marzano, Robert, 136–138, 139, 162
Materna, Laurie, 77, 138
    on the integrated taxonomy, 162
    See also Materna Method, the
Materna Method, the
    analysis strategies, 155–158
    comprehension and understanding
        strategies, 146–149
    evaluation and deeper analysis strategies,
        158–160
    integration of taxonomies into, 138
    strategies for remembering and retrieving
        knowledge, 142, 143–145
    synthesis, creation, and usage of
        knowledge strategies, 160–162
Matteris, M., 78
Meditation. *See* Creative visualizations
Memory
    creation and storage, 27–29
    emotions and, 9, 164–165
    encoding, 28
    the hippocampus and, 8
    kinesthetic, 27, 31
    long-term, 30, 32–34
    loss, age-related, 38–39
    matrix, 117, 118–120, 149,
        150–152, 185
    pathways, 32–35, 167–168
    processing, 30
    research on, 39
    sensory, 29–31
    short-term, 29–32
    types of, 29–34
    working, 31–32
Memory: From Mind to Molecules
    (Squire & Kandel), 8

Mental deterioration, 32
Metacognitive strategies
    active learning promotion, 126–131
    comprehension promotion, 122–126
    graphic organizers in, 95–121
    knowledge acquisition, 94–95
Middle brain
    emotions and, 10
    structures, 7–12
Miller, Bruce, 39
Miller, George, 31, 125
Milner, Peter, 10
Mind calms, 79–84
Mnemonics, 125–126
Movement
    balancing the brain through, 84–87
    the cerebellum and, 5–6
    exercises, 86
    learning and, 7
Multiple intelligence theories, 57
Multitasking, 22
Musical intelligence profile learners, 60–61
Music and learning, 78–79
Myers, Isabel, 54
Myers-Briggs Type Indicator (MBTI), 54

Naturalistic intelligence profile learners, 61
Neocortex, 13
Neural intelligence, 59
Neurotransmitters and neurons, 9
    aging and, 40
    and transmission of thought, 23–25
New Taxonomy of Educational Objectives, The
    (Marzano & Kendall), 137
Note taking, strategic, 123, 124
Novak, J. D., 96
Nutrition and learning, 76–78

O'Banion, Terry, 169
Objective overview diagrams, 112–113,
    114–115
One-sentence summaries, 160
Open-ended probes, 143, 177

Pathways, memory
    emotional, 33–34
    engaging multiple, 34–35, 167–168
    procedural, 34
    semantic and episodic, 32–35
Peripherals used in learning, 74–75,
    166–167
Perkins, David, 59
Personality
    preferences and learning style, 53–54
    types and the amygdala, 9
Personal Learning Strategies Plan, 62, 68
Personal profile of intelligences, 62, 63–65
Pert, Candace, 9
Pfurtscheller, Gert, 22
Physical activity. *See* Movement

Positive learning visualization, 80
Practical intelligence, 59
Preferred learning styles, 48–52
Preskill, Steve, 42
Pribram, Karl, 22
Primary motor cortex, 6
Procedural pathway, 34
Procedure maps, 102–104, 105–106
Process maps, 104–107, 108
Pro/con grids, 158, 159, 197
Protein, 77
Pruning, 24

Questions, concept, 126–128
Quizzes, wrap-up, 161–162

Ratey, John, 93
Ratio breathing, 73–74
Recall, Summarize, Question, Connect
    (RSQC) strategy, 146, 147, 182
Reflective intelligence, 59
Reflective journals, 128–129, 161
Rehearsal strategies, 35–37
Relax, Energize, Activate, and Lead (REAL)
    method, 85
Relaxation and mind calms, 80–84
Repetition and long-term memory, 28
Research, memory, 39
Resourceful state for learning, 72
Restak, Richard, 7, 8, 22, 78
Retention of long-term memory
    multisensory teaching to enhance, 37
    rehearsal strategies for, 35–37
Right-brain teachers, 16
Right-brain thinkers, 15–16
Right hemisphere of the
    upper brain, 13–14
Rituals, classroom, 6–7
Robinson, Francis, 122
Rogers, Carl, 48
Rose, Colin, 25, 27, 37, 72
Rote rehearsal, 35–36

Sapolsky, Robert, 39
Schacter, Daniel, 9, 29
    on aging and the brain, 38, 40
    on learning styles, 48
Semantic pathways, 32–33, 34–35
Sensory information and the
    thalamus, 7–8
Sensory-stimulating mind calm
    exercises, 83–84
Short-term memory, sensory
    memories, 29–31
Show-You-Know diagrams, 142,
    143–145, 176
Silver, Harvey, 54, 55
Silvestrini, M., 78
Simple cycle web, 108, 112–113,
    153, 155, 189

Singular intelligence theories, 56–57
So Each May Learn (Silver,
    Strong, & Perini), 54
Sousa, David, 32, 36
Spatial intelligence profile learners, 60
Spearman, Charles, 56–57
Sperry, Roger, 14–15
Spiker, Ted, 39
SQR3 reading strategy, 122–123
Squire, Larry, 8
Steinberg, Robert, 48
Stem, brain, 4–5
Sternberg, Robert, 57, 59
Strategic note taking, 123, 124
Stress
    hormones, 75
    and memory, 31, 164–165
Study strategies to promote comprehension,
    122–126
Survival mechanism, 4–5
Svinicki, Marilla, 53
Sylwester, Robert, 7, 92
Synergy, brain, 25
Synthesis, creation, and use of knowledge,
    160–162

Taxonomy
    Anderson's updated, 134–137, 162
    Bloom's, 133–134, 162
    Marzano and Kendall's new,
        137–138, 139, 162
    Materna method, 138–162
Teachers
    combination learners/, 51
    left-brain versus right-brain, 15–16
Teaching
    brain-compatible, 41–43
    to enhance retention, 37
    and middle brain emotional balance,
        11–12
    multisensory, 37
    rituals in, 6–7
    and the upper brain learning process, 23
    whole-brain, 19, 20
    See also Learners, adult
Territorialism and the lower brain, 5
Thalamus, 7–8
Transformative learning, 42
Tree diagrams, 113, 116, 117,
    153, 154, 191
Triarchic theory of successful
    intelligence, 57–59
Troisi, E., 78

Upper brain
    processing, 19–23
    structures, 13–16

Venn diagrams, 108, 111, 157, 194
Visual cortex, 27

Visualizations, creative, 79–84

Visual learners, 51, 55

Visual memory, 29–31

Visual processing promotion using graphic organizers, 95

Vitamins and minerals, 76

Walker, Matt, 39

Warm-ups, brain, 171–174

Water intake and learning, 77

Whole-brain learning, 16–19

Wolfe, Pat, 85

Woodbury, M. A., 39

Working memory, 31–32

Wrap-up quizzes, 161–162

Wurtman, Judith, 76

Zamari, Edward, 39

Zeineh, Michael, 8

Zull, James, 93